Public
Libraries
in
COOPERATIVE
SYSTEMS

Public Libraries in

COOPERATIVE SYSTEMS

Administrative Patterns
for Service

RUTH W. GREGORY
and LESTER L. STOFFEL

AMERICAN LIBRARY ASSOCIATION
Chicago 1971

COVER DESIGN: *The design on the cover is adapted from the logo of the Suburban Library System (Hinsdale, Illinois) and represents the interchange which prevails in a cooperative system.*

International Standard Book Number 0-8389-0110-7 (1971)

Library of Congress Catalog Card Number 78-172295

Copyright © 1971 by the American Library Association

Printed in the United States of America

Contents

Preface

This book was written as an introduction to the administrative relationships between small and medium-sized public libraries and the cooperative library system. In this book, the definition of a cooperative system is as follows: A cooperative library system is the combining of the talents and the resources of a group of independent libraries, within a reasonable geographic radius, for the purpose of attaining excellence in service and resources for the benefit of the actual and potential users of all of the member libraries. The plan for the book originated with questions directed to a public library administrator and to a system director. The most pertinent of the repeated questions was, "How does system membership change local library administration?" The sharpest question was, "Will the system ultimately take over local rights and responsibilities?"

The authors intend to answer these and other questions by restating the responsibilities of the local library and by interpreting the ways in which a cooperative system provides its members with resources to meet those responsibilities.

Many of the questions initially asked of the authors came from representatives of communities ranging from 50,000 to 75,000 in population. It was soon evident, however, that the interest in the direction the cooperative system takes is just as strong in smaller communities served by alert librarians and trustees. As a consequence, the audience for this book is anticipated to be librarians, trustees, government officials, and friends of the libraries in communities of 75,000 and under. It is hoped that the approach to the many aspects of system-member library relationships will hold interest also for system directors and students of library science.

It has not been the intent of this book to match the comprehensiveness of Wheeler and Goldhor's *Practical Administration of*

Public Libraries or Bowler's *Local Public Library Administration,* or to replace the pamphlets in the Small Libraries Project. The purpose is to help create an understanding of the separate and joint responsibilities of the member library and the cooperative system in providing quality service. The purpose underscores a conviction that the word "system" in the vocabulary of the library profession is synonymous with opportunity.

RUTH W. GREGORY
Head Librarian
Waukegan (Illinois) Public Library
LESTER L. STOFFEL
Executive Director
Suburban Library System
(Hinsdale, Illinois)

1 A Framework for the Redesign of Public Library Service

The first free public libraries in the United States were established in New England in the early 1800s. They spread across the country through the efforts of women's clubs, hopeful parents, idealistic civic leaders—and the beneficence of Andrew Carnegie. By the mid-twentieth century there were more than 6,500 public libraries to be administered.

In their earliest years small and medium-sized libraries settled down into administrative patterns dictated by the service needs of distinct age groups in a middle-class society. Administrative patterns became administrative traditions. There were periodic innovations, of course. It was the administrator of a small library who inaugurated open stacks.[1] It was the administrator of a medium-sized library who initiated teletype connections between libraries. But in general the typical small library continued the organizational and service patterns devised by library pioneers. Observers of the library scene as late as the 1960s could sympathize with Malcolm Boyd's criticism of "this dreadful sameness"[2] of libraries.

Following World War II, knowledge in nearly every field expanded at incredible rates. The overwhelming bombardment of facts and information, the impact of technology in developing instant communication, and society's insistence on excellence in its educational institutions resulted in a more vital role for and a focus of attention on public libraries. Inequities in opportunities for library service, decent housing, jobs, and education were exposed in every section of the country. Society's needs became quantitatively and qualitatively greater, challenging and rechallenging the traditional roles of all social institutions, including public libraries. At the same time, the nation was completing the shift from an agricultural to an industrial economy; and vast

1

numbers of the population had moved from rural to metropolitan areas.

As metropolitan areas expanded, decentralization and fragmentation of governmental functions developed with the growth in the number of independent satellite communities. The typical method of providing library service—a separate, locally financed and operated library in each community—followed the governmental pattern. The result was duplication of materials and technical processing, idle books, uneven distribution of services, and dissipation of funds. The average citizen was without access to the complete service that was the area's potential.

As the mobility of people increased, various sections of the metropolitan areas grew interdependent, with some supplying employment or shopping centers and others providing a labor force or shoppers. With this mobility and interdependence came interchange of people, until libraries discovered their services were being enjoyed by patrons who found it more convenient to use the library in the community where they worked or shopped rather than the library supported with their taxes. This tendency to ignore political boundaries in the use of libraries was intensified by the vastly increased need for information and the disparity in quality of resources and services among public libraries. The mobile citizen of the metropolis discovered the library in which his informational needs could be satisfied, and the larger, better supported libraries were deluged.

Libraries operating outside the metropolitan area were caught in a net of circumstances that made it difficult, if not impossible, for them to expand their resources to fulfill both the unique requirements of their own communities and the broadening interests of a society dominated by the life-styles of urban complexes. It was readily apparent that the average rural or suburban library could not muster the financial resources to meet the increasing variety of demand. Even if it could, the obvious question arose as to the economic prudence of attempting to duplicate the resources of the great libraries of the central cities.

The Need for a New Approach

Library administration has two basic objectives: to organize library resources and personnel for the advantage of the active patron and to promote library services to the nonpatron. What, then, was the solution to the problem of providing sufficient library resources in suburban and rural America to meet the changing and increasing needs?

One avenue for metropolitan areas might have been consolidation—the creation of a singly governed metropolitan library system with the city library as the core. But great size provokes great problems, as illustrated by the big city school systems that have struggled, during the third quarter of the twentieth century, with the problem of equality in education for all sections of a city and the desire for more neighborhood participation in the decision-making process. Decentralization of public institutions seemed more suitable for the resolution of citizen dissatisfactions. Another obstacle to the consolidation of libraries in metropolitan areas was the determination of suburbanites to remain politically, although not economically, independent of the central city and of other suburbs. The small libraries in metropolitan areas were faced with the necessity to maintain autonomy and to create a climate for cooperation that would open up resources beyond their independent means.

The solution to the public library problem in rural areas, where libraries were serving widely scattered population centers, was even more difficult. County libraries were established but failed to raise significantly the level of local library service in most cases, especially in sparsely populated counties. Nor was the county line found to be, necessarily, a logical boundary for library service areas. Multicounty library units were attempted but were limited in achieving their major goals by the complexities of the political process.

Other schemes were developed in attempts to meet the critical needs of the small independent library. These included voluntary cooperation between groups of neighboring libraries, contracts with the strongest area library for special services, the formation of special taxing districts, and supplementary collections or grants in aid through the state libraries. All these efforts made some contribution to the work of the independent library but fell far short of the goal of equalizing opportunity and improving service. They attacked the symptoms but did not reach the cause of the malaise.

Background of the System Concept

The independent library's inability to extricate itself from a situation created by its own limitations cannot be attributed to a lack of administrative foresight. For decades perceptive librarians and trustees expressed their conviction, through exploratory planning documents, that the time would come when librarians and trustees would be forced to acknowledge that the independent library is not able to stand alone in meeting all its informational, educational, and social responsibilities.

Years of professional searching for workable solutions to the problems of urban and rural libraries focused again and again on the same essentials: cooperation, accessibility, bibliographic banks, reference referral centers, and universal service. The proposed instrument for the realization of these essentials came to be known as the "system."

The most persuasive exponent of the concept of the library system was Carleton B. Joeckel. His *Government of the American Public Library,* published in 1934, was a landmark in the literature on the importance of the larger unit and on the responsibility of the state for total library service. In 1948 Mr. Joeckel and Amy Winslow reemphasized the magnitude of the governmental obligation with the statement, "The great library task of the state is to sponsor the development of an efficient and integrated *system* of public libraries available to all its people."[3] The values of the system concept were further corroborated by the report of the Public Library Inquiry, *The Public Library in the United States,* published in 1950.

The validity of the system idea was accepted by successive professional leaders without controversy. Delays in its implementation were due to a number of factors. The system concept could not be imposed on trustees or community officials by a hierarchy of library theorists. The leadership for the inauguration of a plan for a particular section of the country had to come from the grass roots. In some instances the leadership was lacking; in others the leadership was available, but the times were not right. It was apparent from the beginning that a salable proposal would have to be based on a plan that would not discard the values of the traditional library but would build on existing strengths and open the doors to enriched opportunities.

Improved library service for every individual in every community was the prime incentive in planning for cooperative systems. Paralleling this incentive was the awareness of the indirect financial advantages to the independent library in having access to multiple materials resources and to a superior type of administrative, counseling, and planning center. The financial advantages were not necessarily seen as direct grants to the local library but as collective investments in materials and services, which in effect would augment the local budget. A recognition of indirect financial advantages in system affiliation tended to create a sense of security comparable to the support of a strong credit rating in industrial planning for improved production.

A review of library literature indicates that members of the profession have applied the American genius for organization to the system concept. Library systems have been organized in many ways, from small informal cooperatives to wide-area consolidations and interstate compacts. The differing forms of system organization have been influenced by geography, jurisdictional boundaries, financial resources, area customs, and leadership concepts of the acceptable. There seems to have been no universal compulsion to adopt a single type of system or necessarily to follow the practices of other systems.

The most distinctive characteristic of the system movement in the United States is that all systems have much in common, yet no two are exactly alike. In the mass they present a wide spectrum of laws, governmental structures, membership areas, organizational procedures, services, and rules and regulations. The newer systems have learned much from the trials and errors of the long-established systems, but they have not imitated them. Thus, each system may be said to be unique. This individuality is important to emerging library networks. One of a system's functions is to sustain uniqueness to meet the singular needs of its own area and effectively build up the assets of its member libraries as contributors to national pools of information and cultural resources.

The System

The word "system" has been used several ways in the library profession's vocabulary. It has been applied to the organizational structure of a medium-sized library, with one or two extension units, serving a single municipality. It frequently defines a large city library with many departments, branches, and agencies. It has been used to designate city-county combinations as well as supplementary regional outlets of a state library. The word seems to serve as a relatively understandable form of shorthand to eliminate the need for the writing of a fuller treatise on organization in reports and releases.

It is difficult to produce an exact definition of a library system, not only because of the term's multiple uses but also because library systems themselves vary greatly in government, organization, and range of functions. In 1956, *Public Library Service: A Guide to Evaluation* pointed out that "libraries working together, sharing their services and materials, can meet the full needs of their users."[4] This was a part of a recommendation that did not attempt a definition. Its successor, *Minimum Standards for Public Library Systems, 1966,* emphasized the basic elements of a system but did not define it.

Nelson Associates in the 1969 survey, *Public Library Systems in the United States,* suggested that

> an inclusive definition is required, perhaps along these lines: A public library system is a complex of public libraries in which the resources and services of this complex are made available either to the libraries belonging to the system or directly to the patrons in the system's service area.[5]

Ruth Warncke has pointed out that

> a system exists when a number of independently financed, managed, and staffed libraries agree to establish certain centralized services in order to strengthen each library's ability to serve its own community well.[6]

As noted in the Preface, in this book a cooperative library system is the combining of the talents and the resources of a group of independent libraries, within a reasonable geographic radius, for the purpose of attaining excellence in service and resources for the benefit of the actual and potential users of all of the member libraries.

In their governmental organization library systems are commonly of three types: consolidated, federated, or cooperative. In a consolidated system two or more libraries relinquish their autonomy to form a single library unit under one governing board. In a federated system the member libraries maintain their autonomy and contract for public or supportive services from a designated headquarters library. A federated system may operate under an appointed system board responsible for policy and coordinated service developments. A cooperative system is structured on the concept of building on the strength of the autonomous member library units, in collaboration with a system staff responsible for planning and administering services for the benefit of all member libraries. The governing body of the autonomous library usually, but not always, is an elected or appointed board of trustees. The governing body for cooperative system activities is generally elected from among the trustees of member libraries.

A cooperative library system has been described as:

> a library organization created and governed by two or more authorities operating their own libraries, for the purpose of providing themselves with one or more special purpose library services and, where appropriate, of assuring the provision of general purpose library service to an area for which the system may be responsible. The authorities creating the system may establish a separate authority or may designate an existing organization coincidentally as the organization for the operation of the system. Each participating authority continues to operate its library and have responsibility for library service in the authority's jurisdiction, retains its basic administrative independence, and contributes one or more resources (materials, personnel, services, finances) to the system.[7]

A library system is a planned partnership. The word "system" implies the interaction of the units that make up the whole. The successful systems are those in which the members have vision, understand that cooperation means contributing as well as receiving, and recognize that sharing is a countermeasure to mediocrity. There is no library so small that it does not have the potential to make a unique contribution to system development. Conversely, there is no library so large that it cannot gain by system participation.

The unique values of a cooperative system are products of the level at which it operates. System administration is designed fundamentally to serve member libraries as institutions. The direct clientele of a system headquarters consists of librarians and trustees. The emphasis in the work of the system staff is on the problem areas of concern to the member libraries. But the system staff's approach to problem-solving is broader, being based upon a depth of exploration and research beyond the ability of any member library.

Members of the system staff may be involved to some degree in direct public service through a headquarters library, bookmobiles, demonstration projects, and other activities. The prime role of the majority of cooperative systems, however, is to serve people through the member libraries by strengthening services, coordinating resources for accessibility and quality, and inaugurating programs that will, in turn, improve local service patterns and practices. Systems continuously engage in identifying and analyzing the needs of member administrators and trustees to find the means to suggest new and productive ways of handling old problems.

Access, quality, and stimulus have been underscored as the key words in the system's practical approach to its goals. The cooperative system combines materials and services from a wide area and places them at the disposal of an individual in a single area. The urgency of the need to upgrade continuously this basic function has moved the systems into related activities, which provide opportunities to stimulate the overall advancement of member libraries. Consequently, the cooperative system has become:

1. An instrument of stimulus for the establishment and exceeding of standards in local administration, collection building, and services
2. A coleader, with other agencies, in creating and sustaining a climate for state and federal acceptance of responsibility for library development
3. A channel for the implementation of state and federal appropriations and programs as they apply to member libraries
4. The voice of the member units in library and related planning and research councils
5. A cosponsor of intersystem cooperative programs
6. A testing ground for innovations and experimentation
7. A sounding board for membership opinions and ideas
8. A vehicle for the establishment of special collections and different levels of collection building
9. A continuing education center for trustees, administrators, and staffs of member libraries
10. A bibliographic and reference center in the network complex
11. A medium for the formation and development of networks between different types of libraries
12. A source of advice and referral on legal, technical, and specialized problems of concern to member libraries
13. A recruitment center and personnel clearinghouse
14. A counseling center in areas of intellectual freedom
15. An initiator of essential research studies on problems related to the individual library and system development
16. A catalyst for constructive change and evaluation of system progress.

Through such professional assignments, the cooperative system functions to strengthen member libraries in terms of materials, services, and administrative effectiveness.

The cooperative system begins with the member library as it is. It presents absolutely no threat to the library's local prestige, local responsibilities, program, or personnel unless change and improvement are considered threats. It offers the stimulus of renewal and expansion through an equitable plan for the sharing of resources and through participation in cooperative planning, study, and experimentation undertaken for the benefit of all.

Such rules and regulations as prevail, either by law or by common consent, are a necessary part of good system management and serve primarily as guidelines for orderly growth and as directives to high standards of performance. Membership participation in the planning and continuous development of the system is a fundamental principle. Accumulated experience indicates there are several other elements with implications for all systems.

One of the most important is financing. Some systems are supported through federal funds. Some are state supported. Some are financed by member libraries. Federal support, though temporary, permits demonstrations that give weight to the arguments for permanent funding from other sources. State support, which depends upon the formulas established by the individual states, provides a leverage for equalization and greater opportunities for basic and innovative services. Adequacy in financing often is determined, favorably or unfavorably, by the area to be served. It is obvious that the area must be large enough to provide an adequate base for financial support regardless of the source of the financing.

The strength of the member libraries is of equal importance. The presence of a strong library to serve as the headquarters or central library and as the initial strength on which to build is basic to getting a program off the sheet of paper that records it. Obviously, a group of weak libraries will be unable to move beyond their composite weakness.

It is also generally agreed that a cooperative system must have a realistic plan—one in which measurable steps can be taken within reasonable periods of time and upon which a strong headquarters staff can constantly build. A system is in the fortunate position of being geared to the future with few restrictions from the past, but it should not place the future in jeopardy by overselling or underdelivering at any stage in the development of the plan.

Not the least among the essentials is the charge to the system to serve as a leader among change agents. On the local level change may be perceived as desirable but difficult, if not impossible, for many reasons. There may be deep fears of change at the very heart of the institution. There may be vested interests in long-existing programs or positions. There may be insufficient funds or time to initiate necessary studies of the applicability of new methods. There may be a lack of expertise to interpret data or trends in community needs. There may be reluctance to recommend concepts and ideas to a disinterested board or a fearful staff. There may be misconceptions about the authority to propose new directions. There may be outright reluctance to make the effort.

The system is in a position of strength to assume leadership for change. A cooperative system, adequately funded, inaugurates and carries out its plan of service on the premise that it has an obligation to help its member libraries clear the way to achieve optimum effectiveness. This obligation implies, and in some cases charges, the system with the responsibility to identify areas that will profit from change and to examine the most feasible and economical means to effect such change.

The members of a system staff are, or should be, specialists in their individual fields of competence. The system membership, even though it may include many experienced professionals, naturally looks to the system specialists for the objectivity and the talents to analyze problems and to reach conclusions that make sense in terms of intelligent redirection. A system staff has a time advantage over the member library in being able to move quickly to find answers or to initiate investigations where there are no available answers. Out of its own consultant experience, the system staff has the background to enable it to resist superficial answers, to reconcile conceptual contradictions, and to maintain perspective under the most demanding pressures. Remote from the local critic, it is situated advantageously to brave the risks of experimentation.

The system headquarters staff, in its association with other systems and with nonlibrary technologists and planning groups, acquires knowledge and insights that are prime assets in directing or redirecting membership concerns for essential change. The headquarters specialists have a responsibility not only to promote change but also to stimulate member librarians and trustees to be alert to the fluctuating needs of a changing society and to be active in the cooperative system effort to make the best use of technological advances and emerging professional skills to raise the performance record of public libraries.

Intersystem cooperation has become an asset to cooperative systems. Directors of neighboring systems with common problems have found that the sharing of the negative or positive results of attempted solutions eliminates time- and money-wasting duplication of effort. Intersystem planning and action became imperative with the recognition that systems, like individual libraries, may unnecessarily duplicate specialized materials and services. The economic factors of high-priced research, maintenance of bibliographic centers, automated equipment and communication, contracts with outside specialists, and other sharable ventures reinforce the importance of joint activity by combinations of systems to add to the benefits for all. Intersystem cooperation is fostered in many regions by regularly scheduled work sessions, which bring together the directors of many systems for the purpose of sharing experiences and planning joint operations.

Response to the System

A major thrust behind the relatively rapid growth of the system movement since 1950 was proof, as substantiated by national library surveys and government studies, that the lives of millions of Americans have been diminished by the nonexistence of library facilities or by the poverty status of existing libraries in every section of the United States. The national expectation of a steady growth of a body of informed and productive citizens could not be sustained when there was evidence that millions had no place to turn for their informational needs or for the tools required for adjustment to the fluctuating pressures of daily living. The predicament was compounded by the fact that ignorance and personal ineffectiveness, like disease, spread with a highly mobile population. Modern man may be affluent, or he may be trapped in a ghetto. He may be highly trained for a profession, or he may not have sufficient reading skill to hold a decent job. But he is of concern to the library profession wherever he is, whoever he is, and whatever his background.

The nation as a whole in the last third of the century is changing from an institution-regulated society to a person-oriented society. This trend is evidenced by such developments as the relaxation of rules and regulations on university campuses, the restructuring of policies within the major churches, the extension of personal privileges in the armed forces, and the search in the halls of Congress for just and workable plans for public welfare programs. Visible efforts are being made in most public agencies to understand the needs of the individual and to meet the demands for accountability imposed by the concerned members of society. Library thinking is clearly and positively focused on people, particularly on those many individuals and groups the library has not reached. This is, and probably always has been, the official stand, but performance has not matched professional rhetoric. The small library that quotes the standards in its declaration that "the aim of the public library is service to all the people"[8] is giving lip service to an ideal. An honest reaction is an admission that the small independent library simply cannot meet all the needs of all the people in any single community constantly being remolded by the complex problems of contemporary society.

Conscientious librarians and their boards worry about the increasing use of their collections in relation to the exhaustion of their personnel and their finances. They are aware of unmet needs and may try to handle their problems by limiting the scope of their objectives or by setting priorities in service activities. If they struggle alone, they are akin to professionals in other service agencies who try to put the lid back on the boiling pot instead of trying to find a larger container.

Library literature is replete with references to the nonuser and the unserved in every community. These terms took on sharper connotations with the incredible doubling and redoubling of man's knowledge and with the deepening citizen concern for environmental and human conditions. The needs of the people served by the local library came to be one of the most important factors in a local community's appraisal of a cooperative system and in its judgment of the significance of a system's plan of service. At the center of all thinking about the renewal of the public library through system affiliation stand the man, the woman, and the child who depend upon the librarian to determine what each one wants and to locate the printed, the audio, or the visual material that will satisfy that want.

Modern man lives in a world in which he has learned to expect continuous technological miracles. He reasons that if NASA can repeatedly put men on the moon, the library on his own familiar part of the earth should be able to provide within an hour the special informational material he needs. He believes what he reads in the Sunday supplement about the computer memory banks being within reach of the library world. He is frustrated if he is unable to obtain through his own library the output of a copying machine. The supportive instrument for the local library in meeting the persistent expectations of modern man is the system.

Modern man has become a specialized person with specialized needs that are precise and definitive. Expensive library tools may be required to meet them. Contemporary man also has more leisure and can look forward to longer retirement years than did his forefathers. It is obvious that a wide variety of library materials must be available as productive aids to man throughout his lifetime. The system provides the opportunity for the diversity that can make the use of a public library more completely satisfactory and meaningful.

Margaret Mead's statement that "we are at a point where we must educate people in what nobody knew yesterday, and prepare in our schools for what nobody knows yet, but what some people must know tomorrow"[9] underscores still another imperative contribution to be made to the member library by the cooperative system. All libraries acknowledge an obligation to identify needs and to build collections that anticipate needs. The small library has inherent limitations in fulfilling this responsibility. Anticipating and preparing for the still unknown demands of the future becomes one of the most important assignments to be undertaken by the system on behalf of its member libraries.

A realistic look at the insufficiency of resources in the average small library gave further impetus to the acceptability of the system concept on the local level. Budgets of small libraries as a general rule do not keep pace with the cost of living or the rising cost of books and collection maintenance. The result has been an increasing deficit in the library's ability to acquire substantial collections for normal needs. Limited financing does not easily accommodate urgent requests for specialized materials that are infrequently used. The practice of the independent library is to attempt to invest in resources to meet insistent but limited demands even though they may represent duplications of holdings in neighboring libraries. Those involved in system development recognized that by creating a sophisticated collection for the use of all and by sharing the total resources of its members a more efficient development of local collections was possible.

The sharing principle, operating through the controlled supervision of system administration, made sense to many administrators and trustees. The establishment of bibliographic and reference centers provided the means for further expediting service on the local level. At the same time, the organization of processing centers offered economies in acquisition, processing, and cataloging procedures. The result was a well-established faith in the system's potential for strengthening the fiscal base of the member library to provide for maximum-use acquisitions and for more productive involvement of local staff in person-to-person service, which is acclaimed as one of the finest assets of the small library.

The average small library has some awareness that many of its techniques are outmoded and wasteful of staff time and skills. The librarian of the small community ordinarily has neither the time nor the background to examine modern methods. This points to still another important function of the system—to serve as an adviser or a referral agent in the improvement of methods and the purchase of modern equipment, or even as the initiator of experiments to demonstrate ways of making the work of the small library more efficient.

By the end of the 1960s, systems were widely established and, according to the Nelson survey, had proved their ability to achieve their basic purposes.[10] Many small libraries took advantage of the opportunity to affiliate with systems. Some did not. Slowness in deciding to join a system usually takes the form of time-consuming deliberation rather than opposition.

Delay in the affiliation on the part of a small library may stem from an acknowledged need for further clarification of the purpose of a system and its values to a local library. Rejection may be prompted by preconceptions and apprehensions which, on further examination are seen to be baseless. But a negative response must be respected on the grounds of the right of self-determination. The system staff and the system members seek to understand rather than to force the removal of the blocks that keep any library out of the mainstream of modern library service.

The safeguarding of the independence of the community library is a matter of genuine anxiety for many trustees and librarians. An introduction to the system concept temporarily evokes fears of losing local authority over the use of tax funds, the management of personnel and policies, and the choice of books and other materials. There is a very human tendency for the boards and administrators in small communities to consider their institutions symbols of personal and corporate achievement. This is understandable. They have conscientiously provided and maintained their libraries by the tight allocation of limited funds and a rigid scrutiny of expenditures and bookkeeping procedures. They have worked out rules for public use that seem reasonable to them. Such boards and librarians operate under a guardianship theory of library management. It takes time and many reinterpretations of the system's objectives to reassure them that within a system affiliation they will not only have control of their own administrative setup but have even more opportunity for corporate honor and achievement on the local level.

Another deterrent to joining a system is the home-grown conviction that the local library is already giving outstanding service and there is no justification for improvement to the extent of seeking access to outside resources. The board and the administrator may or may not run a good library. They may be unaware of their failure to fulfill the library's potential. They may have a performance record that is the result of operating on a minimum standards achievement theory of library management.

There is a certain satisfaction in exceeding the standards of one's neighbors or of the nation, but there is also a trap. The exceeding of minimum standards may create a mutual admiration society on the local level in which judgments of performance become subjective rather than objective, in terms of the needs of people. Self-isolation also denies the fact that good libraries have professional obligations as leaders and as contributors to the improvement of library service for all Americans.

A failure to understand the purpose of libraries in a world of gargantuan social problems and incredible technological advances is sometimes responsible for a slow response to system affiliation. A small-town library, for example, is locally judged good if it takes care of the children's curriculum needs and their summertime reading. A heavy concentration on service to children and young people, particularly students, is a publicly appealing use of limited tax dollars in those communities where the adults have not been alerted to the importance of the library for their own age group. Library policies and activities become centered on the needs of the young. The adult—the voter, the homemaker, the contributor to the Gross National Product, the human being—is shortchanged.

The idea of giving prime service to children and students may go back to the declarations of the early 1900s that the library was a handmaiden of the schools. This theory, although it lingers in some communities, was deemphasized long ago with the acceptance by school boards of their responsibilities for providing curriculum-related materials and developing good school libraries. The library profession today is guided by the principle that "public, school, and academic libraries should work together to provide coordinated service to students."[11] A child- and school-oriented public library may insist that coordinated programs do not stop the flow of student demands and that they cannot afford to do much or anything for other age groups. Such a library cannot afford to abstain from system affiliation. A simple matter of a decision provides the means to improve service for all ages.

Devotion to the traditional duties carried on by generations of librarians, and perennially reinforced by state library institutes and graduate library school extension courses, is a factor contributing to the myopia of some administrators toward systems. They seem to like what has been called the "housekeeping busy-work" of librarianship and the custodial routines of administration. They regard cataloging as a particularly sacred province, giving no thought to the values of a processing center in releasing time and talent for more productive purposes. Collaboration with fellow librarians within a system may very well convince time-pressed librarians that expendable routines can be eliminated and staff knowledge of books and materials intensified for a highly professional approach to working with people.

A persistent fear among the decision-makers in communities that have supported the library well enough to allow for good collection building is that they will be overburdened and undercompensated by affiliation with weaker neighbors. In suburbia this fear is fed by a natural resentment against the claims for library privileges made by families who deliberately choose to live outside incorporated areas in order to escape taxes. An anticipation of serious drains on any member library (other than the headquarters or central library, which is ordinarily subsidized for its assumption of responsibilities for the system) is not justified by experience records.[12] These examples illustrate the kinds of reactions that at the outset hinder affiliation with a system. They soon disappear as librarians and trustees focus their attention on the needs of the people they serve.

The cooperative system is a framework for the resurgence of the public library. Resurgence depends upon several elements: skill in the art of probing the status quo, the ability to identify and interpret needs, a willingness to engage in continuous stock-taking for professional growth, a responsiveness to changing human conditions, an abhorrence of the mediocre, and hospitality to new ideas and techniques. These are elements that fuse the system and its member libraries into the planned partnership.

The small library operating in areas where cooperative systems exist has two choices: affiliation or nonaffiliation. Each has consequences. The decision to remain separate from the system is a vote for the status quo. The decision to join is a vote of confidence in the profession's capacity to reinforce itself to meet the demands of a constantly changing society.

Essentials for System Relationships

Certain preconditions are recognized as essentials for productive system membership: the involvement of the membership in developing the purpose and plan of a particular system, understanding of the relationship of the system to its members and to other systems, acceptance of the need for cooperation as a means to achieve professional aspirations, willingness to participate in joint ventures designed to implement service improvements, recognition that involvement means mutual trust, appreciation of the urgency of attaining maximum standards, a high degree of patience, and the courage to face the necessity to redesign the public library to meet the needs of people.

An understanding of the purpose of a system involves an awareness of what the system is and what it is not. The system is one answer to the problems that have been acknowledged as insoluble on the local level. Its promise rests not only on its immediate objectives but also on its flexibility in responding to new situations and crises. Its future depends not only on a creative plan and a high degree of professionalism but also on its ability to avoid the rigidities characterizing so many levels of library administration.

The system is not a panacea. It is not to be equated with utopia in the administrator's office or with euphoria at meetings of the library board. It is a "summons to greatness," with all the implications of that phrase: a clear vision of attainable goals, a capacity for hard work, an abandonment of vested interests, and the training and retraining of librarians for eminence in the pursuit of a profession dedicated solely to the needs of people. The cooperative system is not a crutch for the underachiever among its institutional affiliates. It is an instrument to help the weakest of libraries rise to a position where they can become reliable links in the national network that is slowly evolving to meet the known needs of humanity and the unknown requirements of the future.

Cooperation is an absolute essential for a workable system program. Boards of trustees and librarians who are not willing to cooperate should not even bother to join a system. Informal reports on professional behavior indicate that some librarians do not really want to broaden their services through the channels of cooperation. Attitudes toward cooperation, however, have become a test of the veracity of the claims of librarians and trustees that they have a concern for the unmet needs of potential and active users of their libraries.

Cooperation is a human response that meets with universal approval. It has been the subject of exhortation by speakers and the professional press for years. Actually, it is not an unfamiliar activity for individuals working in libraries. With little or no reservation, they cooperate with all kinds of citizens and all types of agencies on their home territory. Distance in miles and differing jurisdictions need not change the complexion of cooperation. If the needs of the men, women, and children to be served by libraries are placed above all other considerations, cooperation becomes meaningful and indispensable.

Cooperation means more than generosity in sharing materials through interlibrary loans and more than kindly receptivity to the ideas of the system director and his staff. It is the means whereby the system itself can become more sensitive to the needs of the member libraries. Real cooperation can be a source of the creativity that makes the evolution of a system an exciting and provocative experience for the participant who is willing to work through the vexations and delays that inevitably accompany a forward moving plan subject to the consensus of the hypercritical, the doubters, the overly optimistic, and the impatient.

Cooperation calls for a coordination of membership ideas and directives and a determination to resolve essentially minor differences to provide major benefits. It calls for membership voices in system planning councils and for membership engagement in the execution of system services and programs. There may be occasions when a member library, exercising its right of autonomy, does not wish to participate in system services. A member library may feel, for example, that it has a grave staffing problem that precludes the addition of one more performance requirement, such as the booking of films from system headquarters. A cooperative system does not require conformity in the use of its unique resources. Cooperation is not a form of insistence. It is, instead, an invitation to each autonomous library to join in a professional effort to create attitudes and conditions that encourage full use of cooperative system services.

To the uninitiated, cooperative effort within a system may give rise to the fear of losing the right to independent action. In any cooperative arrangement, rules and procedures must be devised for considerate and equitable treatment of the recipients of the service. Rules and procedures seriously affecting the local libraries are determined democratically, that is, by majority vote. Therefore, any diminished freedom of independent action is no greater than that suffered by citizens in a democratic society and is not apt to be significant if service to the individual library patron is the primary consideration.

The cooperative systems throughout the United States have moved their programs forward through concentrated efforts on involving membership in planning, two-way communication, and joint action. There is no doubt of the advantages. The question is how members with a wide range of educational and experience backgrounds may be involved effectively in terms of the cooperative system's own governmental structure, the program time schedule, and the energy and work loads of the staffs in member libraries and system headquarters.

Undoubtedly it would be easier for a system staff to go ahead on its own and set up a program that is to the obvious advantage of all. It would be simpler for the member library to just accept the product of that action. But something is lost in such a relationship.

The cooperative system staff must come to know the characteristics, the goals, the attitudes, and the headaches of each constituent in the system. The member libraries, as the constituents, must be involved in order to understand the "art of the possible." Most librarians are apprentices in the system business. Some expect too much. Some expect too little. Others are fearful of their competence to participate. But involvement is more important than personal expertise. Competence grows with exposure and group experience. A passive participant who quietly acquiesces in the decisions of his peers runs the risk of betraying his own community by cutting off a source of system insight into ways to improve the system.

Communication is essential in a cooperative system. Communication is a two-way exchange. The system administrator needs the questions and the value judgments of the membership. He needs them firsthand and not by way of the grapevine. The member administrators need up-to-date information on progress, *good or bad,* to retain their sense of community and their pride in participation.

Communication changes its form and purpose as a cooperative system matures. This can be seen when a system is designing a service and establishing procedures. Considerable communication with the membership is required in the planning stages. Once the service is initiated and tested, membership advice may be limited to periodic evaluation of its scope and effectiveness. But communication related to a well-established service does not cease. It changes in intensity, allowing time for other communication needs. Both library representatives and system staff may come to resent the tyranny of the telephone, frequent meetings, conferences, questionnaires, reports, bulletins, and all the other communication devices. The alternative is simply little or no communication and a return to the dark ages when librarians in small communities worked in varying degrees of professional isolation.

Sluggish lines of communication lower the potential for mutual understanding by opening the door to paternalism at the system level and indifference at the community level. Good communication is closely correlated with the enthusiasm and genuineness of cooperation. As in all other walks of life, the success of the system depends largely on the faithfulness of people. Excellence in communication is an absolute in sustaining the spirit and the drive that will advance the cooperative system to its maximum potential usefulness to the member libraries and their patrons.

Vitally important in cooperative system development is the administrator of the system and his conception of the system's role in strengthening the libraries within his sphere of influence. In designing the structure of the system, the system executive is a traditional administrator. The system staff will be organized to provide services to the system's clientele—the member libraries. Organization charts, job descriptions, classifications, salary scales, supervision and other personnel practices, and budgeting will follow the normal patterns. In his role, however, the system administrator will always be aware of member librarians and trustees looking at the system's performance as an example to be emulated. His relationships with the system board will influence library board/librarian relationships among the membership. In meeting the requirements of traditional administrative functions, the executive will always be conscious of working in a glass house.

In relationships with the member libraries the system director and his staff have a unique role. Not only do they serve as examples, but they must be patient, tactful, and expert leaders who know when compromise is necessary. The system staff must maintain high standards and expect them to be met by the member libraries. Nevertheless, the system director must develop the sensitivity to know when he should insist on performance at the local level and when he should only suggest or recommend.

Member libraries obviously will present a variety of problems. One local board may be extremely weak; one librarian may be a barrier to the extension of local service; in another library the board and librarian may be working at cross-purposes. The system director will be alert to the problems and idiosyncrasies of each member library. Lacking authority over them, he will develop a sense of timing and await the opportunity unobtrusively to offer solutions to their problems. Such opportunities will arise when he is asked for advice in one area which opens the door to conversation in the problem areas, or when he designs workshops to stimulate thought at the local level about problems previously ignored. The wise system director takes advantage of every invitation to attend local board meetings and encourages such invitations.

The cooperative system director must work through the local administrator while remembering a responsibility to the local library board or other governing authority. Professional ethics will be kept in mind, and pitfalls of involvement with only a part of a local board will be avoided. The local administrator should be kept informed of system contacts with his board members if his inclusion is not possible, and local boards should be informed of system contacts with local community leaders. The system director must be aware of the local political implications of his work with member libraries and must remain above partisan politics. This is always a sensitive area, particularly in dealing with local officials in unserved areas and in assisting in the establishment or merger of libraries.

Although all member libraries will not be treated alike (for they are different to begin with), they can be dealt with equitably— without favoritism or partiality. Each member library has its own problems, which occasionally grow into conflict situations. Mediation may be the most satisfactory avenue for their resolution. If the system director has established a reputation for fairness, he will be asked to serve as the mediator. The value of the system director in this role rests upon the depth of his understanding of the legal processes, the administrative practices, and the management principles through which controversies can be objectively and constructively resolved.

Situations in which a system director may mediate range from minor, but continuously troublesome, disputes to serious controversies. System directors have had experience in mediating controversies between the administrator and the board, between the board and governmental authorities, and between boards and citizen groups. Examples of system mediations between the librarian and the board have ranged from frictions over the inadequacy of salary schedules to objections to policies on dress codes and staff activities in the community. Legal and budgetary problems have been mediated in controversies between the board and local government. Organized moves toward censorship and protests over gaps in service have been mediated by the system director in confrontations with community groups. The resources used by the system director in mediations, aside from experience and the counsel of the system attorney, include the state statutes, local ordinances, data from local library records or community studies, and the library standards and other professional material pertinent to mediation.

The process of mediation through the system presents the system director with opportunities to interpret the duties of the library board as defined by law, and to explain the board's relationships to the librarian, the staff, and the community as indicated by recommended practice. At the same time, it provides an opening to guide member libraries in redirecting their employee, governmental, and community relations. It may also provide an opportunity, if the local board concurs, to use the system's consultant staff as a task force to concentrate on alternative approaches to various aspects of local problems exposed by the mediation studies. An example is system staff assistance in arriving at recommendations to improve service to community groups that feel they have been neglected.

Mediation of member library controversies is a confidential matter, and all records in the system headquarters office are closed to examination by unauthorized individuals. The one possible exception is the community censorship controversy, which may be publicized by the local newspaper. In this instance the spokesman for the library is the librarian or a representative of the library board, unless the local library prefers to ask the system director to prepare official releases.

In all dealings with the member libraries, the system director and staff avoid placing the local librarians in an embarrassing position with their clientele. Even though a patron receives less than the best system service as a result of local staff error, the system should accept the responsibility. Any system regulation or procedure that in its application is found to make the local library look incompetent in the eyes of the patron must be corrected. The system director must involve the member libraries in the improvement of system programs and services. He must be aware that member librarians are on the firing line in direct public service and welcome their recommendations to improve procedures.

System services are designed to be adaptable to differences in local library policies as far as possible. But while member participation in service design is vitally important, the director, as the one person with the overall point of view, should not feel inhibited in making decisions that will result in improved services to the public. The member librarians in a cooperative system will prevent the system director from developing an ivory tower complex, but the system director will lift the sights of the members beyond the daily routines of traditional library service.

2 Patterns of Responsibility and Interrelations

The public libraries in a majority of the fifty states are governed by boards of trustees. An analysis of the legal basis of public libraries by S. Janice Kee and M. G. Toepel reveals that the laws of 44 states define the powers of boards of trustees as legal authorities for public libraries, and that in 35 states all types of public libraries operate under the authority of boards.[1] Libraries not governed by boards may be responsible to city managers, county commissioners, or other officials in local government. The powers of existing boards vary. Some have extensive responsibilities, including the authority to levy taxes. Some are advisory. Variations also prevail in the government of cooperative systems. Many involve trusteees of member libraries in system boards. Others include librarians or laymen or both. Still others, such as the cooperative system in California, do not have system boards. Nevertheless, the trustee concept seems to predominate and consequently is an important element in the relationship of the autonomous library to the cooperative system.

Autonomy

The independent public library as a member of a cooperative system is the same governmental unit that it was before affiliation. It is an entity responsible for its own funding within the provisions of the law, for the welfare of its own staff, and for establishing quality standards for its own resources and services. The cooperative system was not intended to supplant local financing or decision-making in administration or programming. The system may be of major assistance in strengthening the means of fulfilling local responsibilities, but it does not assume those responsibilities.

Consequently, the cooperative system is not an authority superimposed on the governmental structure of the independent library.

24

It is not a regulatory office that requires its members to carry out solutions to administrative problems under uniform rules and regulations. It is an instrumentality set up with legal directives aimed at the orderly achievement of goals that are beyond the capacity of a single library to reach unaided.

Autonomy is an element in the cooperative system structure that applies to both the member library and the system as distinct organizational units. A mutual respect for the responsibilities, rights, and independence of each partner is essential. Autonomy provides a base for equality in a collaboration devised to raise the standards of performance of not only the member libraries but also of the system itself.

Autonomy implies more than a command over current practice and policy in any institution. Autonomy is power to control environment and performance. It is also power to transform an institution with a new or renewed emphasis on quality contributions to the life of the community and the nation.

The malfunctions in the library world, which have beset the autonomous library, are complicated because they are not primarily financial or demographical or sociological, but a combination of intermeshing influences. Frequently inseparable, problems peculiar to libraries do not seem to lend themselves to being checked off one by one in a search for solutions. Library history indicates that only by a united front and through cooperative processes can libraries develop the machinery to examine restrictive problems that they experience in common and to work out solutions compatible with the goals the profession has set for itself. The principle of autonomy adds strength to the practice of cooperation—to the extent that those who govern recognize that neither autonomy nor cooperation is static.

Self-government in local communities has been subject to as much change as have the personal lives of those who govern. To ignore this fact is to lag behind in advancing toward realistic and productive practices in library administration. Change in the concepts of library government is to be seen at every level. Librarians of small libraries, once excluded from board meetings, are expected to contribute to board deliberations. The reactions of the members of the staff, once a silent minority, are solicited in the processes of planning and evaluation. In the world of library systems the ideas of middle management and of the general assistant attract as much attention as do the opinions of the administrator and the trustee representative. The doors of administrative offices and the sessions of the board are open to the public.

Changes in the government of local libraries reflect the emphasis on accountability expressed by government at large. Accountability is not consistent with insularity. Consequently, the independence of all local governmental units has evolved into an unavoidable interdependence between neighboring communities, between a local community and its county or its nearby metropolitan center, and between the local community and its state and federal government. The day has long since passed when a local community and its public library can exist in isolated independence, content to drift from one day to another, giving no thought to the means of handling new obligations imposed upon them by a changing society.

Most trustees and library administrators are dedicated to the principle of home rule despite the proliferation of problems. A cooperative system reinforces that principle in its firm placement of the responsibility for local support and administration exactly where it belongs—in the hands of local officials. Since a cooperative system is composed of a number of autonomous units, a congenial framework of policies and regulations is necessary for orderly provision of services to the local library user. Some regulations will, of necessity, accompany state or federal funding and the inevitable requirements involved in the expenditure of such funds. The guiding principle behind cooperative system policies and regulations is that the autonomous library may serve its people better because the cooperative system exists.

Responsibilities of the Member Library

An independent library is a public agency created to perform several unique tasks on behalf of the men, women, and children who are unable to accumulate for themselves the products of the human mind and the creative spirit that have been recorded in print and on tape, film, and discs.

A broad grouping of the library tasks most visible to the public points to five general areas common to all types of libraries: (1) acquisition, preparation, and maintenance of collections of communications materials; (2) assistance to the public in the use of those collections through the application of appropriate techniques; (3) arrangement and distribution of collections and equipment for effective use; (4) implementation of reasonable controls for fair use; and (5) development of methods to stimulate greater use.

For those unique tasks to be carried out, certain legal and administrative responsibilities must be met by each library. They are not diluted by system membership. A checklist of the responsibilities of the independent library as a member of a system may include:

1. Local financial support
2. Budget preparation and defense of appropriation requests
3. Reexamination of local objectives
4. Employment and development of personnel
5. Provision and maintenance of adequate housing for collections and people
6. Identification of community needs for building book and materials collections
7. Selection of materials to meet local needs and interests
8. Preparation of materials through local cataloging or by contract
9. Maintenance of collections through schedules of withdrawals, mending, and binding
10. Establishment and review of policies for administration, personnel, service, and use of materials and facilities by residents and nonresidents
11. Organization of circulation and other departmental procedures
12. Upkeep of public catalogs and bibliographic services
13. Programming for book-related activities for children, young adults, and in the field of adult education
14. Extension of services to neighborhoods, the handicapped, and the disadvantaged
15. Publicity, displays, and promotion
16. Maintenance of statistical records for reporting purposes
17. Evaluation in terms of minimum standards
18. Maintenance of governmental, interagency, and intercultural relationships
19. Long-range planning
20. Cooperation with system libraries in interlibrary loan, reference, and other system programs
21. Representation and involvement in system meetings and workshops

22. Membership and participation in regional, state, and national professional associations
23. Involvement in studies and action related to library legislation.

Some of these duties are mandatory by law in the several states; all are parts of administering a library to assure smooth operation for access and stimulation in the use of its constantly growing and changing resources.

Some of the problems of small libraries result from a struggle to carry on these activities with insufficient funds, inadequate help, and entangling alliances with cherished but outmoded procedures and outdated equipment. Other problems linger on because of rusty concepts of administration, which do not admit that some of these duties have become specialties that are handled more efficiently by specialists. A case in point is the preparation of books, which is the specialty of processing centers. Another example is reference service, which most definitely has become a specialty in an economy requiring a precise and rapid flow of information. The specialist is to be found in the system reference center, which has become the major referral resource for hard-pressed local reference librarians. Emerging administrative concepts are receptive to those cooperative practices and system resources that create opportunities for the local staff to become more expert in direct service to the people of their home communities.

The public has a right to expect the librarian to be an expert. The publicity releases of recruiting centers, of National Library Week committees, of library associations, and of individual libraries and systems contribute to this expectation. Those members of the mobile population who have experienced the expertise of skilled librarians in one section of the country expect to find their counterparts in another. In some communities this public expectation of good service has turned to bafflement as requests for service outstrip staff knowledge and library resources for meeting them.

The provision of an opportunity for librarians to become experts and to maintain quality of service on the local level is the concern and the responsibility of local library officials. Affiliation with a system does not alter this fact. The foremost obligation of the independent library is to do everything in its power to improve its own condition through its own efforts.

An inadequate library may reflect early twentieth century attitudes toward library finance; sound financing was then equated with an appreciable balance at the end of the year. At one time the prevailing theory was that the chief duty of a trustee was to save money. It is now generally accepted that the trustee's responsibility is to make certain that excellence in library service is guaranteed for the community through prudent expenditure of the funds required. For decades librarians themselves were busy spreading the Melvil Dewey doctrine: "the best reading for the largest number at the least cost." Not until after World War II did service concepts transcend cost concepts in a realistic approach to the use of funds that would meet the needs of individuals of all ages and in all socioeconomic situations. Contemporary theories of money management in libraries begin with the realization that government financing is justified only by the needs of the citizen and is made manifest only through the performance of an institution.

Some libraries may be bogged down financially by the reluctance of library officials to increase appropriations to the maximum allowed by law or to make the effort to convince village, city, county, or other appropriating bodies that it is necessary to keep up with the growth of knowledge and the diversity of human interests. Many communities pay a high price for government- or trustee-imposed insufficiency in library support.

Exhaustive examination of ways to improve the library's financial situation may indicate that a referendum for an increased rate in tax support seems obligatory. This is a difficult step to take in periods of threatening taxpayers' revolts; however, it is a step in which the community at large should be involved. Library officials, even with the counsel of informed community leaders, often shun the democratic prerogative of the taxpayer when they assume that their fellow citizens would not be interested in overcoming adverse conditions that affect their own library. It is true that this is an age of tax resistance, but it is also an age of increasing citizen insistence on involvement in decision-making. Defeat of a referendum is not a disgrace; withholding from the people the knowledge of community problems and the opportunity to solve them is a disgrace.

Some communities have reached their funding peaks because they have dormant economies or because they have small and scattered populations which result in low tax bases. Even so, no library can afford to carry over a penurious attitude from a blighted environment into the era of systems. Insufficient funds are not necessarily responsible for closed minds, but a very small budget can inhibit thinking about ways to get out of predicaments, financial or otherwise. It is not easy to look beyond the obstacles of building, budgeting, and staffing deficiencies in an attempt to visualize improved services. Nevertheless, one of the obligations of modern librarianship and trusteeship is to recognize service needs and to take the necessary steps to secure adequate financing to provide for those needs.

An investigation into sources for adequate revenue may lead to proposals for the formation of a special district that may include neighboring libraries and adjacent areas without libraries in the interest of both a broader tax base and the improvement of services for all the people of an area. A library board that initiates or participates in discussions of the values of special library districts also assumes a position of leadership, which can pay dividends in local library development. The search for sound bases of area support for local libraries may also direct attention to weaknesses in state laws and, as a consequence, lead to close collaboration with those legislators who have concern not only for the voters in their district but also for the welfare of people at large.

Local improvement efforts also address themselves to the quality and capability of the personnel who translate resources into services. A good staff can be the dynamo that converts a small collection into a powerhouse of utility and stimulation for the community as a whole. All too often the trustees look at personnel in terms of what they cost in the aggregate of a salary budget rather than evaluating their present or potential contributions. An examination of personnel possibilities may suggest a long-term advantage to the small library in subsidizing a younger staff member for further training. Apprehensions of resignations and retirements, intensified by the lack of suitable replacements, may be resolved through system help in working out a contract for sharing the services of a trained librarian with a library board in a nearby community. A study of gaps in service may result in contracting for special personnel such as an itinerant children's librarian. In short, the frustrations of a local library in solving its personnel problems may be alleviated by system advice and counsel.

Other avenues for upgrading local services include an investigation of operational practices. A library may find through a self-study, or a system survey, that it is spending a disproportionate amount of time recovering overdue books, adapting catalog cards, or changing classifications of materials prepared by a processing center. Sarah Vann describes such activity as "tinkering within a 3 × 5 mentality."[2] It leads to an overload of work that does not count. Relief from unproductive routines allows more time for direct work with people. This may lead to another overload, but it is one which will be exciting and productive in fulfilling the local library's objectives.

Most small libraries have professional associates in the school libraries or media centers in the area. By initiating cooperative school and public library planning, the public librarians have an opportunity to further strengthen local library service. Joint planning is a means to formulate and test policies, practices, and communication channels that may ultimately eliminate unnecessary overlapping in materials and duplication of services, which neither the taxpayer nor the routine-burdened librarians can afford. Local public library responsibility for this role is explored further as a coordinating function in chapter 4.

The independent library can do much to help itself. Its resources for help range from the literature of the profession to the advisory and referral services of the cooperative system. The independent library remains in the current of upgrading service to the extent that it keeps in touch with the sources of professional knowledge of trends and improved methods and makes use of them.

Experienced system directors have found that initially it is the weakest member of the system who retains a reserve toward full system relationships after affiliation. For example, the small library with the most critical problems may completely ignore such assistance available through the system consultant staff. Statistical reports on member use of system services seem to indicate that the weaker libraries may lack even the energy to draw on system collections for the needed strength in materials to meet daily needs. The cooperative system has a responsibility to foster in its member libraries an awareness of their obligations to know and to use system services for the sake of their own patrons. No system staff member is to be expected to coerce an administrator or a library board to use system facilities. They suggest. They make every effort to establish friendly working relations. They may never go through a member library town without stopping at the library. One system director's regular salutation is, "I was just passing by." Through an acquaintance with system personnel and through system communications or informal reports on how neighboring libraries use the system, the weaker library begins to sense the meaning of system service and to make the effort to know more about how it works.

There are many ways to find out what cooperative system services exist and what services are in the planning stage. The simplest way is to ask. The system director and the consultant staff thrive on answering questions. Their days and nights are spent in attendance at meetings of local boards and in conferences with librarians, trustee representatives, and government officials, singly or in groups. They do not expect everybody in the system circle to react with understanding or enthusiasm. They have infinite patience for interpretation and in-depth explanations. This is an important part of their job since the process of interpreting tends to clarify their own thinking and gives them better insight into points of possible ambiguity in communication.

Still another step to be taken in the process of understanding the functioning of a system is to participate in meetings, workshops, and training courses. Forward-looking member libraries send representatives to group meetings because they are certain that their attendance will ultimately be translated into improved library service. Librarians and trustees of independent libraries contribute in some measure to their own communities, or they would not be in positions of responsibility. The cooperative system offers them an opportunity to enlarge the scope of these positions through the assumption of their rightful place in system affairs. Whitman pointed out that poets to be great need great audiences. The system meetings, too, need great audiences to generate the thrust for wider and more active participation. Originality is not necessarily required at system meetings; involvement is.

Member libraries have a major responsibility to contribute to the system. Skeptics may wonder what a small handicapped library can possibly add to a vigorous system program. Size or apparent limitations are not necessarily important criteria for judging potential contributions. The very small library may be the holder of an unusual collection of regional history. It may own a rare book collection important to scholars. It may have a staff member who is a specialist in some field of knowledge. It may be the home library for a key legislator. It may be an important source of prepublished information on socioeconomic change in the area. It may become a testing ground for system innovations. Its participation will reinforce the principle that system programs and operations are designed for all member libraries regardless of size or strength. The small library's greatest contribution may be in its own utilization of system advice and help in becoming a model among member libraries.

Responsibilities of the System

Systems of all types are shaped by their own individualized plans of service. A plan of service, by any name, defines the role of the system in library development and the scope of its responsibilities. An individual plan of service may be considered as a broadly conceived statement of program reflecting the objectives of the system and its framework for basic supportive services and experimental flexibility.

In some states the formation and subsequent refinements of a plan are correlated with a statewide development program. In others, a plan may evolve through the interaction of permissive legislation, recognition of needs by a concentration of individual libraries, and leadership for organization. The plans of service that exist throughout the country represent divergent approaches and emphases. Two elements unifying the many system plans are the principle of universal access to the wealth of materials available in the nation's libraries and the ambition to improve direct service at the local level.

A plan of service, to have an impact on library development, must be backed up by solid financing and a high degree of professionalism in staffing. Obviously a system will not aim at goals far beyond its current financial or human capabilities. Sometimes, however, a system is unable to aim high enough. An example is a system, circumscribed by inadequate funding or insufficient strength among member libraries, that is limited to a program so low-pitched that it makes very little difference whether the system exists or not. Projections for the future indicate that there may even be a merging of relatively strong systems to take advantage of consolidation of funds, personnel, resources, and plans to improve existing system services and to prepare for the most advantageous use of forthcoming and costly products of technology and highly specialized research facilities.

A plan of service may be considered first among the continuing responsibilities of the system. A plan at the system level requires both stability and changeability, which on the surface may seem to be contradictory elements. Nevertheless, it is a system responsibility to take the lead in implementing the plan with such standard and innovative services as may be agreed on as essential ongoing benefits. It is also a system responsibility to condition the plan, with membership help, so that it can be adapted to the unexpected and thus open up untried opportunities.

Systems, whether newly formed or well established, are as vulnerable to the risks of preoccupation with narrow interests and devotion to established programs as are the individual libraries, which were accused in the 1960s of "doing nothing but more of the same." However, many systems in their reviews of annual accomplishments seem to be asking, "What is the system not doing that it should be doing?" At the same time the Nelson survey reminds the profession that "system trustees and directors need to give much more attention to identifying and analyzing the library needs of their communities."[3] The plan of service in appendix A is an example of a plan revised by joint evaluation and planning by a cooperative system and representatives of its member libraries.

The cooperative system, distinct from its member libraries, is capable of finding out directly and systematically what the needs of its clients are and of forecasting what they will be in the immediate future. Systems have a responsibility to get behind the static picture of library conditions depicted by the annual compilation of statistics taken so seriously by many librarians and their trustees. Statistics tell nothing about obsolescence or currency in collections or about the quality of performance in an individual library. A system must correlate facts with human contacts. It has a responsibility to get out in the field, to observe, and to consult with member librarians and trustees. Field visits have no bearing on a system policy of nonintervention. They are a means for deepening system insights into membership problems and fostering effective working relationships between the system staff and the member librarians and their governing boards.

The investigations carried on by systems to identify member library needs that are compatible with cooperative system planning uncover many concerns librarians hold in common. These naturally vary from system to system, depending on the degree of sophistication in the member library situations. They may be as simple as the need for comparative cost analyses of bookkeeping methods. They may be as complex as the demand for cost figures on the conversion of library circulation records to a computer. The more complex needs lead to the research responsibilities of the cooperative system, discussed in chapter 4.

It is a system responsibility to make clear to the member libraries the channels through which any project or activity must go to become a reality. A membership-supported proposal involving policy or financing may have to go through one or more governing bodies for approval. It may be temporarily blocked for comparative investigation because someone at some level of authority thinks he has a better idea. A project may cost more than was estimated and may have to wait for a budget review or for a search for additional sources of funding. The process of implementing a system project may be identical to that experienced by the independent library administrators in inaugurating new local services. However, it does not necessarily follow that they will recognize that the "miracle workers" at the system level have an order of business similar to their own. Once a cooperative system has been established, the members seem to experience a low pain threshold. They need to be reminded that a system has some kind of supervision or government. They need even more to be informed by the system headquarters staff of the justifications for delays. The patience of the membership is never more critically required than at the point at which it is exhausted.

A major responsibility of the system staff is to reinforce the collaborative nature of the system. The success of a cooperative system depends not only on visible services and evidence of cooperation but also on collaboration in viewpoints and ideas and on sharing the background detail of the evolving program. The system staff must master the human touch in seeking participatory reactions from the membership. A "we-they" attitude on the part of the system staff or the member libraries is indicative of a loss of vision and understanding of the purpose of the system.

It is a system responsibility to keep alive the sense of mission that stimulated library pioneers and inspires the outstanding among contemporary librarians. The significance of modern library philosophy has yet to be translated to the small library that seeks system affiliation just for the sake of a spruced-up status quo. Consequently, another responsibility of members of the system staff is to assume some of the functions of library educators. One of their assignments as educators is the continuous reinterpretation of the objectives of the profession, not just in relation to the distant goals of a national network of all types of libraries, but in the practical context of what their system intends to accomplish to help librarians become ever more expert and professional in their daily work with patrons.

Another educational responsibility of the system is to make certain that the system's plan and mode of operation, the scope of its consultative and material services, and the values of its fact-finding procedures are understood not only by its charter members but also by the newcomers among administrators and trustees. A system staff, like their colleagues in the administrative ranks of the independent libraries, cannot take it for granted that all of their associates have grasped the total content of an informational meeting, or even that they have listened.

A system staff serves in many ways as a synthesizer. Their operational responsibilities involve the combining of ideas, resources, professional knowledge, technical expertise, communication skills, and transportation facilities to fulfill the plan of service. It is their job to order such combinations at a pace that will stimulate but not overwhelm their own office force or the member libraries. Synthesis may involve financial agreements for services from strong libraries within and outside the system for the benefit of all of the public served by the members of the system. It may lead to contracting for the services of specialists outside the library field. It will involve the state library and other public library systems. In working with government officials and area planning groups it is a system responsibility to keep alert to the merger potentials for libraries. The function of the system in an overall process of synthesis is to keep libraries moving to meet the needs of the ordinary and the extraordinary man faced with new and compelling sociotechnical problems.

Obviously the intent of a system is to relate all of its efforts to the needs of all of its members. Criticism of some systems in general has brought out at least two points of controversy, which indicate that the intent of systemwide service has not been made clear. One is the opinion that some systems seem to focus undue attention on the problems of the weakest member. The other is the certainty that a strong library in the system that holds contracts for service to all members has an advantage over a neighboring library of comparable service potential. The first example underscores the importance of equality in distributing system services. Anything less serves only to support the opponents of the system movement. The second example points to the responsibility of the system to maintain a balance between competing membership units. Emerging needs for services may be handled by more than one library in the system. Specialization in collection building, for example, provides an opportunity for member libraries to share in providing prestige services on behalf of the system. In the last analysis, however, the deciding factor in resolving of system problems is the welfare of the total system and of all of the people who may use system facilities.

Another responsibility of the system is to distinguish between popular fads and those creative innovations that have real promise. Librarians in general do not know too much about innovations. The word itself has different connotations for different people. The experienced administrator knows that not all of the so-called innovations publicized in the sixties are necessarily suitable for every library and that long-established projects are not necessarily obsolete. Some librarians with experience in inner city projects have expressed doubts about the capacity of the profession to innovate.[4] It is possible, however, to read into those doubts a challenge—one that the system can accept.

Thus, a system has a responsibility to clarify the meaning of "innovation" for its own membership. Is it a label for novel solutions to small problems, or does it stand for significant change that contributes, perhaps in successive stages, to the overall plan of service? The cooperative system has an opportunity to clear away the mystic aura associated with innovations. It is in a position to take planned risks in a search for methods that will more quickly fulfill its plan of service. A part of its job is to experiment with ideas, with new forms of materials, and with new types of equipment in order to have a reliable pool of knowledge for the guidance of member libraries and for its own use.

The cooperative system has an opportunity, because of the widespread professional interest in innovative programs, to develop guidelines that may give greater assurance to the development of suitable and productive innovations for either the member libraries or the system. These guidelines should emphasize the following major points: (1) the specific purpose of the innovative program; (2) the identification of the people it is intended to reach; (3) the quality of materials, physical facilities, and procedures built into the plan of operation; (4) the qualifications of personnel expected to handle the program; (5) the projected costs on an experimental or continuing basis; (6) the potential for community participation in counseling and evaluation; and (7) the specifics in the objectives and anticipated results that lend themselves to measurement and evaluation.

A cooperative system is responsibile for helping its member libraries meet and exceed recognized standards of service. The system provides a structure through which its own results can be evaluated and, by means of continuous feedback, improved and refined. The corporate knowledge gained from the experiences of all the systems in the country provides an opportunity for libraries through their systems to make direct contributions to the periodic revision and upgrading of standards on the national level.

A cooperative system has a concern and a responsibility for extending library service to areas where the public has no ready access to libraries. Library service may be non-existent in an existing community, in new suburbs, in a small unincorporated village, or in the vast expanse of farm country. In cooperation with areawide planning organizations, a cooperative system may assemble the necessary data on which to base recommendations on alternative methods of closing the gaps in library services.

Planning organizations, governmental or private, have strong interests in the provision of excellent library facilities as part of a master plan for an area. The relationships between trained planners and system directors are good because the objectives of both deal with the improvement of the quality of life for all people. Professional planners borrow library building standards and other pertinent professional literature from the system for background understanding of what the library specialists are saying. Some governmental planning departments request occasional reports from community library boards to ascertain their thinking about future library outlets at the periphery of an incorporated area. At the same time they open up their files to library planners. Planning organizations are able to provide cooperative system specialists with detailed studies in demography, land use, tax revenues, zoning, economic forecasting, population characteristics, and estimates of when an area will change.

The system specialist uses this type of information together with a knowledge of professional problems, in guiding interested officials and citizen groups to the most effective means of providing library services to an unserved area.

In working toward the extension of library service the system can be more than a catalyst. By bringing representatives of neighboring communities together and by interpreting both the data and the values of combined efforts, the system can help to create larger and more viable libraries. Following the principle of building on strength, these larger units often will include existing libraries as well as extending service to formerly unserved areas.

Where the population is scattered, the benefits of library services may be demonstrated by the system through bookmobiles and/or library study center outlets. Such efforts need thorough planning, with participation of community members. Specific goals and timetables should be established for achieving community financing of the realistic costs of services provided. When practicable, the demonstrations might be provided by an existing nearby library, with system financing during the demonstration period in order to create a basis for continuing relationships.

Many additional system responsibilities, though correlated with official plans, may not be spelled out in a formal way. These include: (1) the interpretation of significant trends in the profession, such as those related to the concern for defensive measures in support of intellectual freedom; (2) the provision of background understanding of environmental and social problems which alter concepts of service, illustrated by the profession's emphasis on service to the disadvantaged of all races; (3) the participation in long-range planning with interdisciplinary and cross-professional groups, for example, in the field of adult education; (4) representation on behalf of the system's interests in legislative councils, at intersystem meetings, to the communications media, and at ceremonial functions; and (5) leadership in the establishment of networks comprising all types of libraries.

Joint Responsibilities

A cooperative system has many advantages in an organizational structure that gives the system staff and the system members responsibilities in common. Joint responsibilities lead to an involvement that fosters the understanding, loyalty, and enthusiasm that are requisites for fulfilling professional aspirations exemplified by system programs.

A prime responsibility that systems and their members hold in common is the nurturing of an environment in which the role of the public library as well as that of the system may be periodically reexamined and redefined. A currently unanswered question faces the library world: What should the public library be? This is a difficult question to be answered by a profession scattered throughout the nation and subject to disparate local or regional attitudes toward solutions of social, educational, and economic problems. It is a question the partners within a system have a responsibility to probe for themselves and on behalf of the many publics they represent. The answer has a bearing on the future of both the system and its member libraries.

Relationships within a cooperative system are guided by a plan through which both the system staff and the member libraries can exercise equal influence in recommending new directions, policies, and projects that are of major importance to the greatest number. It is a basic principle of a cooperative system that it concentrate its energy on programs of universal benefit and in an order of priorities that will give the quickest returns to the people who use public libraries today or who may be motivated to use public libraries tomorrow. The establishment of these priorities is a joint responsibility.

It should be obvious to all thoughtful participants that a co-operative system program must be grounded in the surety of knowledge gained from studies of actual conditions. The establishment or refinement of a system program requires a body of facts that will expose the nature of each problem and will perhaps give a sense of the best alternatives for solution. Requests for detailed information from local library records are acceptable to cooperative system members when the purpose of the research is made clear. One of the values of joint responsibilities is the fact that librarians who understand their problems can serve as the intelligence corps for the system specialists. An appreciation of the local library's potential for matching contributions through sharing its experience creates a professional spirit that assures a base of confidence needed to advance the system program and to encourage local effort.

A major joint responsibility is to protect the general welfare through fair and equal distribution of system services and resources. All system participants must guard against the exploitation of services by a selfish or misguided few. This guardianship is guaranteed by membership participation in the framing of policies and regulations, which will not be considered arbitrary if they are reasonable and express the views of a substantial majority.

The cooperative system and its member libraries have a joint responsibility in the identification and development of the talent and special skills of member administrators, staff, and trustees. Member librarians can help identify potential system workshop leaders from the local staff or the board. The system staff can be on the alert to find librarians and trustees from the membership who have the appropriate experience to assist in advising other communities. The system can recognize talent in member libraries by enlisting the help of experienced leaders for on-site, in-service training in neighboring libraries.

The cooperative system can provide a clearinghouse for the placement of personnel and create an informal career ladder for librarians who are ready to move from one library to another. A cooperative system may have a policy of searching first within its member libraries to fill a position on the system staff. System administrators should always be on the alert to find interested and articulate trustees who are willing to take positions of leadership in the system or on state and national levels. The system can establish data files on personnel in member libraries who have the background to serve as consultants on building programs, adult education projects, or special services. The system should have an interest in the talents of both the experienced and the newcomer. In the last third of the century, the profession is characterized by a social concern and a social energy unmatched in library history. The system has an obligation to the future to make use of this energy as a vital resource for developing excellence in library service and for building a corps of leadership for the decades ahead.

Interpretation of the objectives, the program, and at times even the problems of the cooperative system is a joint responsibility. The system staff may be the most articulate among the interpreters, but informed system members are likely to be the most convincing in their home territory. As the system matures, its staff and representatives of the member libraries can serve as a team of interpreters. An integral part of this joint responsibility is to carry the message of system services to the local staff, who may be the last link in the chain of communication but are the most actively engaged in direct service to the public.

The audience for interpretations must include the staff and the boards of directors of the member libraries. It may include nonmember library neighbors, legislative and government officials, and the press. The public at large is also a natural target.

Subjects for interpretation multiply with the expansion of the system program. They may range from an explanation of what a system is to descriptions of specific services. Interpretations of system developments add new dimensions to public relations in a local community and in the system area.

As the cooperative system develops, evaluation of system services and their use becomes a joint responsibility. System headquarters will provide the methodology and machinery for evaluation in specific areas. Evaluations are likely to be systematic and objective. A less formal aspect of evaluation comes into the picture when the member librarian makes every effort to ascertain how much library service has been improved in the local community because of the local library's knowledge and skill in the use of system resources. Proof of the effectiveness of joint responsibilities comes at the point where system members do not wait for formal evaluations but consciously engage in a continuing appraisal of the quality of their own use of system services.

The administrator of the member library and the director of the system are independent agents working at different levels. Their individual responsibilities, as will be seen in following chapters, are complementary rather than competitive. Neither position is superior. As Andrew Geddes has pointed out, a cooperative system does not have a systemwide director, in the usual sense of this term, "to take charge of, to dominate or influence, to handle, direct, govern."[5] The local administrator and the system director have separate and joint responsibilities, to which the trustee adds perspective and objectivity in moving forward to meet the precise library needs of contemporary society.

Interagency and Intergovernmental Relations

The library system provides a unique opportunity to bring about cooperative activities with other public service agencies, representatives of government, and the academic community. As a representative of its combined membership, the system is in a position of considerable influence. In addition, the system knows what cooperation is and the benefits that result from it.

Area offices of public service agencies, such as the fields of mental health, conservation, service to the blind and the visually handicapped, are staffed with experts who are counterparts of a cooperative system staff. Referrals, communications, and interchanges of special skills are possible areas of cooperation with them. A system staff may provide public agencies with fresh insights into the services available at and through the community library, to which the agencies can direct their own clients. The system also may serve as a center for materials, such as cassettes for the visually handicapped. It may be a distribution point for the dissemination of information bulletins on conservation and other subjects of immediate citizen concern. The agency and the system may cooperate in planning workshops for librarians and agency personnel on the literature of a special field such as mental health or in planning demonstrations of such unique equipment as the talking book.

The relationship between the cooperative system and units of local government vary from system to system. Many systems involve mayors, city managers, tax experts, and area planners in their workshop programs. In other parts of the country, local government has sought the assistance and advice of the system director in organizing new libraries. System initiative has led to meetings of representatives from two or more neighboring jurisdictions to examine the feasibility of forming multicommunity library districts.

The state library may use the cooperative system as its liaison with individual local libraries and communities without library service. In this relationship, requests to the state library from the local community for assistance on library problems are referred to the appropriate system for investigation and probable solution. The state library may also use the systems for funneling information to or gathering information from the local libraries. With this sort of cooperation, the state library staff is able to concentrate on the broader problems of libraries in relation to the responsibilities of the state government for library service.

As the representative of the general public libraries of the area, the system can explore cooperative sharing of resources with area college, junior college, school, and special libraries. The public library cooperative system has the responsibility for establishing the local and area foundation for a national network of libraries of all types.

Trustee-Administrator Relationships

Trustees of libraries and librarians are coleaders in one of the most promising ventures in public service: the transformation of public libraries in all communities into indispensable resources for every individual. This effort involves not only the trustees empowered with specific legal duties but also the trustees with advisory functions. There is much to be done. The Nelson survey, for example, emphasizes "the special responsibility of public libraries and public library systems to exercise their full capacity for leadership in bringing about an effective articulation of all segments of the library effort in the communities and regions which they serve."[6] This recommendation points to a promising era of collaboration at local, system, and state levels between trustees and librarians of differing backgrounds, experiences, and philosophies regarding service.

It is foreseeable that the trustee-librarian collaboration will also deal with social issues and technological developments as they relate to library methods, which may seem to be far removed from current concerns of the small community. This shift in problem areas will enhance rather than diminish the rights, powers, and prerogatives of the citizen serving on governing or advisory boards.

An assessment of the potential of trustee contributions indicates that the most important responsibilities related to planning and collaboration in the immediate future, aside from those made mandatory by state law, include: (1) selection and/or support of a competent administrator, (2) continuing appraisal of the strengths and weaknesses of local library services in relation to standards and the needs of people, (3) purposeful participation in all opportunities to strengthen the cooperative system and its member libraries, and (4) involvement in legislative activities and other types of planning for a comprehensive and effective national network of libraries.

The distinction between the roles of the system director, the librarian, and the trustee in collaborative efforts to improve library service are determined by a combination of elements such as the provisions in the law, policies on the division of responsibilities, and opportunities provided in a plan of service for effective working relationships. In oversimplified terms, the role of the system director may be defined as that of a stimulator, an investigator, a planner, and an initiator. The role of the trustee is that of the representative of the people, a transmitter of information, a friendly critic, and a knowledgeable judge. The role of the librarian is that of an administrator and an advocate of any program that will really move the library forward in the achievement of its goals.

The responsibility for taking maximum advantage of these roles is generally assumed at the cooperative system level. At this point all of the techniques of encouraging collaboration come into play, with a major focus on getting the three types of role players into communication. An illustration is the type of brainstorming sessions used by the Illinois Suburban Library System to bring the system staff, the trustees, and the member librarians together to pool every possible dream of ideal service. The ideas at one session ranged from recommendations for a twenty-four-hour reference center to a proposal to use a helicopter for quick deliveries. Brainstorming is followed by a practical evaluation session, which once again necessitates a meshing of roles in setting priorities for new steps in the system program. It is at the system level that the librarian-trustee collaboration finds its greatest stimulus for carry-over to local library service.

The Library Board of Trustees

The board of trustees is the traditional foundation stone in the structure of public library administration. Library board members are generally appointed or elected, although there are some self-perpetuating boards and privately controlled boards.[7] Trusteeship is regarded by some observers as being part of the establishment. Trusteeship may be more correctly viewed in the 1970s as the conscience of the community, as more and more trustees act on a conviction that extraordinary efforts must be made to provide access to strong library resources. The concern of articulate trustees has been a major support factor in legislative action, which has been the legal and financial backbone for system development. In many instances trustee evaluation of the merits of shared responsibility canceled out the initial apprehensions of the professional staff. The capacity of the trustees to change to meet the changing dictates of their communities is not to be underestimated. On balance, trusteeship has become an effective asset for change.

Consolidation of the tangible and intangible benefits of trusteeship for the library of tomorrow is dependent on a number of factors: (1) the spread of sensitivity to the changing values of society, (2) a confident and harmonious working relationship between trustees and librarians, (3) maximum exposure to new ideas and trends in library management and services, (4) openness in communication for the assessment of changing needs, (5) the availability of dependable information for analysis and problem-solving, and (6) genuinely productive opportunities for trustees to share in the planning and the action of library development programs.

Citizens become library trustees through a variety of political or socioeconomic circumstances. Rarely does an individual assume the position with a complete understanding of trustee responsibilities or with a recognition that trusteeship has become a trust involving unprecedented opportunities to contribute to the effectiveness of all libraries as information and cultural centers.

Introducing new trustees to their duties as members of the board of an independent library is the joint responsibility of the librarian, the experienced members of the board, and, upon invitation from the local board, members of the system staff. The framework many libraries use for this introduction is an orientation meeting scheduled separately or held in conjunction with a series of regular board meetings. The purpose of the orientation session is simply to inform. It is designed to provide background knowledge of procedures and an understanding of the philosophy of the board as reflected in policies and services and in its working relationship with the librarian, the staff, and the system. A successful orientation shortens the time a new member needs for knowledgeable participation in board affairs.

The orientation agenda naturally varies from library to library. The basics commonly needing interpretation include:

1. Requirements of state law regarding
   a. Duties of the board

   b. Tenure, as determined by appointment provisions or election laws
   c. Extent or limitation of legal authority
   d. Directives for open meetings
2. Board-librarian relationships
3. Organization of the board
   a. Bylaws and rules of order
   b. Committee functions and relation to the board as a whole
4. Board responsibilities associated with
   a. Library objectives
   b. Library financing and budgeting
   c. Policy formation and review
   d. Library standards
   e. Intellectual freedom
   f. Public and governmental relations
   g. Evaluation of local library resources and services
   h. Long-range planning
   i. Participation in system planning and activities
   j. Library legislation
   k. Membership in trustee associations.

The materials to be distributed at orientation meetings may include:

1. Copy of the library law
2. Bylaws of the board
3. Roster of board members and staff
4. Policy statements
   a. Book or library materials selection policies
   b. Personnel policies
   c. General administrative policies
   d. Use of auditoriums and meeting rooms
   e. Gifts of money or materials
5. Job descriptions and salary schedules
6. Copies of recent annual and monthly reports
7. Sample publicity materials
8. Trustee manuals
9. System bulletins and communications.

The job of informing the new trustee about the affairs of the local board does not end with the completion of an orientation series. Details of verbal explanations fade with the passage of time and under the pressure of the trustees' nonlibrary obligations. It should be anticipated that renewed interpretations of orientation topics are a normal part of a continuing dialogue between librarians and trustees.

The duties of a board of trustees in a small community in a system age have risen from the plane of repetitious routine to a level of interlibrary collaboration that has created absorbing new subjects for trustee exploration and has changed the fabric of board agendas.

System affiliation, however, does not remove the following basic responsibilities of the boards of member libraries:

1. Complying with the terms of state law
2. Selecting and supporting an administrator
3. Delegating authority to the administrator
4. Securing maximum financing for effective operation
5. Supervising the use of funds and other assets
6. Establishing and reviewing goals and policies
7. Establishing salary schedules and personnel benefits
8. Supporting a climate of intellectual freedom
9. Serving as a court of last resort in areas of personnel problems and public criticisms
10. Evaluating the library program
11. Identifying changing needs of the community
12. Interpreting the library to the community
13. Interpreting the system program to the community
14. Representing the library in governmental, civic, and cultural affairs
15. Participating in trustee workshops and trustee association meetings
16. Planning for future library developments
17. Studying and engaging in legislative activities designed to strengthen libraries.

The System Representative

An independent library board joins a cooperative system from a conviction that system affiliation will have cumulative benefits for the men, women, and children who depend on the facilities of the community library. It is a voluntary act. It is usually signified by an affirmative vote recorded in the minutes of the board. This usually is followed by some form of contractual agreement for membership in the system within the terms of the law and the rules and regulations established by the system for the benefit of all member libraries.

Many cooperative systems require that the independent library board appoint or elect one member to serve as a representative at meetings of the system board, which may be elected from the body of these representatives. This sort of member representation guarantees the independent library a voice in system affairs and an opportunity to share in planning for expanding services and in the evaluation of established services. It also serves as a training ground for representatives who may be willing at some time to run for a position on the system board.

Representatives from libraries of all sizes can make valuable contributions to the system board by presenting insights and viewpoints on the needs of those sectors of the system area with which they are familiar. Their role at meetings of the local board is to keep their fellow trustees informed, to interpret system developments, and to gather local information or opinions for the system board as needed. In short, representatives are responsible for promoting two-way communication. Both system directors and member librarians usually make provisions in the agendas of their respective board meetings for reporting, for observations, and for suggestions. In some cooperative systems the area of communication is widened through the scheduling of meetings for neighboring trustees and staff people so that they can hear progress reports from representatives on policy changes, expanding system services, and long-range planning.

In those systems without a formal framework for local representation other than the system board itself, attendance at system board meetings by representatives of member library boards should be considered an obligation of membership. Each local library might appoint one of its board members to be responsible for liaison with the system board. The system board should not be expected to work in a vacuum and act on behalf of the membership without the advice and participation of each member library.

The system director, like the independent librarian, plans orientation meetings for system trustee representatives to improve their understanding of the system level of operation and its approach to problems of growth and change in relation to membership needs. An agenda may include:

1. A review of the history of the system and its plan of service
2. A statement on the organization and responsibilities of the system board

3. An explanation of the system financial structure
4. Introduction of the system staff
5. Progress reports on existing services
6. An introduction to projected plans
7. A discussion of intersystem relationships and projects
8. An interpretation of system relationships with the state library
9. An explanation of rules and regulations
10. A discussion of the role of the system representative in communication, planning, legislation, and evaluation.

System Board

The official board of a cooperative system is customarily composed of active trustees who represent the member libraries. Membership on the system board is a position of major importance. When a trustee of a member library also becomes a director on the system board,

> he retains all of his original responsibilities and adds a number more. Not only is he required to attend meetings regularly, but to assume the obligations attendant on governing the system organization. By law the board is assigned the duty of determining and directing the course toward the objectives of the system; on it rests the responsibility for its success. This calls for more than one's mere presence; it means informing oneself in many fields of library concern, studying carefully all issues, exercising sound judgment in voting for pending measures, evolving imaginative solutions to knotty problems, extending one's influence not only into the community but into high places of professional organization and state government, and finally maximizing one's own capacities for leadership both unofficially and in official roles. To perform these tasks excellently calls for time and energy allocated in quantities sometimes inadequately planned for by prospective board members.[8]

The specific duties of the system board include the standard responsibilities of all boards regarding finance, control of assets, development of services, and policies. (An illustration of bylaws developed by one cooperative system is to be found in appendix B.) The major responsibilities of the system board include:

1. Selection of a highly competent director

2. Continuous development of a plan of service to supplement the work of all member libraries
3. Coordination of the plan of service with the laws or directives of the state
4. Establishment of priorities in the plan of service
5. Approval of budgets for system services and activities
6. Promulgation of contractual services
7. Interpretation of the system and its services
8. Initiation of needed research
9. Periodic evaluation of the system program
10. Approval of project proposals for state or federal funding
11. Maintenance of a balance between competing constituencies
12. Encouragement of intersystem and interagency cooperation
13. Analysis and study of the current and anticipated needs of the member libraries
14. Development of guidelines for dealing with problem areas
15. Development of recommendations for the strengthening or clarification of state and federal library legislation
16. Participation in legislative networks.

A number of basic tenets have been found to be effective guidelines for cooperative system boards:

1. The system will be strong and effective to the extent that it encourages and makes maximum use of professional competence on its system staff and among the member libraries.
2. The system will more quickly achieve its goals as it builds on the strength of member libraries.
3. The system plan of service should be designed to provide services that are beyond the funding or operating powers of the independent library or can be more efficiently provided cooperatively.
4. Rules and regulations should be kept to a minimum and established only for economy, efficiency, or equity in services, programs, and procedures.
5. The system program is of maximum acceptability when it is designed to benefit all participating libraries or when it adds to their collective effectiveness.
6. The system is justified in serving as an experimental laboratory for library development as a means of preserving the best out of the past and of inaugurating innovative programs that may have value for all members.

7. The system has an obligation to seek solutions to library problems through research.
8. The system must be cognizant of the possibility that it may have to deal with two authorities in any member library: the librarian and the board. Consequently, system policies and practices must focus on objectives and programs that encourage unity in purpose and action on the part of local authorities and the system.

Advisory Councils and Committees

A potential source of strength for cooperative system development is to be found in the diversity of experience, personal philosophies, and conflicting opinions among adminisrators of member libraries. It is a strength that must have outlets if it is to have any constructive bearing on the democratic processes of a cooperative system. These outlets take the form of advisory councils, advisory boards, and committees.

A librarians' advisory council, which has been organized by some systems, has a purely advisory function, as its name suggests. Its members are head librarians or their appointed representatives. The council meets as a body several times a year to react, to question, to criticize, and to make recommendations to the system director and board. Advisory council meetings have a number of side benefits. They can be a focal point for the dissemination of information, for the interpretation of the rationale behind system board decisions, for the generating of new ideas, for the clearing up of misunderstandings, and even for rechanneling of the energy to be found in opposition. Advisory council meetings set up an environment that stimulates a natural two-way flow of advice and opinion among professionals working on various levels for a common purpose.

The specific functions of an advisory council may be:

1. Advising the system director and system staff in:
   a. Identifying service needs
   b. Establishing priorities
   c. Recommending modifications in the routines of ongoing services
   d. Selecting subject fields for in-service training and workshops
   e. Determining areas for research

    f. Planning for evaluation of specific services
2. Relaying communications to the personnel in individual libraries
3. Assisting the system staff in the execution of system programs, such as in-service training workshops
4. Serving as support task forces in legislative networks
5. Supporting the system staff in interpretations of the system's objectives, programs, and plans to school and special librarians, trustees, and the public
6. Making specific recommendations to the system board.

In their bylaws some advisory councils also provide for elected executive committees to expedite the consultative and advisory functions of the council between meetings.

Regional advisory committees, made up of representatives of the administrators of member libraries, are a modification of advisory councils. They are used chiefly in areas where transportation or schedule adjustments are difficult. The purpose of a regional advisory committee is again chiefly advisory. Its advantage is its small size. Its disadvantage is the danger that communication might become limited to the small group.

Serving on an advisory council may be a learning experience. Participation will broaden the librarian's understanding of the theories, principles, and problems of system operation—necessary knowledge for sound decision-making. The system that provides the opportunity for each local administrator to serve in an advisory capacity from time to time will have knowledgeable and understanding constituents.

Objectives of Library Service

Library objectives are goals that have been identified by trustees, administrators, and staff as valid and feasible within the capabilities of an individual library or a system of libraries. The goals of public librarianship were subject to spirited probing in the late sixties and early seventies. Two dominant schools of thought emerged. One emphasized redefinition of library goals to concentrate on involvement with social problems and domestic issues. The second underscored the conviction that it is not necessarily the goals that need changing but the emphasis placed on their implementation.[9]

Local Library Objectives

The formulation of objectives is a responsibility of each independent library. To be useful to the small library, objectives must be: (1) achievable in terms of the skills of the staff, who will be charged with their fulfillment, (2) feasible in relation to cost, and (3) directly relative to the needs of the people who use or will use the library.

A model set of objectives is to be found in the text of *Minimum Standards for Public Library Systems, 1966*.[10] These objectives are basic and have universal application. Their excellence has encouraged some libraries to adopt them rather than to work out their own. The adoption of a published and professionally approved set of objectives in its entirety has drawbacks. It requires little effort, but it cuts off a process of self-examination. It tends to perpetuate the traditional. It places subsequent decision-making in a category of improvisation on words that were intended to describe universal rather than individualized objectives. It provides no opportunity for the involvement of staff and trustees in an examination of the status quo or in exploration of new directions.

A board-staff discussion approach to objectives provides a channel for sharpening not only the objectives, but attitudes and vision. The charge that the public library faces either a challenge or a catastrophe must initially be faced at the level of objectives. The examination and reexamination of local objectives are the first steps in developing a sensitivity to respond to society's problems.

One of the difficulties in the establishment or review of a library's objectives to meet the needs of both the served and the unserved is the reliance on assumptions or incomplete knowledge of the needs of the total population. A system has an advantage in that it is able to poll its constituents—the member libraries— to quickly determine the value of a particular objective. The process for gaining insight into public satisfaction with existing or changing library goals on a community level is more involved. Techniques designed to test public reaction to the goals of the independent library and their implementation have included: questionnaires distributed with the cooperation of the billing department of the local water works; house-to-house interviews conducted by the library staff or in cooperation with community study groups; involvement of community leaders from racial, national, or occupational groups in evaluation; and the use of organizations such as the Friends of the Library as sounding boards. The most familiar technique is the analysis of statistics and studies of community trends.

Factors Affecting Library Objectives

Among the traditional factors that have influenced the formulation of objectives for the independent library are the laws establishing the nature and the government of the library organization; the available or potential funding; characteristics of the population; and the economic, cultural, and educational status of the community. The problems of a mobile, demanding, and confused society have projected additional elements into any consideration of library objectives. These are many, but prime among them are the economic and cultural gaps between the affluent and the disadvantaged; the quality of human relations in the community; barriers in communication and cooperation; citizen response to shifts in morality and mores; change in educational methods and curriculum content; the existence or lack of opportunity for continuing education; and the rights of majorities and minorities in an age of high taxes, group pressures, and fears for the future.

The critical problems of modern society are found in all communities, large and small. Differences lie in the individualistic approaches to problems which are evident in every region. The objectives of an individual library reflect that individualism. They must be appropriate for the times. They must be realistic. They must be understood and acceptable to all who work for their fulfillment.

Trustee and staff exploration of the objectives of a library frequently stays on an idealistic plane of relating the values of the library to mankind at large. This can be a heartwarming and sight-lifting experience. The examination must also be undertaken in the practical context of finances, personnel, resources for material, and space. There must be answers to such questions as: What qualifications are needed in a staff to attain the library's objectives? What kind of materials is needed? What does adopting a specific new objective do to the work load? Does an old objective still have merit? What changes in goals are possible because of system affiliation?

Objectives of a Library System

The base for a statement of objectives for a library system often is the broad goal expressed in the law establishing the system. From this base the system develops its operating objectives.

Objectives, to be useful to the cooperative system, must be (1) compatible with the objectives of the member libraries; (2) achieveable through adequate funding, staffing, and cooperative effort; (3) flexible in approaches to problem-solving and (4) measurable.

A statement of objectives probably gathers less dust than any other document produced by the independent library or the system. Objectives are an essential in the establishment of specific goals, the preparation of budgets, and the development policies. They provide the impetus for unified effort in all units of an organization. They are the starting point for the preparation and maintenance of procedure manuals. They serve as directives for coordinated planning. They aid in restoring program balance at times when a single goal may be receiving undue emphasis. The statement of objectives is particularly useful to new administrators, staff, and trustees in getting an overview of the scope and direction of the institution's programs and activities.

Financing

Independent control of finances is a well-established principle of management among cooperative systems. The board of a community library is responsible for securing and budgeting funds from local taxation. The board of a cooperative system has authority over the use of funds allocated to the system. Funds received from the state government ordinarily are controlled by formulas adopted by the state legislature. The usual formulas are based on population and square miles of area served by a system. Cooperative system funds are appropriated for the purpose of generally raising the general level of library service and equalizing such service throughout the area served. System funds are not for direct financial aid to local libraries as is equalization aid provided directly from the state to libraries that have insufficient tax bases in relation to the population served. System funds are to be used for the benefit of the system as a whole and not for an individual library's benefit.

Budget Planning for the Local Library

The factors bearing on budget planning at the local level are those that give each community its distinctive personality and at the same time may result in the creation of its unique problems. These factors are geographic, demographic, economic, social, cultural, and sometimes political. There is interplay among all of them. A major alteration in a single factor may jeopardize other factors as they relate to library service. One illustration of the interplay among community factors can be seen in situations where a governmental authority relocates a major highway. This relocation may affect land use, the distribution of population, the economic welfare of small businesses, and public access to library facilities. This decision initially may be geographic in nature but it has ramifications for all of the other factors. Some major factor inevitably changes in every community in a fast-moving society. Consequently, budget planners must look not just at the factor that has noticeably changed but also at all of the factors as they interlock and influence planning for public service.

MAJOR FACTORS IN BUDGET PLANNING

A. Characteristics of the community
   1. Area to be served: square miles
   2. Density of population: population per square mile
   3. Predominant nature of the community: metropolitan, suburban, rural, retirement, college or university, recreation-centered, or other
   4. Dominant economy: commercial, industrial (light or heavy), agricultural, research-centered, military, or other
   5. Land use: heavy concentrations of population (apartments, multiple dwellings), single-family residences, or combination
   6. Types of neighborhoods: racial, national, or denominational groupings or mixed
   7. Physical growth potential: restricted by proximity to neighboring jurisdictions or open to annexation
   8. Position as, or in relation to, natural trading or political center of area
   9. Transportation: convenience and availability of daytime and evening public transportation; access to public parking
   10. Opportunities for continuing education: night school, community college, or library-sponsored or cosponsored activities

B. Characteristics of the population
  1. Rate of growth or decline
  2. Number of people by age groupings: children, young adults, adults, and the retired
  3. Levels of education
  4. Categories of manpower in relation to job opportunities
  5. Levels of socioeconomic advantage and disadvantage
  6. Ratio of migratory to stable population
  7. Cultural, educational, and recreational interests
  8. Percentage of library users in relation to population growth or decline
      a. Number of registered borrowers; geographical origin
      b. Estimate of users of on-site services, such as information and reference service, special programs, or reader guidance
  9. Changes in library use, such as heavier reference use, specialized interests, or volume of student use
  10. Changes in community development, such as the spread of retirement or nursing homes, expansion of health, welfare, and antipoverty agencies

C. Sources of funds
  1. Direct tax support
      a. Determined by state law
      b. Subject to approval of local government
  2. Endowments or gifts
  3. Income from auditorium rental fees, sale of government documents, fee cards, and other incidentals
  4. Income from contracts for provision of system services or through contracts to supply services to neighboring libraries
  5. Equalization funds or other forms of state aid

D. Characteristics of the library
  1. Governmental structure: municipal, school district, township, county, multicounty, or regional
  2. Board powers and responsibilities: appointed, elected; limits of power
  3. Administrative organization: single library to be administered, or shared administration and/or staffing with neighboring libraries
  4. Age of physical properties: extent of needed repairs
  5. Adequacy of hours of services to meet unique character of community

6. Number of buildings and outlets
   a. To be administered
   b. To be staffed
   c. To be stocked with materials
   d. To be maintained: serviced, heated, lighted, air-conditioned, insured, and repaired
   e. To be amortized or rented
   f. To be expanded or moved to adequately serve the community

E. Manpower needs

   1. Ratio of work loads to personnel
   2. Ratio of professional to clerical staff
   3. Adequacy of custodial help
   4. Replacement needs in anticipation of resignations or retirement
   5. Number of positions to be budgeted (the number and classification to be determined by the size and program goals of the library); typical positions are
      a. Director
      b. Administrative assistant
      c. Secretarial and business office personnel
      d. Professional librarians: children's, reference, young adult, catalogers, or service coordinators
      e. Specialists: experts in work with the disadvantaged, in public relations, or in adult education
      f. General assistants: circulation and other departmental aides
      g. Clerical aides: typists, file clerks, menders
      h. Pages (shelvers)
      i. Bookmobile drivers
      j. Custodians
   6. Salary levels
      a. Related to comparable positions in area requiring similar training and experience
      b. Adequate to attract qualified professional personnel nationally
      c. Compensatory in terms of unpopular evening and weekend schedules
   7. Fringe benefits
      a. Adequate paid vacations
      b. Cumulative sick leave to provide for prolonged illness
      c. Provisions for accident, hospitalization, and disability
      d. Retirement plans

8. Opportunities for professional growth
   a. Provisions for compensation for professional training
   b. Provisions for expenses at system meetings, conferences, workshops
   c. Provisions for acquisition of professional material for in-service training and for broadening professional background

F. Budgeting for library materials

   1. Age, size, and quality of collection
   2. Number of outlets to be stocked: bookmobiles or branches
   3. Requirements for current additions to match local needs
   4. Subject areas requiring priority funding
   5. Requirements for replacement of basic titles
   6. Fixed and rising costs of bibliographic, informational, and reference tools
   7. Requirements to meet needs of "special publics," such as the disadvantaged and the handicapped
   8. Availability of more specialized materials from system

G. General operations budget

   1. Rising cost of supplies: office, departmental, and custodial
   2. Nonnegotiable fixed costs
      a. Insurance
      b. Utilities
      c. Maintenance contracts, such as for air conditioning or typewriters
      d. Equipment rental, such as for charging machines
      e. Postage and mailings
      f. State and national association dues
      g. Transportation: gasoline, railroad fare
   3. Equipment replacement schedule: typewriters, office machines, or bookmobiles
   4. Contracts: processing, consultant, or legal services
   5. Public relations and publicity.

The Local Library Budget Process

The library budget is, in the last analysis, a plan for library service translated into dollars and cents. It is indispensable. It is the major, and in many cases the only, channel for obtaining financial support. Every trustee has a concern for the budget; every librarian functions within a budget. Few, however, talk about budgets voluntarily or out of the budget season. Techniques of budget preparation rarely raise a controversy in the professional press.

Yet the planning and preparation of a budget are an administrative process that is not only a legal obligation but one that directly relates to the fulfillment of the objectives, the policies, and the program of a library. Budget preparation, consequently, is not an isolated action performed once a year as a requirement for the acquisition and allocation of funds. It is a planning process grounded on current experience and focused on projections for the best use of anticipated funds to raise standards of staffing, collection building, and services designed to meet the needs of the public.

Exclusive control of the library's finances is ordinarily vested by law in the library board. The board, in exercising its prerogatives, delegates the management functions related to this responsibility to the librarian, its chief executive officer. Various trustee manuals interpret the relationship of the library board to the chief librarian as comparable to that of a company's board of directors to its manager. In the case of the library, the board, regardless of its elected or appointed status, is accountable to the taxpayer. The librarian is accountable to the board—and accountable with the board to the citizens of the community—for the strengths and weaknesses of library service. The trustees and the librarian work together on budget planning just as they work together on policy-making and long-range planning. The board and the librarian are mutually dependent on each other for intelligent decisions in financial planning and for "know-how" in justifying financial requests and in interpreting the needs of the library for the fulfillment of its unique functions in society.

A thorough understanding of the laws related to library financing is imperative in budget preparation. State laws provide the guidelines for the collection and administration of library funds. The laws related to library finance may be incorporated with general revenue acts or defined in chapters of library law. The general revenue acts frequently have a bearing on the source of revenue and the method of collection. Library law may differ within one state for small or large communities or for different governmental jurisdictions, such as villages, metropolitan areas, townships, counties, or districts. It is the law which extends the powers of one library board as an independent governmental unit or limits the authority of another library board as a department in local government.

The trustees must be aware of their legal responsibilities in relation to library finance. They must understand the precise obligations of the authority granted to them by law. In addition, they must know the meaning of the terms used by tax collectors, such as assessed valuation. Budget planners must be aware of the law as it may apply to civil service regulations, which may or may not affect library salaries and benefits. They must know the law as it applies to provisions for retirement, disability, hospitalization, and employee benefits. They must know the statutory or local directives for budget presentation. Budgets that do not comply with the law are vulnerable to objections by individual citizens, tax leagues, and attorneys for corporations with nationwide rather than local roots. The system consultants are a major source for interpretation of the law and for guidance in the preparation of a budget. Budget and finance workshops for both trustees and librarians constitute one of the most successful programs of cooperative systems. Often they are repeated annually as introductions for newcomers and as refresher courses for the experienced budget planners.

The first of the budget planning sessions on the local level may advantageously start with a review of the law as it applies to the local situation and a review of tax rates, levies, extensions, and collection costs as they relate to current data on anticipated income as fixed by law or compatible with local funding resources.

Budget planning continues with a review of the library's purpose as set forth in its statement of objectives. Once the objectives are determined, it is possible to establish long-term and short-term goals. Goals should be specific and should indicate "how much and by when." Clues toward establishing specific goals can be found in library standards. For example, a book collection equal to three books per capital might be one goal; a staff of one professional and two clericals per six thousand population might be another. In a community experiencing rapid population growth, the "by when" part of these goals will need to be carefully determined and constantly evaluated. In a new library the goal of book collection development may be a long-term one, but it will only be attained if short-term goals are set and reached.

Once goals are established they should be prepared in written form and disseminated. An essential part in reaching established goals is a plan, and an indispensable part of a plan is the budget. Budgeting follows rather than precedes planning. If the long-range goal is three books per capita and three staff members per six thousand population within five years, how many volumes and staff members must be added each year to reach that goal? What money is needed each year for this purpose?

The growing diversity of community needs has resulted in an add-on approach to budget planning. No one wants to give up established services, and the addition of new services without additional funds all too frequently results in a lessening of the effectiveness of the entire service program. The budget planners need to explore a number of problems: (1) How much money is needed to continue present objectives at their current levels? (2) What financial support is needed to meet minimum standards? (3) How much money for staffing and resources would be needed to adopt new goals to meet pressing public demands? (4) What priorities should be set? (5) Which goals should the budget strengthen to take maximum advantage of system services?

The librarian who stimulates a board to establish specific goals will be supported by trustees who know where they are going and are willing to defend their budget requests. Too often a budget is established merely by determining how much was spent in various categories the previous year. This method does not produce a planned effort to improve services. The budget should be a plan to spend money to reach set goals that will carry out established objectives.

Through goal setting and budgeting with a purpose, the board and the librarian will be working together in a joint effort toward progressive improvement. The board will have confidence in the librarian. Because of this confidence, the librarian will have complete freedom to act within the established budget. The essence of a successful librarian-board relationship is mutual confidence. Mutual confidence is one byproduct of good budgeting.

The amount of time to be allowed for the study and completion of the appropriation budget depends on the complexity of the situation in terms of the library's size or its program, on priorities to be established, and on the kinds of problems to be resolved. Priorities involve choices, such as the comparative and immediate importance to the community of building up services to businessmen or extending service to an isolated neighborhood. Both are important. One may have to take precedence over the other in long-term budget planning. Such choices may involve increased cost factors. The extension of evening service hours, for example, may require funds for guard or police protection. Priorities and problem resolutions, which have an effect on not only the coming year's budget but on those for future years, take time.

Budget planning is a twelve-month procedure in the mind of the librarian. No month in the year passes without notations being made for inclusion in a folder on the budget. A working schedule of five to six months for data gathering, for examination or questioning of plans, and for thoughtful review of any proposal is needed for even the most modest of budgets. Many librarians agree with the frequently expressed view that the less money there is to be spent on books, the more time is required in planning to spend it. The same point of view applies to the total budget. The tighter the budget, the more carefully it must be correlated with objectives and the plans based on those objectives.

The starting date for actual budget preparation may change, but there is one date which is constant. That is the deadline for the library's appropriation budget documents to be in the hands of the appropriate government official. This date depends on the fiscal year observed by the local government. It is the responsibility of the librarian to ascertain any changes in the deadline or in the form of presentation required by local officials for uniformity of presentation by all departments.

An administrative step in budget planning is the gathering of essential data for quick access to information ranging from current costs to future needs in relation to estimated income. This necessitates a deadline, for example, a date when a building and grounds committee must complete its cost studies for some major maintenance project, a date when the inventory sheets of the stock of supplies must be checked and requisitions filled out, a date when requests must be submitted to the librarian by the heads of departments. Many libraries have no departments, but there usually is at least a custodian, who is in a good position to know how much and what kind of soap and wax is needed.

The responsibility for assembling background data normally and logically is a duty of the paid administrator. The librarian is the keeper of the service and financial records that are essential for budget planning and for the building up of an information bank that must be part of the background of all members of the budget planning team. The source of the records needed for budget planning is the librarian's office. These should be simple records, devised to produce the facts as needed—no more and no less.

The monthly service reports of the librarian provide an accumulative body of knowledge for trustees since they record community use and trends in reader interests. The reports may reflect work loads, which give evidence of the need for additional personnel. Budget planning time, which spreads over a reporting period of months, offers an opportunity for evaluation of the quality of existing services.

Some of the most useful materials for board consideration in working on the budget include the following:

1. *A report of current annual expenditures.* Budget planning must start before the current fiscal year has ended. As a consequence, recent annual expenditures for study purposes must cover an arbitrarily selected period. This may be, for example, from September through August or from February through January, depending on the library's budget planning schedule. The important element in this report is the recency of the twelve-month period.

2. *A comparative expenditure statement.* This is a handy record that simply transfers the annual financial reports of a selected number of recent years to a single page. It presents receipts, itemized disbursements, and balances in parallel columns for quick comparison of actual costs over several years. Comparison will show at a glance the amount spent in the same line category from year to year. The comparative statement is useful as an index to rising costs in all lines of expenditure, particularly to changes in fixed costs, such as utilities, insurance, heat, rent, or contracts for services. Examples of fixed costs are charges for maintenance of typewriters or a subscription to the *Readers' Guide*—costs over which the budget planners have little or no control.

3. *A report of income from sources other than the library levy.* Most libraries have some income that is separate from the levy under consideration. Fines, fee card receipts, and money from investments or gifts are income and should be taken into account in determining the amount of money to be levied. Income from sources other than taxes reduces the levy in some states. In others, such income has no effect on the levy. In either case, nontax income is subject to budget planning, unless it is a gift designated by the donor for a specific purpose.

4. *Salary data.* A report on current salaries, the latest information on the cost of living, and the salary schedule are essential documents for the budget planners. The salary schedule is a basic document developed by library boards to determine salary ranges

for different types of positions and annual increments within each range. It is important in computing the total increments to be included in the budget. Without a salary schedule the board becomes involved in time-consuming comparisons with the pay scales of schools or neighboring libraries and risks hasty decisions that are inconsistent with sound financial planning and staff welfare.

5. *Estimates of supply needs.* The reports of an inventory of office, library, and custodial supplies together with a review of anticipated requirements provide the information for a budget item on supplies.

6. *Estimates on building maintenance.* The cost of building upkeep, aside from custodial supplies, depends on the age of the building, the past history of maintenance, and skill or lack of it on the part of custodians. Many boards have buildings and grounds committees that are responsible for the library property and for recommendations concerning its condition.

7. *The budget items.* The report forms supplied by some state libraries provide guidelines to items that must go into a budget. Some local governments require the use of uniform forms for budget requests from all departments. A typical budget requires itemized budgeting for the following: (a) salaries, broken down into categories for professionals, library assistants, custodial help, bookmobile drivers, and other personnel; and (b) general expense, including books, periodicals, newspapers, recordings, pictures, films, binding, supplies, contractual services such as book processing, building maintenance, insurance, sewer and water, heat, light, telephone, bookmobile maintenance, and contingency. Many librarians also include budget items for public relations, convention expense, and professional dues.

After the basic data have been assembled, a preliminary budget is prepared by the librarian for the finance or budget committee or in some cases for the board as a whole. This is the point at which the members of the board evaluate progress and discuss the data received in advance in relation to the first draft of the budget. It is the time to question and the time to make "an appraisal of where we are, where we stand, and how we can cope with a given situation." From this meeting a second draft is prepared for further refinement. There is no limit to the number of budget meetings the board or a committee of the board may wish to hold. Good preparation of background materials, however, will mean fewer meetings. The final draft of the appropriation budget and the levy resolution must be adopted by the board as a whole. The officers of the board are usually required to affix their notarized signatures to all budget papers submitted to the local government.

Some local governments require the library and other departments to have a representative at public hearings to interpret or defend the annual budget, or at least to answer questions about it. This is not a situation to dread but an opportunity to do a public relations job not only in presenting the budget but also in interpreting with enthusiasm and knowledge a program that will justify the financing necessary to strengthen the library's services. These library representatives make their presentations verbally, sometimes using written statements, graphs, and other audiovisual aids and sometimes surveys made by community study groups. Their best line of defense is to be found in the thoroughness of their preliminary studies for the preparation of the budget.

The independent library is responsible for its own budget planning. The system, however, stands ready to provide answers to questions such as the average cost of books or the range of current salaries in the area. Many systems also provide consultant service in the actual preparation of budgets and offer an opportunity through institutes for a better understanding of the purpose of a budget and of the procedures of budget-making within the framework of state law.

CHECKLIST OF BUDGET PLANNING MATERIALS

Category	Background Information	Planning Information
General	Current budget	Objectives statement
	Financial reports	Minimum standards leaflet
	Comparative annual expenditures	Estimated tax and nontax income
Personnel	Staff work loads:	Public service and use reports
	Staff-population ratio	Salary schedules
	Professional-clerical ratio	Cost-of-living data
	Full-time and part-time ratio	Fringe benefit plans
	Maintenance adequacy	Comparative area salary figures
	Personnel qualifications	Estimates of staffing needs for new services
	Staff welfare provisions	Costs of staff replacements
	Personnel policies	
	Ratio of salaries to total budget	

Category	Background Information	Planning Information
Library materials	Size of book collections: Volumes added during year Volumes withdrawn during year Nonbook collections Bindery costs Cost of acquisition and cataloging Insurance Ratio of expenditures to total budget	Goals for collection development Estimate of price increases Replacement estimates Anticipated cost of expanding a particular collection Contracts for processing materials Review of insurance coverage
Building maintenance and service	Current costs: Insurance Heat, light, water Telephone Supplies Needed repairs Ratio of expenditures to total budget	Reviewing insurance coverage in relation to replacement costs Estimates of repairs and improvements Building service contracts
Equipment	Number and condition of typewriters and office equipment Adequacy of files, etc.	Cost of replacement or repair Costs and justifications for labor-saving equipment
Other expenses	Office supplies Publicity materials Travel reimbursements: Workshops Institutes System meetings Library business Convention expenses Professional dues Mailing Petty cash.	Estimates of costs of letter-writing, mailing, etc. Review of policies.

Related Fiscal Responsibilities

Fiscal responsibility implies an understanding of two basic principles: (1) no officer or member of the board of directors of a library has the legal authority to take action on financial matters without explicit delegation from the board as a whole, and (2) the official documents of the board, including all bookkeeping and accounting records, should be housed in the library for central access, open inspection, and protected storage. Fiscal responsibility is also a recognition that there are areas subject to in-depth study by the board and the administrator that may necessitate consultations with community and system specialists. These include insurance coverage, accountability for payroll withholdings, bonding, auditing, contracting for special services, and planning for capital improvements.

Insurance

The purpose of a library's insurance plan is to cover the replacement costs of the physical plant, materials, and equipment; to insure the public from losses due to injury on library property; and to safeguard the staff from losses resulting from illness, accident, or death suffered during the course of employment. Not to be overlooked is the cost of recataloging should the card catalog be destroyed. Since the shelf list provides a record of holdings when a loss occurs, its protection by microfilming or other means should be considered.

Adequacy and the cost of insurance are equally important concerns. Sources of information in this complicated field include library literature, representatives of local insurance companies, and insurance consultation services that may be available through the system.

The types of insurance usually carried by the independent library include:

1. Property insurance, which covers buildings, furniture, equipment, books, and other library materials (Special attention should be paid to the advantages or disadvantages of deductibles for plate glass windows which are a frequent target for vandals. Exceptionally valuable book collections, works of art, or exhibits owned by outsiders are also major considerations in an adequate insurance plan)
2. Legal and liability insurance, including workmen's compensation and comprehensive general liability insurance
3. Vehicle insurance, including maximum liability for bookmobiles, station wagons, other mobile units, and automobile nonownership insurance

4. Hospitalization and medical insurance for the staff
5. Fidelity bonds.

A few general guidelines for an insurance program of value to all libraries are:

1. All insurance policies should be held in the librarian's office for immediate referral in case of questions about claims, exemptions, deductibles, or coverage.
2. A checklist of all policies, including such basic data as names of companies, policy numbers, amount of the premiums, due dates, and policy expirations, should be kept up to date in an insurance file or in the administrator's manual.
3. Policies should be consolidated wherever feasible.
4. The adequacy of protection of the staff through affiliation with group insurance or pension and disability plans should be periodically reviewed.
5. A current data file on hospitalization and disability benefits should be maintained in the librarian's office for the information of the staff and trustees.
6. The installation of fire detection devices, regular schedules for servicing of fire extinguishers, and inspection of the building and equipment for potentially hazardous conditions should be considered as important as the insurance policy itself.

Payroll Withholdings

Fiscal responsibility also includes conformance with regulations governing income tax, social security, or pension deductions withheld from the payroll. This ranges from distributing W-4 forms for determination of employee deductions to the keeping of records for the preparation of summaries of state and federal income tax withholdings for all personnel employed during a calendar year. Withholdings from the payroll also involve matching funds from the library as the employer. Current information on the formula used to determine the amounts of such contributions is essential for correct withholding and transmittal of monies withheld to the authorized receiver. Advice on the obligations related to this transmittal is available from the local municipal offices, the Internal Revenue Service, and consultants at the system headquarters.

Bonding

Laws of the various states specify conditions under which both trustees and personnel must be bonded. Some municipal governments require the bonding of the treasurers of local boards and of any personnel in tax-supported institutions who may be charged with the handling of funds. The directors of systems and treasurers of system boards are customarily bonded. Each individual involved in fiscal responsibilities must determine the legal requirements related to his own duties.

Auditing

An audit is a verification of the proper use of library funds. The independent library may be included in the general municipal audit, or it may be required to furnish its own audit report. In either case, the library is the depository for the ledgers and annual reports, together with supporting documents such as invoices and official minutes of the library board, and other data the auditor may require. As a general rule, a system is required by law to furnish its own annual audit report to the state and to its member libraries.

The role of the auditor in some communities is expanding to include a review of the library board's response to its fiscal responsibilities. The auditor may want to review insurance policies, special contracts, such as a rental agreement for the use of a copying machine, or evidence of the board's conformance with a law requiring bids for high-cost installations. This review, which is usually advisory, is designed to detect oversights or misunderstandings rather than to introduce a new level of regulations.

Contracting for Services

Contracting for services is not a new venture for libraries. Contracts for janitorial services and for air-conditioning and heating maintenance are common. Many libraries have entered into contracts with processing centers for the acquisition and cataloging of library materials.

Contracts are legal business. Each member library should have its own attorney. Many small libraries take advantage of the services of the local corporation counsel or the generosity of a lawyer who happens to be a board member. Reliance on free legal service is not always in the best interest of the library. Both the corporation counsel and the board member attorney frequently have professional obligations that take priority over the claims of the library. In addition, there will be natural reluctance on the part of a board to question or criticize an opinion which is donated.

A system employs legal counsel for services directly related to system business. These services may also entail investigations of questions of systemwide interest, with the results being made available to the members. A system's legal program may also allow for conference privileges involving local trustees and their attorney with the system attorney, under limitations imposed by system policy or budget.

With the creation of systems, many new types of library contracts have come into being. A system, for example, may contract with one or more strong libraries to serve as central or cocentral libraries for the system. A system may contract with a member library to administer a special system project. A member of a cooperative system, on the other hand, may contract with the system headquarters for professional assistance that requires more than the normal consultative services available to all members. Systems may contract with other systems for the establishment of services such as film circuits, bibliographic or last-copy storage centers, and research projects. Contractual arrangements between systems and special libraries for the benefit of system members are another example of the continuing emphasis on contracts as a means of extending accessibility and encouraging cooperation.

Budget Planning for the Cooperative System

The characteristics of the cooperative system will have an obvious affect on the system budget since they will, in great measure, determine the system's service design. A rural cooperative system in an area with little prospect of population growth and widely dispersed member libraries will require a different design of service than a system in a geographically smaller, high-density metropolitan area with rapidly increasing population. Salary levels of clerical and maintenance personnel may differ significantly due to differences in the local labor market. One system may have sophisticated, well-rounded collections in several member libraries while another has less initial strength on which to build. A system in a densely populated metropolitan area will be more apt to see the need for experimentation to meet the problems of the area while the rural system may need to concentrate on basic services that have the potential for an equally dramatic improvement of library service to the area resident.

Additional major factors affecting system budgets include the operational costs of the system's intermember communications and public relations programs, and of such special services as centralized processing, printing and printout facilities or last-copy depositories, which may be unique or sponsored cooperatively with other systems. Each system must determine for itself what factors are significant in developing its philosophy or approach to system budgets. There are guidelines, such as the following Public Library Association outline, that are valuable to system budget planners.

MAJOR FACTORS INFLUENCING SYSTEM BUDGETS

A. Nature of the system
   1. Organizational structure
   2. Number of units to be
      a. Staffed
      b. Stocked with materials
      c. Rented, depreciated, insured
      d. Heated, lighted, cleaned, maintained
   3. Geographic area to be served
      a. Size in square miles
      b. Barriers such as mountains, rivers, limited-access highways, railroads, industrial complexes
      c. Concentrations of population, whether centralized or scattered

B. Characteristics of the population to be served
   1. Rate of growth or decline
   2. Educational levels
   3. Socioeconomic status
   4. Employment opportunities available; level of unemployment: seasonal, cyclical, chronic

C. Staff
   1. Salary levels
      a. Related to other positions in the area requiring similar training and experience
      b. Adequate to attract qualified professional candidates nationally
      c. Clerical salaries equivalent to those paid for similar work in the area
      d. Adequate to attract nonlibrary professionals, such as personnel officers, business managers, computer technicians, subject specialists, and the like

2. Fringe benefits
   a. To cover ordinary illness and vacation needs of staff
   b. To assist in unusually prolonged illness or disability
   c. To enable staff to retire at a mandatory age set to benefit the employee, create promotional opportunities for younger staff, and maintain the efficiency of the system operation
   d. To encourage long tenure of staff exhibiting high potential for growth on the job
   e. To counterbalance necessary but unpopular hours and schedules
3. Opportunities for professional growth
   a. In-system travel to book selection and other staff meetings
   b. Continuing education: time with pay, tuition, and/or travel
   c. Attendance at state, national, and other professional meetings

D. Age and quality of the existing materials collection; is it
   1. New, still being built up to reach the minimum per capita standards for all media?
   2. Up to minimum standards, chiefly needing current additions and replacements?
   3. Inadequate in quality and depth; in need of weeding, extensive additions of basic titles, greater reference strength?
   4. Supplemented by nearby stronger, more specialized collections, access to which is financed by the state or by the system through contracts?
   5. Limited in variety by need to duplicate titles extensively because
      a. There are multiple outlets?
      b. Central collections are departmentalized?

E. Operational services
   1. Those received from other governmental units without direct cost, such as purchasing, processing, bookkeeping, personnel recruiting and examining, maintenance, or utility franchises
   2. Those for which costs must be included in the budget: contractual services such as the above, use of film circuit, interlibrary loan fees and postage, computer time, etc.

F. Costs of transportation
   1. Staff and library materials for short distances only
   2. Staff for long distances to ensure face-to-face contact between headquarters staff and unit staffs
   3. Library materials for long distances or in considerable quantities because

    a. Borrowers may return materials to any branch or outlet
    b. Units exchange substantial proportions of their collections
  4. Bookmobile purchase and maintenance

G. Need for experimental or innovative program related to the social problems of a changing society

H. Planning and implementing long-range objectives for the system.[11]

The System Budget Process

There is little difference between library and system budgeting. The fundamental difference is that the system's source of income is usually the county or state.[12] Funding from the state requires an act of the legislature to raise the level of income to allow for increased services. Basic system services, such as interlibrary loan and central reference, or delivery services consistently expand to meet member libraries' needs. The system budget must provide for these projected increases aside from requests for additional, but less fundamental, services. Usually systems have no source, other than operating funds, for major capital expenditures such as new buildings. The potential for rapid growth in the demand for basic services and the necessity of stretching the operating budget to cover major capital outlays requires anticipative planning. To take advantage of the system's unique opportunity to test methods of solving problems, the budget should also provide for experimental programs.

The system director should always be conscious of the example the system sets for its members. The system budgeting process and the finished budget should be models to be emulated by the member libraries. Setting an example for others imposes obligations on the system director and system trustees. System staff salaries should be realistic even though those of some member libraries are too low. Justifications for increased expenditures should be thorough. Current procedures should be evaluated continuously for improved efficiency. The example provided by the system thus may serve as a guide to more effective financial procedures and standards at the local level.

If the local library as a member of a cooperative system is to retain its individuality and independence, the system together with its members must exercise vigilance in resisting the natural trend of some libraries to seek financial support from the system or to become freeloaders. System funds should not be allocated to member libraries except as legitimate reimbursement of the cost of services performed by a library on behalf of the entire membership. The headquarters library that provides central reference service to member libraries will require additional reference materials, staff, furniture, and equipment to carry out the reference function. Reimbursement to the headquarters library through the purchase of reference materials, furniture, and equipment, all of which remain system property, is legitimate. Contractual arrangements to reimburse the library for staff salaries and fringe benefit costs are necessary. Member libraries should not expect the headquarters library to provide such services without adequate reimbursement.

There is a clear obligation for the system to make thorough studies of both direct and indirect costs incurred by the headquarters library. Such studies, made by impartial outside experts when necessary, assure adequate reimbursement to the headquarters library. Other member libraries are also assured that system funds are being expended for the benefit of all.

In some instances performance of a system service brings additional benefits to the library responsible for it. Housing all or a part of a system's book collection yields benefits in terms of ready access to the system collection by patrons of the library. Although difficult to measure, such benefits should be recognized as an adjustment factor in reimbursement contracts. On the other hand, libraries housing system collections should not be expected to include the system collection in their insurance coverage. Insurance of system property is clearly a system responsibility.

Systemwide borrowing programs providing free access to any library may include methods of system reimbursement to libraries that, because of strength and location, are heavily used. Reimbursement will take into account the "cost of cooperation," which is an agreed-on amount of loans that each library should be expected to provide without reimbursement.

Systems have a responsibility to provide for communications, and communications costs frequently are included in system budgets. Telephone and teletype equipment located in a library for the purpose of providing system services is paid for by system funds. Toll calls are required for normal communication in many systems. The small library with a limited budget may hesitate to make full use of system services because of the cost of toll calls. The system may make it a matter of policy to absorb toll costs by permitting collect calls or use of credit cards or by making other arrangements with the telephone company. However, should system funds be inadequate to provide needed services, the cost of plugging in system services by telephone may have to be accepted as a local library responsibility.

In a cooperative system it is reasonable to conclude that the financial ability of the system to broaden its services will be in direct relation to the willingness of its members to assume some of the costs. Rather than assess members for this purpose, a system may find it more acceptable and in conformance with its objectives to require some degree of local effort to round out a system service at the local level. Central reference service might be cited as an example. The system reference service should be aimed at a level of sophistication beyond that expected of the member library. Yet some libraries may have reference collections inadequate to support even the local function. To prevent the use of the system service replacing the local acceptance of responsibility, the system will stimulate the library to strengthen its own collection. This might be accomplished through consultation or in-service training and by providing basic reference collections on loan in return for a local agreement to purchase other necessary reference materials.

In heavily populated areas where libraries are usually quite close, successful reciprocal borrowing programs provide an opportunity for more efficient use of system funds. For example, libraries may be grouped in service zones, with each library in a zone specializing in one or more types of materials. One library may house framed art prints while another provides tape recordings. The residents of the entire zone then will have access to the specialized collections through reciprocal borrowing and interlibrary loan, thereby eliminating duplication of art prints and tapes in each library. Voluntary subject specialization in book purchasing also lends itself to the zoning technique in some systems. The close working relationship of a group of small libraries in a zone may aid later efforts toward voluntary consolidation of small units into more supportable libraries that are large enough to meet the needs of the current age.

3 Capital Improvements

The necessity to plan for capital improvements is ultimately faced by all libraries. It may be forced on them by the age of an existing building, by insufficient space for growing collections or increased public use, by the deterioration of the neighborhood in which the library is located, or by a combination of these and other factors. Trustees and administrators of independent libraries may wish to consider two major steps in the resolution of a building problem: leasing buildings and equipment from current or anticipated income, or turning to the voting public with a referendum authorizing the sale of bonds for construction.

Leasing Alternative

There are times when independent libraries should consider leasing buildings rather than selling bonds to finance new construction. One example is in communities where traffic, shopping patterns, and social developments are unstable or unpredictable, thus precluding planning a permanent location for the library. Other communities may have financial problems, such as a severely limited debt ceiling, which prevents the sale of bonds to finance construction of a library building. A library system with no bonding power and no other means of financing construction may find the solution to the problem of needed office space by leasing. Mortgaging should be investigated, but legal limitations may not allow this course of action.

Communities in transition may find an advantage in short-term leases, which permit periodic review of the appropriateness of the location. In areas somewhat less fluid but still transitional, it may be possible to arrange for construction of a building designed specifically for library use but adaptable for later commercial use if the character of the surroundings change. Such buildings are constructed by private builders and leased to the library for a specific term, such as ten years, with an option for renewal for an additional period. Lease-purchase arrangements may also be considered. These provide for a portion of the lease payments to be credited toward the purchase price.

By leasing a building, a library board retains the flexibility to adapt more readily to community changes and avoids the large initial investment. Flexibility is not free. It is paid for in the owner's profits and taxes unless exemption from the latter is provided by law. On expiration of the lease, a sharp rise in rent may be faced by the library. The cost of buying flexibility should be carefully calculated before the decision is made to enter a lease arrangement.

If leasing a storefront building that is part of a larger complex is being considered, pitfalls can be avoided by careful investigation of the types of businesses conducted by immediate neighbors and by determining how heating and air conditioning are controlled. Some libraries have discovered too late that there is a music store beyond the reading room wall and inadequate insulation from noise. Others have found that they lack any control over the air temperature because the thermostat is located in another part of the complex.

Some libraries find an immediate solution of a pressing space problem through leasing or purchasing temporary buildings, as schools do. These buildings can be purchased and then sold after the space problem has been permanently solved.

Furnishing and equipping library buildings also may be accomplished through leasing arrangements. Interest payments are generally high compared to rates for library bonds. If leasing is being considered, the added cost of interest charges should be weighed against the purchase price. Long-term leasing of specific equipment may sacrifice flexibility unless provisions are made in the lease for updating the equipment. Some types of equipment, photocopiers for example, are continually being improved. If updating is included in the lease, it should be considered an advantage over purchase. Freedom in purchasing supplies for leased or purchased equipment needs investigation during negotiations. The profit in some lease arrangements lies more in the constant reordering of necessary supplies than in the equipment itself.

Leasing of automobiles is usually profitable for a profitmaking, tax-paying organization that can write off some of the costs in tax savings. It is doubtful that leasing motor vehicles can offer savings for libraries.

Referendum Planning

Large capital improvements for libraries, such as additions or new buildings, ordinarily involve referendums, through which the community as a whole has a share in determining the future of the library. The official move toward referendum planning ordinarily is the prerogative of the library board as a whole. The decision to explore the direction in which the library should go invariably is grounded in long-standing awareness of inadequacies that are fixed blocks to good service. The hour of decision may come about through the cumulative effect of the monthly reports of a justifiably frustrated librarian. It may be touched off by a board discussion of ideas picked up at a system meeting by a trustee representative. It may be a response to a concerned and articulate citizenry. Recommendations and supporting justifications for action that result from an independent and objective survey of the library made by a respected local citizen study group provide an immeasurable impact on the deliberations of a library board.

In referendum planning, the objective of the librarian and the trustees is to produce a proposal that will prove to the electorate that the library has a sound and workable plan to achieve adequacy in physical facilities and quality of service to meet the library needs of the total community.

The roles assumed by librarians and trustees engaged in planning for a referendum are multiple. They are resource investment planners for their fellow citizens. They are analysts of service needs and potentials. They are judges of theories and plans. They are diagnosticians of political reactions, lay interest, and tax resistance. They become experts in internal and external communications. They turn themselves into salesmen and dedicated advocates of their library's cause. They work together as a coordinating unit, which has been labeled by many authors as a "team."

Published commentary on the history of successful and unsuccessful library referendums indicates there is no single formula applicable to all communities that will predetermine the specific responsibilities of a librarian or a trustee in referendum planning —aside from such obligations as are made mandatory for trustees by law. Local leadership patterns differ; human talents differ. Men and women ordinarily take on responsibilities recognized as being within their special capabilities. However, the records also show that many individuals rise to the challenge of an untried activity and far exceed their own or other people's expectations in imaginative approaches to the sound planning that ultimately wins the approval of the voters.

As a general rule, the roles of the members of the board and the librarian in referendum planning are determined by law, by an existing precedent of delegating administrative functions to the librarian, by mutual awareness of individual skills, and by the exercise of common sense. The librarian and the trustees form the core group of the planning team, which is augmented at later stages by consultants, lawyers, architects, and other specialists. The first responsibility of the core group is to recognize that public trust, which is implicit in their positions, demands a decisive attack on problems that restrict the advancement of local library service. Public trust further charges elected or appointed trustees and their administrators with accountability, a factor that underscores the importance of a commitment to a philosophy of planning, in which personal dedication is expected of each member of the planning team.

Librarians and trustees who have gone through the process of referendum planning reflect on their experiences in terms of the following guidelines:

1. All members of the team must know and understand the state law as it applies to: (a) library finance, (b) bond issues, (c) the authority of the library board to plan and initiate a referendum, (d) the legal requirements and the machinery of the local government for the conduct of the election, and (e) the local ordinances and codes.
2. Objectives of the library must be formulated or reformulated, as the case may be, as testing points for deliberations and decisions.
3. Members of the team must have access to the same basic information on current conditions and to the findings of all studies, and be willing to take the time to examine such data as a basis for sound decision-making.

4. Members must go beyond the assumption that they "know the community" to assess possible changes in community values, to determine evolving socioeconomic characteristics, and to identify the needs of the served and unserved people of the community.
5. Members must be convinced, on completion of studies of possible alternatives and of various plans, that a referendum is the only answer to the library's problems.
6. The team must take a united stand on final decisions despite differences of opinions or the diminution of cherished dreams.

A referendum for a new building is the culmination of many steps in planning and long deliberations. The depth and quality of the work that precedes the date of the election is a prime determinant for success or failure at the polls. Few obligations faced by librarians and trustees as a group are as insistent. Successful planning requires unanimous agreement at the outset that the job is worth doing. It further demands a stretching of vision, a discarding of preconceptions and of attitudes of negativism, and a receptivity to all kinds of ideas for consideration on their own merits. It also requires a "plan for planning" worked out to fit local time schedules and to sustain planning momentum with a minimum of crises.

There are many published aids for the inexperienced planning team that wants to know what to do and when. *Local Public Library Administration,* for example, reprints a list of steps in library building planning that correlates actions with corresponding responsible agents.[1] The perceptive planner will recognize that study and action combinations and assignments of individual and group responsibility should be tailored to the local situation. A list of recommended steps is not an unalterable guide. It is only a starting point for the individual community. There are built-in limitations in published checklists. Space restrictions alone preclude focusing on the cooperative nature of successive steps; and the most detailed and logical of all checklists cannot show that many steps and actions are handled concurrently. The important point is that the planning team must know what steps to take and what time schedules to establish.

The role of the librarian on the referendum planning team is one to be expected of an executive, as the administrative extension of the board. It involves professional knowledge, a willingness to take a leadership position in planning and to learn by planning, the capacity to listen and interpret at all stages of deliberation and decision-making, and the ability to develop a methodology to co-ordinate the work of all members of the planning team.

The first responsibility of the librarian in referendum planning is to prepare the groundwork for investigation by all members of the team. This task devolves on the administrator for many reasons: training and experience, access to records for the compilation of data and to materials for research, and professional exposure to ideas about meeting standards and upgrading service.

The librarian's background studies call for identification of areas most profitable for group research and for selection of material pertinent to examination by all members of the planning team. An essential goal of both data-gathering and literature search is the involvement of the core group in concentrating on its results at the earliest productive time.

Building Program Statement

The first major professional assignment following the background studies is the preparation of a building program statement. This is a written document spelling out the requirements of the proposed building in terms of its overall function and its specific service needs. The purpose of the statement is to interpret to the trustees and the architect a concept of the use of space in relation to people, materials, services, and administrative controls. It is the key to their understanding of organizational and functional needs. It is a basic tool in the self-education process entered into by the planners and is an essential for the architect, who must translate function into a serviceable and attractive structure. It is the first creative act in planning, and one on which the preliminary architectural drawings, as another creative act, must build. The building program statement should include:

1. An introduction focused on the library's own philosophy of service, an interpretation of its official objectives, and a brief explanation of the ways in which people use books and non-book materials in contemporary society
2. A chapter of statistics and other factual data on the community for quick reference. This may include pertinent de-details on the development of the community and the history

of the library. It must include population projections and information on governmental, economic, educational, cultural, and nonpublic library developments that have a bearing on the future use of the library

3. Basic service requirements (the major part of the building program statement). Areas such as offices, public service departments, and maintenance and work quarters must be analyzed, and detailed descriptions given of what is to be accomplished in these areas, the number of people to be accommodated, and the furniture and equipment needed to carry out the function of each area. The building program statement allocates space, estimates area sizes, defines area relationships, and establishes stack, furniture, and equipment requirements. It indicates the importance of interior flexibility, acoustical controls, and provisions for expansion, as well as location criteria, site size, and access. This section of the building program statement should reflect administrative concern for the coordination of facilities, for traffic patterns, efficiency in work flow, and the effectiveness of supervision. It is the place to emphasize the common concern of the administrator and the trustee for maximum service at minimum maintenance costs.

The building program statement may also have an appendix that includes such items as:

1. A timetable of steps in building planning
2. Current registration, circulation, and general use statistics
3. Organization charts
4. Work flow charts
5. Checklists of types of equipment to be considered
6. Checklists of construction features to be avoided.

There is general consensus in the profession that the building program statement is the responsibility of the librarian. This is a correct assumption. To label it as an assignment for the librarian alone is an oversimplification. The point is that one person must be responsible for the actual writing of the document. Somebody has to do the job, which in the last analysis is a professional one. Under some circumstances it can be handled by a consultant in collaboration with the librarian. However, the author, whether librarian or consultant, does not write this document in isolation. It is a product of conferences with the trustees and the staff, with fellow librarians, with planning agencies, and with system or independent consultants. It comes out of analyses of problems and their possible solutions. It is refined by information picked up at building conferences and by observations made during library visits. It is clarified by the questions of the trustees and is molded by a very realistic view of the future in terms of financing, maintenance, staffing, materials resources, and the needs of the served and the unserved in the community. It is the library board's responsibility to approve the building program statement when it is satisfactorily completed. It is the librarian's job to use the statement as a reference tool and expand upon it in working with the architect on preliminary plans.

Another role of the librarian is to serve as a guide on inspection trips to new library installations early in the planning schedule. There is merit in the recommendation of some experts that such visits be made after the local building program statement has been drafted in order that the members of the planning team may examine various methods and techniques used by different architects in handling concepts or specific problems.

Libraries to be visited may be chosen because they are in communities comparable to the home community in size or economic character, because of the reputation of the architect or consultant, because the library ranks as a progressive public institution, or simply because the planning team is interested in furniture and equipment selection.

A tour package of materials prepared by the librarian for the visiting planners from both the board and the staff may advantageously include a data sheet covering the names of key people; a brief summary of population characteristics, socioeconomic conditions; the educational and cultural assets of each community to be visited; and selected data on the construction, which may have been published in professional journals or trade publications. The librarian can also consider working out a form for each planner to fill out during the inspection. These do-it-yourself forms have value as a future reference file to serve as a backstop to memory, particularly if there is a time lag between observation and decision. Appendix C provides a sample form that may be adapted to record observations by members of the visiting team.

Policy Reviews

A review of current board and administrative policies is another pre-referendum activity. All existing policies should be examined for their applicability to service in new quarters. New policies should be formulated to complement new opportunities. Policy changes should not be deferred until occupancy of the new building is assured; they should be correlated with basic planning. Policy decisions are far-reaching and affect space relationships, collection building, staffing needs, and expanding services. Evidence that the board has thought through its policies in relation to capital improvements is of vital importance in winning public confidence.

It is important to establish a policy for handling large gifts from organizations or individuals, which may be announced prior to a referendum as evidence of support or after the referendum as a "name" contribution to a new facility. The purpose of a policy on large gifts is to direct the thinking of a possible donor into channels for gift provisions that will aid rather than limit the effectiveness of a planning team. For example, many well-meaning organizations have a private dream of a prominent alcove or a separate room to house their special-interest collections in the public library. Often these collections require special handling or involve problems of supervision that are not consistent with good building planning for maximum service at minimum cost. A gifts policy worked out in anticipation of such proposals may serve to stimulate constructive ideas on the part of the prospective donor. It will also serve to convince the public in another way of the board's dedication to a unified plan for excellence in service.

Major Trustee Responsibilities

Good communication is imperative in planning for the library, not only among the members of the planning team but also with other community officials and agencies engaged in resolving problems of land use, zoning, neighborhood rehabilitation, extension of public facilities, and the orderly and attractive development of the area within their jurisdiction. There is common agreement that the task of keeping government officials and city, county, or regional planning commissions informed of the progress of the library planners should be initiated and sustained by the trustees since they are either appointed by governmental authorities or are elected officials themselves.

The assumption of this responsibility by the trustees does not impose silence on the librarian in meetings with government officials or at interdepartmental and interpublic agency conferences. It is simply a natural extension of the role of the trustees in their dual capacities as library officials and as nonsalaried members of the planning team. The trustees can foster community understanding through their use of nontechnical vocabularies and their citizen-oriented concern for good library service. Most officials of local government do not want to be burdened with the specifics of each planning session but will appreciate being kept up to date and will respond with interest and enthusiasm to informal—preferably, in an age of mounting paperwork, verbal—reports from trustees at reasonable intervals. Communication with the press is frequently delegated by core group planners to the librarian, who should already have a good working relationship with the local communications media.

A number of steps in planning in the pre-referendum period are the responsibility of the library board, which has legal authority to govern the local library. Advisory boards may share the responsibility with government authorities. Both have recourse to the professional knowledge of the librarian and to the system's building consultant service. The legally constituted board's authority ordinarily includes the determination of project costs; development of a plan for financing; contracting for the services of attorneys, an architect, a consultant and other specialists; site selection; adoption of the building program statement; approval of the schematics and preliminary drawings; transmittal of petitions to the local government for official approval of a referendum; and the agreement on a referendum date.

All these responsibilities are of equal importance, but there are at least three that have a special impact from the standpoint of public reaction. These are the recommendations in the program statement, the selection of an architect, and the selection of a site. The building program statement will usually contain some opinions of the consultant, as an outside expert, on the inadequacy of the present facilities and the reasoning behind the specific recommendations on the size of the proposed building. The consultant's opinions and recommendations can be helpful in initial publicity releases. Judicious distribution of copies of the program statement to newspaper editors and others in influential positions may be considered.

The name of the architect is psychologically one of the most important "first facts" to be presented to the public in advance releases on the progress of library planning. Citizen acceptance of the choice of an architect in many cases depends on evidence of the care with which selection was made and the planners' justification for their final choice.

The final choice of an architect will depend in large part on the board's appraisal of the following points:

1. General reputation of the firm for creativity and reliability
2. Availability of the architectural firm to do the job at the time specified
3. Size of the architectural staff and qualifications of key personnel and consultants
4. Background of the member of the firm who will actually design the building
5. Architect's plan of supervision of day-to-day construction work
6. Review of the firm's past estimates in relation to actual construction costs and its record of success in keeping within a construction budget
7. Recommendations of former clients.

Many experts recommend that both the architect and the building consultant be employed prior to site selection to gain the benefits of advice from their separate competencies and experiences. It is particularly important that library boards interview several architects as a background for judging various approaches to architectural concepts and building problems. The following outline may serve as a useful guide for both architects and library boards in an interview situation.

INTERVIEW OUTLINE

    I. Background of the firm
       A. Experience
          1. What types of buildings has the firm erected?
          2. Does the firm specialize in any particular type of building?
          3. Can it supply photographs and references?
       B. Organization
          1. Is the firm large or small?

2. What are the advantages of either?

3. How large is the staff? Will the firm need to hire many new people to handle this project?

4. To what extent will the principals of this firm actively participate in the project?

5. Does the firm have its own mechanical, structural, and electrical engineers, or does it employ consultants? If consultants are used, who are they?

6. What other experts will be called in for advice on special problems, such as heating, ventilating, lighting, and acoustics?

II. What services can the firm provide?

A. Preliminary programming and planning (pre-bond-issue presentation material)

B. Preparation of working drawings, specifications, and detail drawings

C. Drafting forms of proposals and contracts, issuing certificates of payment, keeping accounts and carrying on the business administration incident to the conduct of the work

1. What is the firm's procedure in bidding?

a. Advertisement for bids?

b. Invitation to qualified contractors?

2. Does the firm recommend a single general contract or separate contracts?

D. To what extent does the firm supervise construction?

E. What other services are available from the firm? Does the firm recommend these services be a part of the contract?

1. Furnishing, equipping, decorating

2. Landscaping

3. Demolition of existing building

4. Other

III. Timetable

A. How soon after the firm is awarded the contract can it start the project?

B. What timetable does the firm suggest for items A, B, C, and D under II?

IV. Fee schedule and other expenses

A. What services are included in the fee, and what is the normal fee for this type of project?

B. How is the fee determined for work done should the bond issue fail to pass after the preliminary work has been completed?

C. What services of the firm require additional payment?

D. What other expenses must the board consider in budgeting

for planning the building?
1. Surveys
2. Travel expenses
3. Other
V. Library consultant
    A. Does the firm recommend that the board engage a specialist in library buildings as a consultant?
        1. Librarian of wide experience?
        2. Consulting architect?
    B. Is the firm willing to work with a consultant?
    C. What should be the relationship between architect and consultant?
VI. What preparation should the board and librarian have completed before engaging an architect?
VII. Any other points the architect may desire to bring out

If several architects representing firms of various sizes are interviewed, differing points of view on the problem will be brought to light. The interviewing process will be enlightening to the board and the librarian and will stimulate their thinking about the advantages and disadvantages of a large or small architectural firm, of single or separate contracts, prequalification of bidders, and the time required for various phases of planning and construction. Additional factors to be included in the building budget, such as soil borings and site surveys, will be introduced in these discussions. The board will discover several basic decisions need to be made, including the placing of responsibility for interior color selection and furniture specifications as well as landscaping. A schedule of interviews with several architects will not only assist the planners in deciding on the firm of its choice but will also be an educational experience for those unfamiliar with the details of the construction industry.

Selection of the site stimulates intense public interest. The board's decision is usually made with the help of many advisors, including the architect and the consultant. A natural participant in the site selection process is the librarian, who has professional concerns for public safety, for access to public transportation by staff and patrons, for the potential of the land area for functional planning, and for future expansion possibilities. The librarian who studies professional literature is able to sum up the positive factors that will guide the final selection. Additional advisors are to be found in the offices of the local or area planning commissions. These groups develop projections and statistical records of community change, which are invaluable in weighing choices. The system director or system building specialist may be called on to interpret to the planning team the principles of preferred sites and such professional literature as Joseph Wheeler's *Reconsideration of the Strategic Location for Public Library Buildings,* published as an Occasional Paper by the University of Illinois Graduate School and available in the professional libraries of many systems. Deliberations over site selection become highly cooperative. Accountability for final selection rests with the trustees alone.

After the site has been selected and title to the land has been transferred to the library board, the architect (as a member of the planning team) prepares schematics, preliminary drawings, and cost estimates for the approval of the board and assists the core planners in the preparation of a referendum brochure for use in the campaign. Frequently the architect asks that a single representative of the planning team work with the firm on the implementation of the building program statement, the development of the preliminary plans, and subsequent postreferendum planning. The representative is normally the librarian. This relationship does not eliminate the rest of the planning group from the exciting prereferendum activities. They are drawn in at regular intervals by the architect and the consultant to discuss progress and help make decisions. The use of a single representative is simply a device to expedite the translation of needs onto the drawing board and into ultimate reality. A single representative is also able to take care of small details that are not of major concern to the core planning team.

The library board, whether it decides independently or acts on the recommendations of interested citizens, may want to make broad explorations before setting a firm date for the referendum. These may take the form of feasibility meetings to exchange views with the members of a library survey team, representatives of key organizations, government officials, and leaders of interested civic organizations. A feasibility session attempts to get views on the acceptability of the library program, suggestions on the best campaign leadership, and opinions on good timing in relation to the work load required for good campaign organization.

The mayor of a community or the chairman of a county or regional board should be sensitive to the public mood, and should be in a position to give good advice on the timing of the referendum. As one citizen said in evaluating the progress of a campaign, "The amateur at referendums certainly should listen carefully to the advice of politicians." An elected official is in the best possible position to identify enthusiasm and support for civic change and improvement. He also is aware of pockets of resistance to community development. It is prudent to listen to the counsel of a man who knows from experience how attempts at persuasion may rouse vigorous and sometimes vicious opposition. A campaign for a library referendum can afford a minimum of mistakes. There is no point in deliberately going against the warnings of seasoned campaigners. The referendum campaign period is too short to recover from costly misjudgments in timing by enthusiastic amateurs. As H. G. Johnston has said:

> A library seeking to pass a bond issue ceases to be that fine old institution of culture and learning, and becomes merely one more threat to the taxpayer's purse. To succeed . . . demands talents not usually endowed to a librarian or even to his board—the political savvy and know-how of a precinct captain and the expertise of a public relations specialist.[2]

Referendum Leadership

The leaders who move into public view on behalf of a library referendum should come from a citizens organization. This does not mean that the librarian and the library board abdicate any of their responsibilities. It does not mean they will not share the work load. It is simply a good way to establish the fact that there are other residents who are concerned with the improvement of the library and its facilities and who are willing to stand up and be counted. The key source person for facts and materials, for explanations of library board policies, and for details on long-range planning is still the librarian. The body legally responsible for library development is still the library board. The librarian and the board, however, may find strategic advantages in taking a strong supporting, rather than leading, role in the referendum campaign.

The contributions of Friends of the Library organizations throughout the country have been interpreted in many ways in library literature. A question remains: Is it advisable to organize a Friends of the Library group for the specific purpose of helping with a campaign for a library building referendum? There are opposing schools of thought on the subject of establishing an organization for a function associated so definitely with tax increases. The warning that the establishment of a Friends group solely for campaign help may lead to organized opposition should be analyzed in terms of possible reactions by the local citizenry. One determining factor is the extent of citizen interest in community developments. Another is the presence or absence of known opponents to any form of organized support for public institutions. A sure knowledge of the acceptability of one more organization in a community is also indispensable in making a decision to organize such a group.

A Friends organization may be formed just prior to a referendum with complete public confidence if one or more of the following factors prevail in the community:

1. The library has already made "friends" of large segments of the community
2. There have been repeated requests for the formation of a Friends organization over a period of time
3. The library has had a good public information program, which has alerted the community to its needs
4. An independent organization, such as the League of Women Voters or AAUW, has made a survey of library objectives and needs before the formation of such a group was proposed and has made its findings public.

The public library board and staff must have some kind of enthusiastic, citizen-motivated help behind them to carry out a successful referendum, particularly in periods of intense resistance to tax increases. There are not enough people officially connected with the library to do the job alone.

It is obviously advantageous to start a campaign with a well-established organization behind the library, a going concern that has already adopted a constitution and has working committees and a treasury. One disadvantage of a new organization formed just a few months in advance of the referendum is that some people confuse the issue by believing that joining the Friends and paying their dues is all that is expected of them in supporting the library cause. On the other hand, a new organization with a single goal for its first-year agenda has an appeal to fresh recruits who want to devote themselves to an achievable objective. A new organization manned by a dynamic cross section of the community starts out with a spirit and an enthusiasm that comes only from association with stimulating leadership, new ideas, and exciting new projects.

Friendly critics of campaign plans have varying opinions about the people who should interpret the referendum to the community at large. There are some who never sway from the belief that the board, the librarian, and the staff should stay off the speaker's platform at all times since they are suspect for having a special axe to grind. Others feel that the librarian and the trustees should be preferred spokesmen because of the weight of authority their studies and planning bring to any discussion. The argument can be resolved by an agreement to take the middle ground. The laymen then take the prominent position, with close backing from the core library planners. Actually everybody becomes involved before the campaign is over, regardless of differing opinions of campaign approaches.

Some organizations ask the librarian or a particular staff member to explain the library proposal. Others want to hear what the board members have to say. It would not be sensible to refuse invitations because of a rigid policy created by fears of possible charges of self-interest. Nevertheless, there is considerable evidence that the citizen volunteer has great advantages over a library official in approaching his fellow citizens on the library proposal. In the first place, he is regarded as a fellow taxpayer. Many audiences seem to forget in the heat of a campaign that trustees and librarians are, as a rule, also property holders. A speech by a volunteer also may stimulate freer discussion from an audience than does a presentation by a board member, who is a symbol of officialdom to be regarded with a certain awe. It is good to get the questions out in an open meeting, and this the volunteer can do. In the last analysis, however, the referendum campaign is a community project, and the wise policy is to use the best person available for a job that has to be done regardless of that person's official or unofficial status. Individuals who, by common consent, assume the leadership in the referendum campaign must be those who have a clear understanding of what they are leading.

Referendum Campaign Organization

A referendum campaign team must have a working chairman rather than an honorary chairman. A study of two Philadelphia referendums of the mid-1960s advised that "a campaign chairman should be recruited almost a hundred working days before election if the campaign is to operate at maximum efficiency."[3] Other experienced campaigners recommend the appointment of a chairman six months before the election.

The campaign chairman usually is supported by an executive committee, whose function is to develop campaign plans, including plans for funding, to discover willing campaign talent, to coordinate the work of subcommittees, to handle emergencies, to counter strange rumors, and to keep up the spirits of the worker who is battered down by opposition. The executive committee is entrusted with overall plans for a successful referendum. It is sometimes called a steering committee or a core committee. Often it is composed of subcommittee chairmen to facilitate unity of effort and to expedite the progress of the campaign. The librarian and a representative of the library board are always members of this committee to provide information and direct assistance.

It is the duty of the librarian to help this committee become thoroughly conversant with the facts of the library issue—from details of library history to long-range plans. The librarian supplies the committee with fact sheets, working papers on the library's needs, and projections for the future. All of this material may be assembled and duplicated in the form of speakers' manuals and question and answer booklets for use by not only the executive committee but all participants in the campaign. In addition, the librarian must be available day and night to answer the unanticipated questions. The age-old advice, "never overestimate the public's knowledge and never underestimate the public's intelligence," must be a part of the librarian's working philosophy throughout the campaign.

It is the job of the executive committee to identify every area that needs to be covered in the campaign and to see that each is being handled properly. Each member of the executive committee should serve as a chairman of a working subcommittee. Cochairmen may be drafted from the citizenry at large, but the executive committee can work more effectively if it is kept to a size that allows all members to be discussion participants at executive meetings rather than auditors. A major responsibility of the executive committee may be raising funds to conduct the campaign. In many states tax funds cannot be used for campaign costs.

Campaign Subcommittees

The following committees may be established by the executive committee:

Finance: To raise necessary funds for campaign expenses

Speakers bureau: To help train speakers; to schedule speakers and confirm dates for clubs and organizations

Publicity: To work with the editors of local newspapers and house organs on news releases, feature stories, and special events coverage; to assist in the preparation of letters to community organizations and to the citizenry

Radio and TV: To plan with the local radio and TV staff for live interviews, taped program series, and spot announcements

Coffee hours: To arrange neighborhood discussion groups and establish information centers in collaboration with the chairman of the speakers bureau

Mailing: To address envelopes for bulk mailing of letters and brochures

Library tours: To conduct informational tours through the old library quarters

Arrangements: To secure accommodations and handle related details for open meetings

Telephone: To arrange for telephone volunteers in every ward to get out the vote on election day

Transportation: To supply transportation to the polls.

Some library campaigns have utilized additional committee units such as the sponsors' committee, which includes prominent people whose names are used in advertisements and other types of publicity to show support for the library referendum. Still others have organized business committees and professional men's committees to ensure an aggressive kind of support from these groups. These examples indicate the many possible variations of committee structures to meet the requirements of a particular area. The executive committee may want to appraise the effort it takes to organize such committees in terms of the total campaign program. It may decide, if time is at a premium, to concentrate on the maximum use of a minimum number of committees.

An elections committee is a valuable aid in small communities where the number of polling places is limited to the legal minimum by local government. This committee may be able to secure election judges who will donate their time, thus saving money for the library. This plan is not advantageous in cities requiring several hundred judges and substitutes for the election. Volunteers in this case will use their time much more effectively in getting out the vote.

Campaign Workers

The main corps of workers comes naturally from the Friends organization, federated women's clubs, the League of Women Voters, AAUW, men's service clubs, and other public-spirited organizations. There can never be too many voices or too many hands. Many library patrons not affiliated with organized groups give their offer of help directly over the circulation desk. A systematic plan for recording data on all volunteers should be set up early for the benefit of the campaign chairmen. It may take the very simple form of a mimeographed card on which individuals can write pertinent personal data, such as phone numbers and hours available, and can check categories in which they are interested, such as contacting organizations, addressing envelopes, telephoning to get out the vote, babysitting for voters, or poll-checking to see how much reminding must be done late on the day of the voting.

Campaign Materials

The campaign for a library bond issue is hard work. The period of concentration must be as short as possible for the sake of the volunteers as well as for the cause. Too long a period dampens enthusiasm, upsets the families of volunteers, and allows time for opposition to arise. Three to four weeks is a recommended period for the actual campaign. Several months before this period, however, must be spent in preparation of materials. All of the following communications aids must be prepared in advance to alleviate strain and pressure during the campaign period.

Mailing Lists

A master card file of names for mailing lists is assembled from the library's registration files; from the yearbooks of clubs and organizations; from lists of sponsors of local cultural events and contributors to recent area fund-raising campaigns; from directories of school personnel, interfaith councils, social welfare affiliates; and from lists of newcomers and nonjoiners in the community suggested by the staff and patrons. Sometimes managers of letter-service companies are willing to secure written permission for the library to tap closed membership lists, such as the congregation of a church or synagogue, and will run off addressographed cards for the campaign committee's master file.

Extreme care should be taken to eliminate duplicate cards and to spell all names correctly. The taxpayer is quickly annoyed by the receipt of multiple envelopes from the same mailing, and an enemy can be made by the misspelling of a name. The volunteers who address the bulk mailing should be warned to resist changing the unusual spelling of a familiar name without double-checking for accuracy. Obituaries in the daily papers also should be checked for possible removal of names. This is good public relations in its simplest form.

The library as a nonprofit institution may obtain bulk mailing privileges by application to the local postmaster. An advantage of making at least one mailing at the regular rate is the return privilege, which is a help in weeding out the names of families who have moved without leaving a forwarding address. Addressograph plates may be made for the master mailing file, but this is one expense that can be eliminated if it is feasible to set up "addressing bees" at the homes of willing volunteers.

Fact Sheet

A fact sheet is exactly what it says. It is a one-page document designed to transmit basic information in the simplest, quickest form. It reduces data from all other working papers and informational literature to the bare minimum. It is planned for the patron who reads on the run, for the executive who appreciates one-page reports, and for the campaign worker who wants to carry his facts in his pocket for quick reference.

The fact sheet should include points of information that it is anticipated will be used over and over again. This information will vary according to need, but the most frequently used items include the date of construction of the old building, its current seating and volume capacity related to present-day population and usage, data on critical needs, and projections for the future. The most hard-hitting reasons for the need for the new building should be summarized in simple declarative sentences. The fact sheet should also include the cost of the proposed project and the date of the referendum.

The fact sheet is one of the most heavily used pieces of campaign literature. It is distributed continuously from the first open meeting to the last coffee hour. As a mimeographed job, it is inexpensive and may be easily revised if experience shows the need for additional facts. Its advantage is brevity.

Question and Answer Booklet

There are certain questions asked about a library, its operation, and its plans that are repeated over and over again after the announcement that the library requires funds for a new building. These questions are asked by patrons across a circulation desk, by the man on the street, by audiences in the question and answer period following a talk on the library plans, and even by hecklers in the course of a presentation. They are asked of staff and board members, newspaper reporters, and active campaign workers. It is the responsibility of the librarian to provide the answers in writing as background information for all who expect to give an answer. A prepared answer is a communications device. It does not mean that all the people answering the question necessarily use the same words. It simply means they all have the same information.

The questions themselves can be gathered from many sources. For example, the League of Women Voters or any other study and action group that undertakes any kind of study in depth of library objectives, resources, or needs will be willing to keep a record of the questions asked during the period of investigation. Personnel on bookmobiles or in branch libraries are in a good position to keep a record of the questions asked by patrons who are unfamiliar with the facilities of the main library. Members of the board and of the general staff can produce the kinds of questions to which the head librarian thinks everybody knows the answers.

It is interesting to note that in the initial stages most of the questions deal with services. People are interested in how librarians select books and how library boards arrive at policies such as the cost of fee cards. It is not until the campaign is well underway that serious questions arise about board decisions related to the new building. At this time many of the questions are about costs. A firm answer on the amount of tax increase per $100 assessed valuation must be obtained from the county treasurer's office as soon as the total cost estimate is received from the architect and approved by the board. From this figure the board will be able to estimate the tax increase on property in various categories for the information of the voter.

The question and answer manual is prepared in advance of the campaign, but not all questions can be anticipated. Even though many queries are posed and answered, there will still be some similar to the following:

> Why didn't the library board hold a competition for architects who have had experience in designing library buildings? Why didn't they ask the architects to bid on the job and take the lowest bidder?
>
> Why did the library board have to destroy an historic old school to build a new library? Why didn't they plan to locate the new building in a park? Why didn't they plan to place it near a shopping plaza?
>
> Why doesn't the library provide parking—or if it plans for parking, is it legal?

The question and answer booklet is the most useful tool that can be placed in the hands of the volunteer. The average person's memory is very short, and it is easy to forget details that are outside one's own field. The question and answer booklet is not only a tool, it is a memory jogger.

Brochures

Brochures for campaign purposes are selling devices. They must not be confused with dedication brochures. Each serves a unique function. They are not interchangeable. Preparation of these brochures must be based on what each one can do for the library program. The campaign brochure must serve the concentrated purpose of convincing the voter of the validity of library needs. The dedication brochure, on the other hand, may serve the dual purpose of recording an historic event and of providing an introduction to services available in the new library building.

As a selling device the campaign brochure must be eye-catching and idea-stimulating. It does not need the dignity characteristic of most dedication brochures. The campaign brochure must tell the library story quickly and succinctly. The text must be brief.

The message should include such seed words and phrases as "fire-trap," "crowded stacks," or "dangerous intersections" to fit the problem and evoke images in the mind of the reader. It should be illustrated with photographs, drawings, or graphs that will help get the message across. The brochure also should convey the vision behind the plans that will alleviate the problem, and it must state the estimated cost of the project. It must translate facts into ideas and ideas into favorable public reactions.

The help of a public relations specialist is useful in the preparation of the layout of a campaign brochure. Selling with words and pictures is his business. He can cut through library jargon to the essential words that catch the attention of people. He can prepare the comprehensive dummy, or "comp," in less time than it takes the nonprofessional. He knows instinctively how to relate various elements to each other to get the message off the page and into the reader's mind. The brochure, to be worth the money expended for printing alone, must be effective; otherwise, it is a waste of time and effort. It must attract and hold attention because it has to compete with many other mailing pieces that come into the hands of citizens.

The librarian can state the philosophy of service for the brochure. The architect can provide a floor plan from the preliminary drawings, which suggest the direction of architectural plans. The printer can give advice on paper stock and on provisions for bulk mailing. A good layout man can put it all together into a selling job. There are librarians who can do this kind of job with skill. The trouble with a library campaign is that the librarian's hours are needed for countless activities. The librarian does not, as a rule, have time for more than a compilation of facts and figures for someone else to put into a form that will convince the reader that the library project will be worth the money it will cost.

The subsidizing of the cost of the brochure by the Friends of the Library or some other organization is good psychology. It is substantial witness of their support of the library campaign. A donor credit line printed on the brochure will forestall any public assumption that tax funds were used to print a brochure designed to encourage a rise in taxes.

Sample Ballots

Sample ballots on the library proposition with an X printed in the "Yes" box have been used successfully in many communities as enclosure pieces in general mailings from city departments, banks, or business houses. The specimen ballot is relatively small and adds little or no weight to an individual office or firm's mailing cost, whereas a brochure may cause some handling problems because of its size or weight. Sample ballots have been used in some communities as place mats at local restaurants during the week of the election.

The sample ballot should be obtained as soon as possible. It answers a persistent question from the workers: "What is the ballot going to say?" The wording of the proposition on the ballot is the responsibility of the corporation counsel. He is guided by the law. The ballot may be long and involved in stating not only the basic proposition but also the repayment schedule. It is obviously better to have a simple statement, but the law may dictate or the bonding lawyers may advise a more detailed proposition. In this case it is good to have sample ballots available for discussion groups at coffee hours. A paragraph-long proposition may confuse some voters and lead them to think that the referendum is more costly than it actually is.

Slides, Pictures, Models, and Signs

The old Chinese saying that a picture is worth a thousand words proves to be true in producing visual evidence of crowded and dangerous conditions in an old building. Slides can be used to supplement discussions at neighborhood coffee hours and at more formal presentations before organized groups. They are particularly helpful to campaign workers who are acquainted with the library and its conditions but who need prompting of some kind to do a job of interpretation on those occasions when members of the library staff cannot be present. Slides are not an absolutely perfect device since some of the audience will be convinced that the shots were posed and others will feel that the pictures do not portray a bad situation vividly enough. However, they may prove to be an indispensable aid in getting across a message.

Black-and-white shots of patrons jammed into an old library may be used for bulletin board displays inside the library and on the bookmobiles and will attract a great deal of attention because of the local human interest factor. Glossy prints are also helpful to pass around in small neighborhood discussion groups considering the library issue.

Models of the new building are an excellent visual selling device and will be prepared by the architect if there is sufficient time between the completion of the preliminary drawings and the day of the referendum. In lieu of the model, a large-scale drawing in color of the proposed new building may be prepared by the architect for display in public places and at meetings.

Outdoor display signs advertising the library campaign are sometimes designed and painted by talented campaign workers. Clearance with local unions will circumvent any possible hostility on the part of paid craftsmen. The expense involved in such advertising is frequently borne by the individual artist or his friends.

Paid Advertisements

Advertisements for billboards and newspaper ads in support of the library referendum have been subsidized in some communities by local business and industry or by the Friends of the Library. A decision to solicit this type of support from business and industry must certainly be guided by knowledge of the local situation. It is not good public relations to approach firms that are constantly plagued by requests for door prizes or by demands to make up deficits for worthy causes. On the other hand, there are instances on record showing how a number of firms have joined together to publicly advertise their endorsement of a library referendum. The merits of the Oak Park, Illinois, library referendum, for example, were reinforced by full-page ads subsidized by twenty local firms.[4]

Referendum Campaign Techniques

The number and variety of campaign methods and activities to be undertaken in a concentrated campaign period is determined by the time schedule and the number of volunteer workers who can be counted on to produce results. It must be remembered that all campaign activities take time. The simplest of techniques is probably the coffee hour for small neighborhood gatherings. Planning this quiet little event takes long telephone conversations to arrange for homes and additional calls to arrange for discussion leaders, but it is indispensable in an effective campaign.

It is important that ambitious projects be assessed from the viewpoint of the probability of completion within a relatively limited campaign period. A case in point is the excellent, but obviously time-consuming, idea of establishing an organization contact committee, through which campaign leaders arrange to attend the executive board meetings of all clubs and organizations in the city. The purpose of this effort is to secure an opportunity to explain the library story with enthusiasm to the officers and directors of each organization, with the hope that they will put on a miniature campaign among their own members. The trouble with this idea is that most small and medium-sized cities have too many organizations, and time runs out.

Kick-off Meetings

The prime campaign period may start off with an open public meeting under the auspices of the Friends organization or the campaign committee. It should be a well-planned meeting which will attract an audience. The program committee must not rely on a name speaker or on a lively agenda to get out a crowd. They should work at it. Every organization in the community should be officially represented. This first, and perhaps only, open meeting will attract the attention of government officials. Politicians are sensitive to the direction and strength of public interest. They will work for a community project if they see that it is of sufficient concern to lead outstanding citizens to give up a free evening and to offer weeks of time for campaign duties. Widespread representation from the citizenry at this opening session will lead to an enthusiastic response on the part of elected officials.

This meeting offers a major opportunity to present an overall explanation of the library problem, the board's plans for resolving it, and the ways in which organized and unorganized citizens can help. It should be planned primarily as a background information program even though there may be a featured speaker. It is a good time to use the "big-name citizens" idea that so many volunteer advisors constantly urge on a referendum planning team. Prominent men and women who are overburdened with civic obligations will be willing to serve as masters of ceremonies or speakers for such an occasion, whereas they may not have time to participate in the promotion of the campaign itself.

Letters of invitation to individuals and organizations to attend this meeting should frankly state its purpose as the stepping-stone to a bond issue. It is no secret when the library needs a new building. The proposed referendum will be the agenda item. A frank statement of purpose is preferable to references about getting together for an interpretation of library problems or organizing for cultural development. A forthright statement will challenge the citizen, particularly the one who is reluctant to join just another organization.

This open meeting is the place to introduce the campaign chairman and the key workers in the campaign organization. Introductions should be brief. Essential business should be handled with dispatch. The meeting should begin at the announced time and should last no longer than one hour. The library problem and its proposed solution should be interpreted through slides and the persuasive words of knowledgeable speakers. Every moment should be used to get across to each person in the audience that there is a community job to be done, that it is in their own self-interest to get it done. This campaign kick-off session is the generating point for building up citizen convictions and for firing enthusiasms that lead to willing participation in the campaign. As Abraham Lincoln said, "With public sentiment, nothing can fail; without it, nothing can succeed."[5]

Speakers Bureau

A speakers bureau is composed primarily of friends of the library, organized or unorganized, who are willing to take the time to study thoroughly the supporting data for the library cause and then to take even more time to talk about it to their fellow citizens. Enthusiasm, knowledge, and sincerity are the most important attributes for any participant in a speakers bureau. Some campaigners believe in recruiting only the best known citizens for this job, a theory that has its merits and drawbacks. Sometimes a leading citizen is too busy to do the necessary reading of campaign documents; he can be cornered by a heckler if he has not studied the facts. On the other hand, the library campaign may be just the opportunity that capable young unknowns have been waiting to make their mark in the local cultural scene. Members of service clubs and Toastmasters International are excellent recruits.

It is important to remember that all communities are made up of people of differing social, economic, and educational backgrounds. Those with similar backgrounds, interests, and tastes tend to group together. In many instances, representatives of these groups are more convincing in an interpretation of library needs to their own membership than are representatives from another group. A good example is the section of the community made up of people with foreign language backgrounds. A member of their own community is a more acceptable interpreter of civic issues than is an outsider. Ethnic groups have been effectively approached in some areas by a team made up of the librarian, a campaign leader, and a leader of the foreign language society making presentations of the library story in English, followed by a translation for the benefit of those who do not understand English well. In short, the chairman of the speakers bureau must enlist not only good speakers from all walks of life but also those with special language skills.

Training for the speakers should be conducted in informal but informative sessions that will familiarize each person with the facts and needs but not overwhelm him. A cup of coffee and a discussion often set the pace for productive training. The basic materials used in training sessions include a speakers manual made up of fact sheets, sample speeches, and answers to questions; and visual aids such as slides, pictures, and tape reproductions of interviews and programs. The librarian is in a key position to lead in the training discussions designed to inform the articulate and willing speaker and to give him confidence in developing his own approach and style of presentation.

The Press

The local newspaper editor or some sympathetic member of his staff can be one of the first citizens to see the tentative draft of the library's building program statement—not for publicity purposes at this point but for background information and as a foundation for understanding a proposed civic improvement. It must be admitted that editors are individuals and that this approach may not work in every community. Ordinarily, the quicker the press understands the problems and the decisions the library board has to make, the better the relationship is. Editors and reporters who have a genuine concern for community development appreciate the importance of keeping early deliberations off the record until definite decisions are made. They are much more knowledgeable about the psychological values of timing for release dates than are amateur publicists. Often they are more than willing to help establish publicity time schedules. The better the understanding of journalists, the more unlikely that a headline will hurt the library's cause even though the story that follows supports it.

In the view of some observers, newspapers can overdo the library story. Constant coverage on the same theme for too many weeks may bring about reader boredom. Yet, at the same time, very young reporters are eager for one more story, and campaign workers justifiably want newspaper support. It is up to the library staff to suggest newsworthy ideas that will catch the attention of various segments of the general public. Sometimes these stories tie in the library with the achievements of people or the interpretation of the work of specialists and do double publicity duty, which does not hurt the library in any way. A useful suggestion is a story on newly naturalized citizens touring the library with a language specialist to become acquainted with materials that will help them understand the American way of life. The photographer can take a picture of them in an area needing improved facilities or more space.

Letters to the editor offer a popular public forum in small and medium-sized towns. When plans for a new library are announced, a surprising number of people, often nonresidents, write to the editor. Seldom have the letter writers inquired about the investigations made by the library board or found out what the thinking was behind a decision. They just sound off. The library board should have a policy not to answer such letters. An official answer from the board simply prolongs an unprofitable dispute; however, an answer from a qualified "Friend" can be effective when the editor feels that a response would be helpful and requests an answer.

Community newspaper editors take seriously their responsibility to provide their readers with facts and opinions. They are usually receptive to the proposal that a series of articles be prepared under the sponsorship of the referendum planning team. Articles published during the last few weeks of the campaign can obviously cover many subjects. A suggested series includes:

Article by the adult education director of the local schools on the public library's role in the adult education movement

Articles by school specialists, such as the school psychometrist, on the advisory functions of the children's department

Column by the director of a parochial high school on the educational and reading-counseling services of the young adult department

Article by the president of the Chamber of Commerce on the economic assets of good library service

Article by a senior citizen who has a genuine concern that younger generations get the library habit as one of the prime resources in preparing for retirement.

The possibilities for involving articulate citizens are endless. Individuals from all walks of life seem pleased to be asked to express their views. The series can be planned under the general editorship of a talented campaign worker in collaboration with the newspaper editor. It is advisable, however, that the librarian see the articles before publication—not for the purpose of revision or censorship but to be certain that there is not a sentence that misinterprets the library's concept of service. A case in point is a glowing column on the public library's relationship to the parochial schools, which stated that books for classroom use were delivered from the public library to the school. Since the library under discussion does not provide delivery to any school, parochial or public, this unqualified statement implied that the public library gives preferential treatment to a particular type of school. A preview of the copy before publication would have permitted addition of a single phrase explaining who picked up the books, thus eliminating a possible point of misunderstanding and potential trouble.

Still other outlets for planned feature stories on the library's needs and plans are the house organs of local industries. These publications will do an excellent job on the library story for a special audience, which is certain to read a publication designed for them. Industries will frequently offer to provide reprints for wider distribution by the referendum team.

Arrangements should also be made for short articles in the monthly releases of unions, cooperatives, the Chamber of Commerce, and other organizations that have publications with space to allow for an interpretation. Briefer notices are welcomed by the editors of newsletters of clubs and organizations.

Radio and TV

Interview programs on local radio or television stations are excellent vehicles for the dissemination of information on the library board's plans for a new building. A typical live interview broadcast lasts one hour, with the usual interruptions for station identification and the advertisements that sustain the program. One type of radio interview incorporates direct phone contact with the radio audience, who can ask a question by phone but do not have to identify themselves. The library participants must be prepared for some wicked questions since the questioners are shielded by anonymity. The interview participants must remember the public relations aspects of the program and not become unduly exasperated by heckling or irrelevancies at the other end of the telephone. A postmortem over one interview program suggested that articulate campaign workers be alerted to join the rebuttals by phone since they, being cloaked in anonymity also, could answer a heckler in kind without repercussions to the library cause. However, the interviewer, ordinarily is accustomed to handling difficult people and is adept at getting the discussion back to productive information and solid discussion.

A series of radio programs on tape offers an opportunity for the campaign committee to present a complete library documentary to the public, ranging from past history to long-range planning. Radio spot announcements on the regulations of absentee balloting, on the hours that the polls will be open, and on the needs of the library are, of course, a part of scheduling for the climax of the campaign.

The Telephone

The telephone committee bears one of the heaviest loads in the library campaign. The chairman selects committee members from every precinct. Long files of names and telephone numbers can be compiled from the reports of committee members and from the suggestions of the library staff and campaign leaders. This committee also asks for "sure" lists of potential voters from key people, who agree to remind these individuals to vote on referendum day. These are lists that are divided by precincts for use by the committee members who live in those precincts. The critical time for the telephone committee is the day of voting when busy citizens must be prompted to go to the polls.

Essay and Poster Contests

The idea of essay and poster contests conducted in the public and parochial schools on behalf of the library is one of the most popular promotion projects suggested by referendum planners. Articles in the professional literature indicate that this device has been used successfully in many small communities in the past; however, there are increasing objections to this type of activity in the schools. Many administrators and teachers believe, with justification, that they do not have enough time to teach, and they have some resentment toward any encroachment on their plan of study. It would be well to explore the extent of receptivity for this type of project before it is formally proposed. There is no point in losing votes over a poster. It must not be assumed that any referendum activity, even distributing bookmarks to be carried home by children, can be handled through the classroom teacher without the permission of school authorities.

Library Tours

A tour of an antiquated building is one of the most convincing demonstrations of the need for a new building. Even the regular patrons of a library are ordinarily unaware of the deficiencies of an outmoded building because the staff of most libraries go beyond the call of duty to make service as convenient as possible for the public. As an editorial writer of one county newspaper said during a campaign, "If the librarian and her colleagues would fall down on the job once in a while, it might be a lot easier to convince patrons of the urgent need for a new and expanded library."

A general announcement of the availability of library tours usually does not attract large numbers. A tour chairman must extend special invitations to busy people to get them behind the scenes in a crowded library building during the campaign. Some campaign committees, for example, have used the technique of coffee breaks at the library, to which people from all walks of life received personal invitations. Members of civic organizations and the library board were present to conduct the tours, to explain problems, and to answer questions in the library setting.

In another type of tour, the campaign leaders visit bookmobile stops to explain the importance of the referendum to bookmobile patrons, who may see no relationship between an improved main library and their mobile facilities. This type of tour seems to be enjoyed by members of the speakers bureau who like an occasional change from the platform to the person-to-person approach.

Absentee Votes

There is no time of the year when all of the library's supporters are in town. Absences on the day of voting could very well be a decisive factor in the outcome of the referendum. A file of individuals whose travel plans are known should be established early in the campaign, and several follow-ups should be made to remind these voters of the importance of applying for an absentee ballot by mail or in person. Another source of absentee votes is the college student of voting age who has not changed his residence. These students are day-long library users in vacation periods and are consequently familiar with service and space limitations that their vote might help to alleviate. Favorable absentee votes have been known to total several hundred affirmative votes. The effort to publicize dates and procedures for the absentee voting privilege is well worth the effort.

The Referendum and the Library Staff

Many librarians have been told at the peak of a campaign that the library's finest asset is the staff. It is not necessary to elaborate on the thesis that the staff is at the focal point of all public relations for the library. There are many good books and articles on this subject. The important factor for the campaign is that the staff be given the tools to maintain its excellence. Every member of the staff, including the janitors and the pages, must be given copies of all campaign literature. Channels of communication to the staff must be kept open regardless of how time-pressed the librarian is. It is mandatory that the staff be fully informed of unusual difficulties, of decisions on campaign procedures, of the speakers bureau calendar, and of dates for absentee voting, as well as ways to meet citizen objections to the preliminary drawings. They must have full and up-to-date information in order to handle questions and over-the-desk conversations intelligently.

Staff members obviously have skills for organization of materials and setting up of files. These skills should be offered to the lay campaign chairmen who are inclined to set up overly elaborate systems for carrying out their jobs. Daily staff assignments provide natural opportunities for direct interpretation of library plans and person-to-person discussion of points in the campaign literature. The staff effort will involve everyone from the clerks at the circulation desk to the children's librarian, whose annual visits in school classrooms may coincide with the campaign, to the adult education specialist, who goes out into the community for library-related programs. In the last analysis, the person-to-person approach is the most effective of all campaign techniques, and the library's own staff is in an unparalleled position to use this technique on the spot or with a follow-up at a more convenient time.

Every campaign has its time schedule, in which there are three major periods. A checklist of duties within those periods appears below.

SCHEDULE OF REFERENDUM CAMPAIGN DUTIES

Organizational period	Organization of campaign committees
	Establishment of target dates and time schedules
	Preparation of master name files for bulk mailings
	Preparation and duplication of fact sheets, question and answer manuals, and other campaign documents
	Picture-taking for slides
	Planning series of newsletters to Friends organization for progress reporting and pep talking
	Scheduling newspaper and radio information program
	Planning layout and printing of brochures and bookmarks
	Training sessions for speakers bureau
Campaign period	Open kick-off meeting
	Speakers bureau in action before organizations and at coffee hours and teas
	Distribution of bookmarks and campaign literature
	Radio interviews and programs
	Library tours
	Daily newspaper coverage
	Follow-up for absentee ballots
	Mailing of special letters to ministers, priests, rabbis, educators, and opinion-makers
Final days	Mass mailing of brochures
	Distribution of maps with polling places
	Mailing of reminder cards to vote
	Joint service club/library programs
	Concentrated telephone campaigns
	Radio spot announcements
	Poll-checking to spot precincts where light voting indicates need for telephone reminders
	Providing for transportation to polls
	Announcing results of referendum
	Thank you notes or other appreciation notices to campaign workers and supporting organizations

The System and Capital Improvements

Housing the system staff, materials, equipment, and services presents a unique problem that requires the determination of a basic philosophy of the system's organization and the answering of searching questions. The organizational philosophy will usually be established during the initial stages of the system's formation. Three patterns of organization appear to have developed: (1) joint administration of system and central library, (2) independent operation of each, with the system as a tenant and sharer of central library services, or (3) complete independence, with minimal system involvement at the central library. Any one of these choices demands from those involved the utmost in objectivity and single-ness of purpose—service to people.

By means of construction grant priorities, at least one state encourages the combined system and central library building. More easily merged collections, more closely coordinated staff, and generally more efficient public service should be the advantages of housing both under one roof. Nevertheless, potential problems are inherent in such close affiliation. Usually the central library is so designated by common agreement, but contracts should be specific. If the agreement is not renewed at some future time, what problems does this present to each party? Do the personnel policies of the library and the system differ enough to cause confusion or friction between the staffs? Will the system, although it is housed with the central library, be able to maintain objectivity in providing services to the other member libraries? Who holds title to the building? What potential problems exist in the future space needs of either party? Is the headquarters library central enough geographically for easy membership access to the system offices?

Some systems have found satisfactory answers to at least some of these questions by hiring a joint director of the system and the central library. Other systems have decided separate quarters are necessary in their particular circumstances—especially if the central library lacks sufficient space. At least one system and central library attempted a compromise by proposing a single building with a clear physical separation for the two functions. The failure of the central library's bond issue referendum prevented the compromise from being tested.

When the system is a tenant and sharer of central library services, whether it is jointly or separately administered, it has an obligation to avoid becoming a liability to the central library. The system must pay its own way and the costs being reimbursed should be clearly set forth in the contract. A central library sharing its physical space and services must be in a position to defend itself from local taxpayers' objections, which may arise at any time but are certain to be raised during a referendum campaign. With equitable reimbursement, the central library should be in a position to point to the system as a distinct advantage to the local patron.

Being a relatively new concept, the system is especially subject to the peril of underestimating the space needed to house future services. Flexibility and easy expansion are vital in planning a system headquarters building. The experience of systems that have built in the past should be investigated to enable the building planners to profit from those who have preceded them.

The system may have its own problems of physical facilities, but it also has a responsibility to assist its member libraries in building programs. This assistance may range from recommendations for rearranging the interiors of old buildings for more effective use to advice at various planning stages for a new building. Building consultant service may be provided, either directly by qualified system staff or indirectly through assistance in selection of a consultant and partial payment of the cost as a stimulus to local boards, which may hesitate to seek expert consultant service. Public relations advice and assistance may be provided in relation to referendum campaign planning in member communities. Lists of new library buildings as suggestions for local boards to visit can be prepared. Files of building program statements, building plans, and construction cost figures may be assembled for the perusal of the local librarian and board contemplating a building program. It is a system responsibility to provide encouragement and advice on capital improvements whenever requested to do so by the local library.

4 Administrative Responsibilities

Library planning in many local communities was revived and redirected in the late 1960s and 1970s by the voices of the people. The dominant voices were those of community leaders who spoke for the neglected. In addition, there were the voices of members of the profession who criticized traditional library attitudes and goals.

Planning Responsibility

Most publicly supported institutions have been challenged by taxpayers. Trends in public reaction point to the day when citizens may demand specific planning from all tax-supported agencies. One may wonder, along with David Ewing, "why Americans have not demanded more planning . . . from government agencies in order to improve public control of them."[1] Most communities are aware that segments of the public are demanding participation in planning for public institutions. They know of organized and unorganized citizen groups that question the merits of continual requests for increased revenue. Some are aware of the occasional public official who suggests that all tax-supported agencies be required to return to the polls each decade or so to determine public interest in their very existence.

The purpose of planning is to set the stage for the fulfillment of objectives. Planning has the potential for creating an understanding that objectives are more than words. Objectives, correlated with planning, represent an opportunity for interpretations that lead to self-initiated, talent-stretching contributions from a staff. Planning may also lay the groundwork for future evaluation of staff contributions and performance. The general literature on planning emphasizes that the exercise of the plan-

115

ning function tends to increase efficiency, lift morale, and provide the background of information and understanding necessary for sound decision-making. Planning is an instrument that prepares a library board and staff to accept change, which is the inevitable consequence of living in a complex world of continuing pressures.

Planning, according to management theory, is "the process of determining a course of action." Planning in libraries has been defined by Kemper as

> the dynamic process of *committing* library resources systematically and with the best possible knowledge of the future, *organizing* systematically the effort needed to utilize these resources, and *measuring* the results of planning decisions against the expectations through organized systematic feedback.[2]

It is an unusual small or medium-sized library that has a plan of service stretching into the future. Some small libraries have long-range plans incorporated in city, county, or regional planning documents. These, however, usually deal with buildings and land use rather than with projections of the needs of people for expanded library resources or with the possibilities of new directions in service. Many small libraries are handicapped in their ability to plan because they are insecure in a planning role or are unable to see beyond current staffing or financial limitations. Others may engage in planning, but their ideas are rarely communicated to the public. It is believed far too often that the public would not be interested in a library's venture into the field of planning. This belief has led to a marked degree of outrage from the activist population and from the ranks of quieter study and action organizations.

The interested citizen of the average small or medium-sized community usually finds only two documents on which to base an assumption that the local library has a plan. One is the budget, which may be published in the local paper or discussed at a town meeting at the beginning of a fiscal year. The other is an annual report, which may be summarized in a news story or in a mimeographed leaflet at the end of the year. These two documents are separated by a time gap of at least twelve months. Any connection between them is not apparent to the citizen. The citizenry is entitled to stronger evidence of the planning abilities of those chosen to direct the future of the library.

The planning responsibility is no longer the exclusive domain of a board or a committee. Many libraries involve all members of a staff in planning for the library as a whole, and for their own areas of competence in particular. This can introduce an element of challenge into planning sessions. It certainly provides an opportunity to capitalize on staff knowledge of community needs. Using the staff as participants in the planning function substantiates the Herbert Gans theory:

> Planning must . . . be user-oriented; the goals which planners work toward must relate to the behaviour patterns and values of the people for whom they are planning, and not just their own values.[3]

System affiliation may be a stimulus for planning by the independent library. System meetings are a source of ideas, techniques, and advice. Participation in system planning broadens the planning experience of each member librarian. There are mind-sharpening differences between planning at the local level and at the system level. The planning of an independent library is confined to a single community or service area and to projections conceived as feasible and uniquely appropriate for that jurisdiction. The system, on the other hand, is concerned with many areas and with a level of planning that is capable of changing attitudes and removing obstacles in a movement toward improved library-centered opportunities for all citizens. The distinctions between the two levels of planning responsibility can be summarized in this way:

Local level

1. Defining the planning function of the local board and staff
2. Perceiving changing needs of the served and unserved in the community
3. Reappraising local long-range objectives and short-term goals
4. Determining and evaluating policies as aids to fulfilling objectives
5. Examining library standards and their local application

System level

1. Identifying the scope and requirements for systemwide planning
2. Analyzing areawide environmental, economic, technological, and social conditions as barometers of requirements for advancing system services
3. Exploring and selecting feasible and appropriate goals for systemwide service
4. Establishing and evaluating policies for building system services and procedures
5. Interpreting standards and providing guidance for their implementation

Local level

6. Examining advantages of centralized processing or other contract services

7. Establishing priorities in collection building

8. Planning innovations to meet needs of the unserved

9. Developing local orientation and in-service programs for trustees and staff

10. Sustaining publicity and public information programs

11. Planning for local interlibrary, interagency, and system membership cooperation

12. Planning for evaluation of local services

13. Determining needs for community studies or library surveys

14. Encouraging staff creativity in the fulfillment of the library's objectives

15. Communicating with system

16. Visualizing role of the independent library in system

17. Participating in the community's planning process.

System level

6. Providing for technical and administrative advisory services

7. Coordinating channels for access to multinetwork collections

8. Expanding services to areas without library service

9. Developing comprehensive continuing education programs for trustees, administrators, and staff

10. Sustaining systemwide public relations programs for public understanding of system services

11. Planning for intersystem and interdisciplinary projects and service contracts

12. Planning for evaluation of system services

13. Determining areas of specialized research for benefit of the member libraries and the profession

14. Supporting professional growth in member libraries through the provision of leadership and participation opportunities

15. Solving problems of communicating with member libraries

16. Visualizing role of the system in a nationwide network of libraries for services to member libraries

17. Participating in the area and state planning process.

The cooperative library system has been called a planned

partnership, and, to paraphrase John Dewey, it is a partnership that plans together. A participative organizational structure is needed to assure the involvement of the membership in sound system planning. Four cornerstones of this structure, aside from financing, are: (1) continued opportunities for system and membership collaboration on the determination of the appropriateness of changing goals; (2) a mechanism whereby the system staff can quickly convert their specialties and the benefits of research into programs and services desired by the membership; (3) channels through which the member library can feed back into this mechanism the insights that will help the system become increasingly more useful; and (4) incentives for the member library to build on existing strength. Planning for a cooperative system consists of two major phases: the strategic or goal-setting phase and the implemental or carrying-out phase. The system staff and the member libraries are involved in both.

The system has the advantage of being able to concentrate an appreciable share of its funds and the time of its staff specialists on planning. The system staff is in a position to take an objective, long-range, broader view. They are able to take Toynbee's advice: "Don't plunge in precipitously; think before you act; give yourself time to see your subject or a problem as a whole."[4]

The 1963–66 evaluation of the New York state systems found that "those systems which are most successful in their service programs are doing the best jobs of planning."[5] If this pattern prevails in other parts of the country, it is highly possible that systems, as planning leaders, will inspire the member libraries to broaden the scope of their planning. There may be other influences. A community library, through the benefits of system services, will be identified in the public mind as a source rather than as a site for all resources. Such identification will reinforce the essentiality of local planning beyond artificial corporation limits. It is conceivable that neighboring libraries, especially in suburban regions, may decide on the basis of a close geographic relationship and joint planning to offer to cooperate in innovative programs or special research studies on behalf of the system. The cooperation of member libraries in system planning is profitable in those cases in which the system requires comparative data to ascertain the potential of public interest in an innovative service. An illustration might be a member-inspired, but system-directed, study designed to test, in different population areas, public acceptance of fee charges for in-depth reference or abstracting services provided by member library-system collaboration.

Study and Research Responsibilities

According to Alvin Toffler "anticipatory democracy"[6] is needed to cope with the modern pace of change. In order to anticipate changes and to plan to meet them, continual fact-gathering for planning and research purposes must be standard operating procedure for the local library and the cooperative system. Research is an area rarely touched by even the most affluent of autonomous libraries. Their resources and energy must of necessity go into all of the ramifications of work with the public. Lack of training in research techniques adds still another barrier to any meaningful research on the part of independent libraries. However, local libraries must study their communities constantly to keep abreast of changes in current and potential clientele and to anticipate changes in the economic bases of their service areas. No community is stagnant. Although changes are sometimes so gradual as to be unnoticed without purposeful community study, they are going on persistently and inevitably. As a part of its planning process, the local library must gather data to shed light on the changes that have already occurred and that predictably will occur. Community information-gathering is of inestimable value not only to the local library but also to the system, which must determine areas of research that will be productive in terms of the local library's services. A system gathers data from its member libraries on salaries, fringe benefits, hours of service, fines, fees, tax rates, per capita support, and use. Annual compilations of data distributed to the member libraries in graphic form assist them in comparing themselves with others. The system also may compile current information on technological developments which may offer more efficient methods of performing usual functions, such as central computerized circulation control, or possible new library services, such as electronic video recordings.

An in-depth professional library is customarily developed by a system for the use of its consultant staff and its members. In the process, publications based on library research in the state and from other areas of the nation are assembled and culled for information pertinent to the member library. Digests of research findings are often sent by the system to the individual libraries to stimulate the thinking of the local staff and board members. When feasible, the system assists a member library in the application of the products of research in a pilot project. Research at the system level may yield justifications for the voluntary merger of two or more inadequately supported small libraries to yield a more realistic tax base and improved services.

The types of problems lending themselves to system research are the massive problems of the profession, which cannot be explored successfully by any one library. They may include questions of human response to be answered by research into reader habits. They involve problems of feasibility and the cost of adapting technological advances to library use. Two examples of research initiated by systems are comprehensive reports on natural library service zones in a system area, and feasibility studies of bibliographic banks and information retrieval systems.[7]

Research starts with the identification of a problem and an appraisal of the most appropriate techniques to expose its roots. It involves the collection, processing, and interpretation of data and the building up of a body of information to serve as a foundation for the knowledge that may be the springboard for remedial action. The cooperative system has a responsibility to remind the membership of the distinction between data and knowledge. The membership will participate in many aspects of research, if in no other ways than by completing questionnaires or checking lists against card catalogs. The degree of their confidence in research undoubtedly will be in direct ratio to their understanding of the rationale in research methodology and in their being forewarned that an accumulation of data is not immediately transmuted into wisdom. The results of research may be positive or may be negative. The cooperative system and its member libraries learn from both.

The cooperative system's role in research is multifaceted, and the system is unusually well structured for it. It has the freedom and the capacity to engage, by employment or contract, the services of research specialists from all disciplines to examine the origins of library problems and to work toward the alleviation of those problems. Outside research agencies also may be engaged by the system to determine the feasibility and design of a new system service. They may study various library operations to provide a means for member libraries to evaluate policies and procedures. Current trends indicate moves toward increased inter-system action in planning and financing research and toward involvement in regional or even statewide research projects. Research is recognized as an essential responsibility and an outstanding opportunity yet to be fully exploited by cooperative systems on behalf of their member libraries.

Policy-making Responsibility

Policies are guidelines that point to directions for administrative decisions and for carrying out service procedures. They should result from a consensus that a policy directive will be advantageous to the people it affects and that its implementation will expedite management and service operations.

Policy development is part of library planning. Sound policies correlate with the objectives of the library. An objective aims at an accomplishment. Policy formulation offers an opportunity to establish the best possible framework in which to move toward that accomplishment. Every policy has some bearing on the objectives and their achievement. For example, personnel policies that are fair and compatible with staff welfare indirectly support the library's goals by removing the personal frustrations that inhibit a total response to the challenge of the library's objectives. Correlation of objectives and policies helps to eliminate inconsistencies that may be expedient but are disastrous because they erode public confidence. A simple illustration is a policy on emergency use of noncirculating reference materials outside the library. Such a policy must recognize emergency situations but protect the on-site user.

The final authority in policy-making is the board of trustees. A board in a small community considers policy development on its own recognition, on recommendations from the librarian and staff, and occasionally through the prodding of an articulate public. The system aids the member library in its policy-making responsibility by scheduling workshops on the policy function, by gathering sample policy statements for examination by interested librarians and trustees, and by direct consultation at the request of the local library.

Staff involvement gained acceptance in the 1960s and early 1970s as an asset in policy development. The staff are the people who know the most about the public they serve, who are able to identify an area in which a new or improved policy would be helpful, and who have the insight to assess its potential usefulness. The formulation of a workable policy is dependent on a free flow of information about the nature of a policy proposal and on a mutual respect for divergent viewpoints on approaches to make it effective. The value of a policy is to be judged by its acceptability to a staff, who must interpret it, and to the patrons, who either understand it or are alienated by its effect.

Policies are not isolated guidelines. They interrelate with rules, routines, and standards of day-by-day operation. Every institution has some rules. For a library, a rule is a regulation governing a stable situation. A rule may be, in a sense, the implementation of a minimum standard, such as the number of hours a library shall be open to the public. Or it may be associated with penalties prescribed by local ordinances, such as the loss of library privileges due to the destruction of library property. A rule in the strict sense is mandatory. Typical library rules that are fixed—at least until they are revised—cover such conditions as areas of service, hours of service, borrowing provisions, number of paid holidays, and terms of employment.

However, some rules in a library are subject to policy interpretations. An effective policy allows for the exercise of judgment, common sense, and a realistic appreciation of the purpose of a library on the part of the staff. For example, a rule may state that no person may borrow library materials if his fines have accumulated to more than a certain amount. A policy, molded by an objective, may modify this rule under exceptional conditions. There is justification, for example, in reducing or canceling a large fine to encourage a child from an economically deprived home to make a fresh start in the use of books and other library materials.

A policy is not an excuse to break rules, however. A rule that is broken constantly should be reexamined. The application of a policy that on occasion allows for a modification of a rule must relate to an objective. In fining a child, the objective is not to make money but to help him learn the reason for rules as he grows in skill in the use of the library's collection. Policies that modify rules serve as instruments to correct alienating factors that grow out of misunderstandings. Staff skill in the interpretation of the modification reestablishes public confidence at all age levels in the justice of reasonable rules.

Most policies in a library came into being not in relation to rules but in conjunction with plans to fulfill the goals of the library. Advantageous characteristics of library polices are flexibility and a positive emphasis of policy reliance upon library objectives. In addition, effective policies for the 1970s indicate a response to the behavior trends in the community and reflect the broadening concern for a definition of social responsibility on the part of the profession.

Policy Statements

Policies must be in written form to be used effectively. The preparation of a policy statement is not complicated. A single individual, many times the librarian, is charged with writing the first draft. This draft becomes a working paper which, when duplicated and distributed, is the starting point for generating ideas and for encouraging examination by trustees and staff of the ramifications of the total policy program. A working paper has several values: it is a time-saving agenda that keeps the discussion moving in a direct line; it serves as a medium for illustrating the broad range of areas that need policy coverage; as a black and white presentation, it makes visible those proposals that cry out for clarification in terms of semantics.

Policies should be written simply and concisely. Particular attention should be given to those words or phrases subject to several interpretations. A case in point is a personnel policy stating "A leave of absence of one week with pay is allowed at the discretion of the librarian upon the death of a member of the immediate family of a staff member." The phrase that raises unnecessary questions in this policy is "the immediate family." Obviously it was assumed when this policy was written that there would be general agreement on the relationships covered by the term "immediate family." Human obligations and dependencies are not that easily categorized. Consequently, this phrase and others like it should be spelled out to prevent misunderstandings and resentment.

Policy writing may involve several revisions, with contributions from all members of the policy writing team. The final policy statements are subject to the approval of the board, as the policy-making authority. They are then duplicated and distributed to trustees and staff members for convenient referral. At a later date, an active policy statement becomes the working paper for revisions. A decade ago policy-makers could believe that their policies might meet a large proportion of problems without need for major revisions for approximately five years. But a fast-changing society has imposed the need for constant alertness to the currency of policies and their relationship to public expectations.

Types of Policy Statements

Many areas of library administration merit policy treatment. The major ones are general administration, personnel, public use of buildings and equipment, major gifts, and selection of books and library materials. The latter is discussed in chapter 5, "Collection Building and Maintenance."

General Administration

General policies are those that provide direction for decisions affecting overall library operation rather than separate functions or departments. General policy needs vary from library to library. Points commonly covered in a general policy statement include:

1. Adult education: the library's responsibilities toward the initiation of or cooperation with adult education programs in the community
2. Community leadership and involvement: the library's position on the use of library time for staff participation in civic, educational, or cultural activities outside the library building
3. Freedom to read: the library's response to the concepts of intellectual freedom in a democratic society
4. Public communications: the library's judgment of the kind and content of public announcements, nonlibrary posters and hand-outs that are appropriate to display in relation to the library's informational and educational function
5. School-public library relationships: the public library's recognition of the distinction between school and public li-

braries and of its obligations in cooperative planning and programming
6. Area library resources: the library's awareness of the strengths of other types of libraries in the community and its responsibility to create reciprocal relationships
7. Confidentiality of borrowers' records: the library's position on governmental investigations of patron use of materials.
8. Petitions and solicitation of funds: the library's position on patron rights to freedom from public solicitation of signatures or donations for worthy causes
9. Affiliation with library associations: the local library's recognition of its leadership and contributory obligations to the profession
10. Standards: the library's awareness of standards as an aid in measuring progress and achieving degrees of excellence.

Personnel

The dominant elements in a personnel policy statement are the objectives of the library and the people who are expected to implement those objectives. A study of personnel needs and working conditions raises questions that must be reflected in these policies: What are the board and the administrator doing for and with the people who are on their payroll? What kind of policies indicate a consideration for the welfare of the staff? What kinds of policies provide incentives for initiative, creativity, and competence? Both trustees and staff can contribute answers to these questions.

A personnel policy statement may cover the following subjects:

1. Criteria for selection
2. Channels for advancement
3. Staff opportunities for participation in management
4. Staff responsibilities to the library in engaging as citizens in political and social action
5. Working conditions
   a. Hours per week
   b. Schedules
   c. Free days
   d. Frequency and length of rest breaks
   e. Holidays
6. Vacations
   a. Year-round or limited to summer
   b. Accumulation privileges

7. Sick leave provisions
   a. Annual
   b. Accumulated sick leave
8. Injury on library premises
9. Hospitalization and medical insurance
10. Released time for voting
11. Compensation related to jury duty
12. Leaves of absence
    a. Study
    b. Travel
    c. Funerals
    d. Maternity
    e. Acceptance of teaching invitations
    f. Military duty
13. Compensation plan for overtime
14. Limitations, if any, on moonlighting
15. Resignation notification requirements
16. Severance pay
17. Dismissal procedures
18. Channels for grievance
19. Pension procedures
20. Payment of professional dues for staff and/or board
21. Conference and system workshop time and expenses
22. The relationship of staff organizations to library administration
23. Parking privileges
24. Discount privileges for personal book and library materials orders.

Public Use of Library Facilities

A library with meeting room facilities needs policy decisions on:

1. Types of meetings to have priority: educational, civic, cultural, and public information events or library-sponsored programs
2. Possible exclusions inconsistent with the library's objectives, such as bingo games or religious meetings
3. Use of the library name in distributing partisan literature or for an organization's mailing address
4. Smoking or food distribution privileges
5. Admission charges, fees, and tipping
6. Storage of records or equipment belonging to organizations meeting regularly in the library
7. Closing hours and holiday limitations
8. Responsibilities of groups using the facilities.

Major Gifts

A major gifts policy statement provides guidelines for the consideration of important gifts of money, books, or art objects offered with conditional reservations. The most important factor in this policy is the determination of what in the long run will be for the best interest of the library. Equally important is the policy recognition that library personnel are not assessors and consequently are not qualified to establish monetary evaluations of any gift they accept.

System Level Policies

Policy development at the system level is influenced by many factors, among which are: the guidelines of *Minimum Standards for Public Library Systems, 1966,* the explicit and implicit directives of the system's own plan of service, the characteristics of member libraries, the quality of resources at the headquarters library, the level of service requirements, and the example provided by the experiences of well-established systems. In many areas, system directors exchange policy documents and have an opportunity to alert each other to the consequences of inadequacies or gaps in policy development.

A system has policy statements paralleling those of the independent library, such as personnel policies. In addition, a system must have policies relating directly to services, such as collection building, interlibrary loans, reciprocal borrowing, or project demonstrations. The sensitive policy areas for a system are those dealing with the eligibility of nonresidents to use system services and with the rights of nonparticipating libraries in the area to use system services.

Administration and Management

The administrative function of the member library, exclusive of fiscal responsibilities, consists of: (1) organizing material and human resources for effective service, (2) interpreting policies and recommending policy change as needed for the fulfillment of objectives, (3) determining the range of activities feasible within budgetary limitations, (4) providing guidelines for the management of the library, (5) reviewing operations for satisfactory performance or needed improvements, (6) stimulating staff initiative, (7) executing leadership responsibilities in the library, the community, and the profession, (8) reporting current activities and progress, and (9) planning for the future.

Administration involves routines, as do all other library occupations. However, all aspects of administration, from organization to planning, can be reduced in the last analysis to human relationships. If they cannot be, there is a chance that the administrator is preoccupied with operational details rather than with the skillful use of staff and time. There is a distinction between creative administration and routine management. The fact that the distinction bothers the profession is reflected in library literature, which repeatedly gives warning that far too often professional talent is diminished by either the assumption of or the assignment to nonprofessional duties.

Library administration necessitates professional vision, judgment, and decisions related to the unique objectives of the library as distinct from any other institution. "Management" means carrying out the operations and procedures normally determined at the administrative level to be the most efficient means of meeting the goals of a library. Management involves operational techniques not necessarily unique to the library.

The term "administration" is sometimes used to designate both a level of responsibility and the people who work at that level. The head librarian, as the chief executive, traditionally bears the burden of overall accountability. The administrative function in practice, however, is becoming a shared responsibility. Administration in a library is made up of segments that focus on differing types of services and draw on differing kinds of skills and specializations. The general components of the administrative function, such as organizing, interpreting, planning, and leading, are the work of the individuals who are in charge of them. Consequently, the coordinator of work with children, the coordinator of extension services, and others have an obligation to contribute the benefits of their experience and specializations to the total administrative function.

The philosophy of sharing the responsibility of the administrative function within the organizational structure of the library has changed the role of the chief administrator from that of a "boss" to that of a stimulator, a trainer, a coordinator, and an enabler. In the average library, this change does not lessen the accountability of the head librarian for decision-making or for the effectiveness of the overall library program. Shared responsibility serves to multiply leadership capabilities and promotes a high sense of personal and professional responsibility at key points in the library service program.

Evolving management theories point to an administrative obligation to create a climate conducive to broadening the base of staff involvement in the improvement of work productivity. This responsibility involves an old-fashioned concept, morale, defined in contemporary terms as a "mode of participation." This term is translated to mean a process of effective or ineffective participation.[8] Sustaining a productive mode of participation means the application of such motivators[9] as the stimulation of challenging new relationships between the staff as members of a working group, and increased opportunities for achievement through the organization of the creative and analytic abilities of all the members of the staff. Participatory administration requires learning new terminology for leadership skills. The cooperative system, through its workshop programs, is able to lay the foundation for understanding and implementing approaches and techniques to achieve excellence in the mode of participation.

Communications is the one area of responsibility related to the mode of participation that is perhaps the easiest to overlook. Conscious effort must be made to involve the members of the staff who work part-time, who man the desks while staff meetings are in process, or who never look at a staff bulletin board. Communication within the library, as within the system, must be a two-way interchange. Clerks need information on such details as who is in charge if all supervisory personnel are out of the building. Administrative personnel need to know what the staff is thinking and how they judge public reactions to new policies or programs.

The devices used to keep the doors open for communication include regular staff meetings, departmental meetings, newsletters, and suggestion boxes. Overcommunication is rare. It may prevail in situations in which the administrator prematurely shares a worry, such as a threatened budget cut that may never materialize, and thereby starts a chain reaction of anxiety and frustration. This kind of overcommunication is probably not so prevalent as the overcommunication that is staff-generated and takes the form of gossip, rumors, or even undue worry over an outburst of dissatisfaction from a single employee. The administrator or supervisor has to learn to distinguish between a real problem and the human habit of griping and to act quickly to cancel out both cause and effect of either gripes or rumors with facts and interpretations. Planned communication, deliberately built into administrative practice, offers a constructive approach to the resolution of many human and professional problems.

Administrative Innovation

In administration, as in all other aspects of the library profession, innovation is now the order of the day. Participatory management[10] has been attempted with some success in industry and has been tested with reported success in at least one library. In participatory library management, the entire full-time staff is organized into various committees that meet regularly and reach decisions only by consensus. The benefits of participatory management are improved communications, increased interest in the library's problems and needs, and stimulation of staff initiative. Management by committee is limited to the extent that responsibility for standards, performance, and results still rests with the administrator.

An innovation that seeks to replace the traditional hierarchical pyramid organization structure is the matrix, which "diffuses decision-making, responsibility, and authority"[11] throughout the library staff and limits the administrator's function to that of coordinator. Staff members in the matrix organization become specialists in their fields and are paid in recognition of superiority in their areas of expertise rather than on the basis of increased responsibility. Responsibility is not vested in the administrator; the entire staff is held responsibile for the organization. Full use of staff abilities, talents, and decision-making by those most closely involved with the problems at hand are cited as advantages of the matrix organization (see figure 1).

Administrative innovations are a recognition that management reaches its objectives only through the efforts of people and that people function at a higher level when they are given an opportunity to contribute to management. Cooperative library systems are able to help librarians understand the evolution of management theories through workshops that draw on the expertise of innovative managers in other fields.

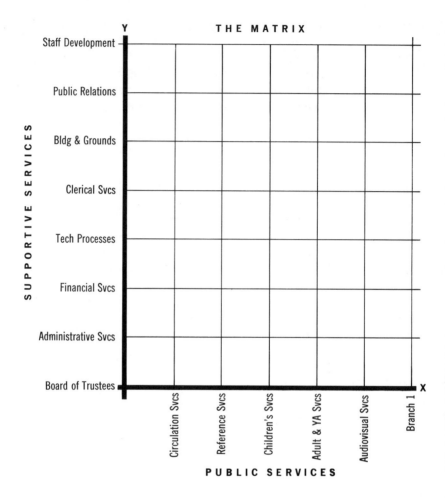

Fig. 1. A matrix developed by Don Sager (Elyria Public Library) for experimentation in a small library system, with supportive services located on the Y axis and public services on the X axis. (Reprinted with permission of *American Libraries* and the author)

Coordinating Responsibility

As the agency responsible for serving the entire community, the public library accepts the responsibility of initiating efforts to coordinate the services of various types of libraries in a community. The types of libraries existing in the average small community differ from region to region but may include elementary and secondary school libraries, junior college libraries, armed forces libraries, special libraries from industry and business, church libraries, social agency libraries, and regional planning or other governmental libraries. The motivation for coordinated planning is a concern for the quality of and accessibility to the total library resources to be found in the community.

Problems of coordination between publicly supported community and school libraries and privately supported libraries may seem insurmountable to some librarians. To others the idea is a challenge. One example of the acceptance of a public library's coordinating function is the enlistment of an existing committee from representative types of area libraries to serve as a task force to examine attitudes, barriers, and future needs for coordinated service. The cooperative system in the area participates in the local effort by providing panelists and resource people for open meetings, which focus on cooperation. System participation in a local area conference underscores the system's responsibility to work toward a network made up of all types of libraries.

The so-called student problem is considered by many to be crucial and has priority in most communities. Curriculum-related pressures prevail in all areas. The 1969 survey of the Chicago Public Library found that this metropolitan library "is to a significant extent an agency for formal students."[12] This statement could apply to almost every public library. The problem in smaller communities is compounded by citizen confusion over the necessity for taxpayer support of both curriculum-centered libraries in the schools and individualized services for the child and his parents in the children's departments of public libraries. The rapid spread of adult evening school programs, junior colleges, and new state universities have produced additional pressure points where they did not exist before.

Many public libraries have attempted to rebalance the pressures of student use by establishing formal and informal relationships with school authorities and school librarians. Some of the methods used include:

1. Establishment of councils or coordinating committees composed of school and public library administrators, school and public librarians, and representatives of special education departments (The objectives of such committees are to attempt to clarify the proper role of each institution in serving the student, to encourage maximum use of the school libraries, and to eliminate duplication of resources and overlapping services)
2. Exchanges of personnel, sometimes called "job swaps," to create a climate of real understanding of the practical realities that face both types of libraries in their daily work
3. Appointment of a public library staff member to serve as a liaison between the public library and the schools through clearinghouse functions such as exchanging information on acquisition plans for the purchase of expensive tools, ascertaining schedules for mass assignments, and resolving misunderstandings as they occur
4. Inauguration of experimental summer and school-year reading programs for the disadvantaged or the gifted in cooperation with special education faculty
5. Orientation of school faculty through public library programs and open-house affairs to enlist the interest of teachers in new books, subject bibliographies, and the effective use of books and other library materials
6. Preparation of leaflets and brochures for students and parents, explaining the distinctions between school and public libraries and describing the types of services available in each with suggestions for their use
7. Planned interuse of school and public library information distribution centers, communications, and delivery services to sustain a continuous flow of information and to improve an interlibrary loan program
8. Participation in advisory councils established by junior colleges for curriculum development and cooperation with all types of libraries in the area.

School districts often encompass more than one community, and students from a university, college, or junior college, may range over a wide area, using several public libraries within a system. A cooperative system is in a position to provide the necessary leadership in efforts at cooperation between the libraries of the educational institutions and the affected public libraries. The system may initiate meetings of the librarians to plan a coordinated program in order to avoid wasteful duplication and improve overall service. The system can provide the stimulus for exploration and experimentation by setting up a pilot project in a member library's community. The system has the responsibility to begin the long-range planning necessary to bring all types of libraries into active membership in the system network.

The coordinating function extends also into the area of special libraries in local industry and business and to libraries maintained by churches, hospitals, or social agencies. Special libraries came into existence because the public library was unable to afford the specialization of interests they served. They have remained outside the library community partly because of their specialization but more often because no one has asked them to participate in professional interchanges that are mutually advantageous. The custom of some army and navy libraries to invite librarians from all types of libraries to audit or participate in their annual workshops provides a worthy model for public librarians and systems to emulate. Formal agreements between special and public libraries may be limited by the sophistication of the special library collections or by the policies of the parent organization. Informal cooperation, however, is always possible. A cooperative system has a promising opportunity in its responsibility to explore ways for the special and public libraries to be of mutual assistance in reference, bibliographic search, materials selection, and in-service training.

Public Relations Programming Responsibility

An examination of available surveys of small or medium-sized libraries reveals a general weakness in the area of public relations programming. A library may have excellent publicity through outstanding on-site displays, spot announcements on the radio, attractive reading lists, and a regular newspaper column. Publicity, however, is only one part of a public relations program. Surveys indicate that despite good publicity the typical library has not been notably skillful in informing the total public about its capabilities to serve their needs. As a member of a cooperative system, the average library frequently interprets system services in a limited fashion and with a librarian's vocabulary.

Public relations is a broad function that deliberately aims at deepening public understanding of the objectives and the resources of the library and their potential in making a difference in the lives of every individual in the community. Various ways of achieving this aim have been explored by various libraries: (1) employment of an experienced public relations specialist, not necessarily a librarian, as a member of the staff or on a part-time basis, (2) joint sponsorship by neighboring libraries of a public relations program conducted by a specialist, (3) consultations with a public relations expert on the system staff, or (4) a contract with a public relations firm.

The public relations program at the system level differs from that of the local level in that it is designed to serve all the member libraries in informing and selling the public on the benefits of the resources available through system services and through the additional resources afforded by the information and materials network. The system public relations program is usually handled by a public relations firm or an experienced staff specialist. It provides the member library with brochures on system services for public distribution and utilizes all areawide communications media: newspapers, regional periodicals, television, and radio.

There is an understandable interest on the part of system members in the possibilities of expanding the system's public relations service to include individualized service for member libraries. Such an expansion would give added support to the total public relations program and guarantee professional treatment of public relations matters on a local level. System-subsidized public relations for each member library depend on the system's plan of service and on the cost of employing a public relations firm with a field staff large enough to handle effectively the job at the local level and at the system level.

Priorities in the system program, approved by the membership, may necessitate financing by the system and the member libraries on a shared cost basis. Regardless of the source of funds, a public relations program covering both the broad needs of the total system and the specific needs of the member libraries must be carefully defined. The system staff, the public relations specialists, and the member librarians must join together to examine member expectations and to determine what is possible. There will be questions about the meaning and the elements of such a program. Some librarians may think in terms of posters and displays. Others will have a more sophisticated image of public relations. There may be a problem in the allocation of the time of the public relations specialist in serving the very active library and the quiet library. A successful system-plus-membership public relations program must recognize the diversities of member library needs and the principle of equity in treatment.

Responsibility for Evaluation

Librarians and trustees of independent libraries often exhibit some anxiety about the way their library "measures up" to libraries of similar size. They turn to statistics printed in state bulletins in the hope that they may find an answer. Unfortunately, the use of published statistical compilations without expert interpretation has relatively little value for local evaluation. These compilations are usually out of date by the time they are published. The annual reports that provide the data are subject to misinterpretation at the point of origin. Still another handicap in the use of published statistics is that they provide no insight into the quality of library collections or any measure of public satisfaction with available services. This situation has improved, however, since cooperative systems have assumed responsibility for gathering statistics, particularly for the use of their members. A system's statistical service has the advantage of being based on current data. A most important element in the system's statistical work is that the system staff has the background to provide interpretations, which are essential for any meaningful use of comparative tabulations at the local level.

The profession has not found measurement tools that have application to all situations in all parts of the country. The national standards are set at minimum levels, and the 1966 version is geared to the system. A limited number of statistical standards have been prepared as an addenda to the *Minimum Standards for Public Library Systems, 1966*. These standards are expressed in percentages. They state, for example, that of the materials used regularly in the local library, a minimum of 80 percent of the juvenile material requested should be available locally; communities of 25,000 to 49,999 should own 65 to 80 percent of the adult nonfiction material requested regularly; and communities of 50,000 to 99,999 should own 80 to 95 percent of the adult nonfiction in regular use.[13] These percentage figures are helpful, but they still do not satisfy many trustees or librarians, leaving a very large challenge to the cooperative systems to help develop yardsticks that will be of value to the membership for self-evaluation.

One available tool in the local assessment process is the library's own statement of objectives. Of course, some excellent objectives are too broad to be measured with the techniques available to the small or medium-sized library. An example is "The library shall provide materials to help all citizens educate themselves continually."[14] However, the library's statement of objectives may include goals which are narrower in focus, such as "The library shall initiate programs that will provide information on problems of local and national importance." This more specific objective may be examined in terms of the action taken. The satisfaction of citizen-participants with the results may be ascertained through interviews or questionnaires.

Another form of measurement is a study of the cost of a particular service. An analysis of the time and cost factors in hand-charging compared to machine-charging may result in the acquisition of labor-saving machines and the adoption of techniques that will provide more reliable or quicker service. The system consultant staff may play a very important role in helping member libraries measure the effectiveness of service techniques and analyze operational costs.

Many libraries attempt to determine user satisfaction. Lawrence Powell pointed out that "if a library is staffed by cheerful, willing and intelligent people, the public will be well served."[15] Librarians accept this statement with some reservations. They rarely have reliable insight into the functioning of their co-workers in terms of the library patrons' self-oriented objectives. Administrators try to gauge the intangibles of person-to-person service through attitude surveys and analyses of verbal and written complaints. Attitude or opinion surveys are used by many institutions to obtain an overall measure of the quality of service. Questionnaires can be devised to obtain a usable sampling of public attitudes, interests, and degrees of satisfaction. If the full value of a survey is to be realized, it should be designed, conducted, and interpreted by qualified personnel. Surveys repeated every five years or so are particularly useful as cumulative case studies to provide data on the rate of library improvement and trends in public judgment.

A complaint may be, in a sense, a compliment. It may indicate that a taxpayer cares enough about the library to take the time to explain his point of view and the reasons for his dissatisfactions. On the other hand, it may simply reflect the personality of the complainant or a crisis in his personal life. The recommended technique is to request that the complaint be put into writing. A complaint without sufficient grounds may dissipate with the effort of putting it in written form. A legitimate complaint, in writing, may be studied and corrective action taken as needed. At the same time, a legitimate complaint may be considered a contribution to the background knowledge needed for change in service techniques or collection building. Some complaints are to be expected. If there are none, the impact of the library on the community is probably at a low level. Too many complaints should be regarded as symptomatic of the need for a review of policies and procedures.

A useful gauge in measuring public relationships is the press. As a general rule, the newspapers of the community feel a kinship with the library. The library and the press have a common cause. The library usually is not the subject of critical editorials, but it is occasionally the subject of a letter to the editor. When such letters appear and are critical, there is something to be learned about the library's failure to communicate and to interpret its objectives, its resources, and its limitations. The lesson to be learned, however, should not involve a defensive answer for publication but rather a constructive move toward improvement in the regular public communications programs and in services.

Areas in which an independent library may advantageously direct its self-examination through staff and board collaboration include:

1. Logic and convenience of arrangements of material for easy public access, with an examination of rationale for any restricted-use collection
2. Quality of the collection in terms of use and community needs

3. Reference and information services to pinpoint weaknesses in the collection or in-service training
4. Arrangements of public service desks for optimum work flow
5. Effectiveness of efforts to coordinate resources and services with other types of libraries and referral agencies in the community
6. Extent and effectiveness of programs to reach the unserved
7. Channels used to inform the public about existing programs, additions to the collections, and add-on services from the system
8. Effectiveness of individual reader guidance services for all age levels
9. Effectiveness of services to groups in terms of leadership, supply of materials, or reading lists.

The system may undertake the evaluation of a local library on the request of that library. Requests for evaluation should be in writing and should include a definition of the scope of the evaluation desired. System evaluations of member libraries require a staff with expertise in the area to be evaluated. Areas in which the system may be of assistance include:

1. Study of the book collection to analyze subject fields that need strengthening or weeding
2. Survey of furniture, stack, and equipment layouts to recommend rearrangements for improved service and more efficient use of space
3. Studies of existing or potential cooperative activities with other types of libraries in the community or nearby
4. Studies to provide suggestions for reaching the unserved segments of the community or for serving the unincorporated area beyond the community's boundaries
5. Review of the library's methods of publicizing its services and those of the system
6. Studies to recommend methods for a community self-study against which to measure the library's effectiveness
7. Review of the library's policies with suggested revisions
8. Review of the library's budget and budgeting procedures
9. Review of the library's personnel organization, classification, and pay plans
10. Consultations on the use of compilations and tabulations of library statistics illustrating the strengths and weaknesses of comparable libraries

11. Studies to help in the formation of a Friends of the Library group.

Evaluation of the system is a joint responsibility. The methodology for system evaluation may be devised by the system or by the state library. In the interim between formal evaluations of system services, both the system staff and the member libraries should ask such questions as: "Are more books and library materials available because the system exists?" and "Are more citizens being served more effectively because of the library's affiliation with a cooperative system?" If the answers are hesitant or vague, the system and its members should perhaps take a sharp look at the system plan and at the ways in which libraries do or do not take advantage of it.

In every service area there are some residents who do not use the library's services. Although many of the unserved may lack the simple ingredient of motivation, the alert librarian and board of trustees will want to be certain the library has exhausted all methods of stimulating library use by all segments of the population. Any doubt about the library's lack of effectiveness in communications or provision of services to any portion of the population should be countered by an analysis of the characteristics of the nonusers and the efforts made to relate local and system services to them. This does not necessarily imply that the local library should engage in a missionary program. Rather it indicates that nonuse should be from choice rather than from lack of awareness of what the library has to offer or dissatisfaction with services already tested.

As tax-supported public service institutions in a society in constant flux, neither the local library nor the cooperative system can justify assumptions of currency, relevance, adequacy, or universal awareness of its materials and services. Periodic self-examination is necessary to assure those responsible that the library and the system are fulfilling their roles to the fullest possible degree. Each has its own role in self-evaluation. The library will be examined and evaluated by those locally responsible to the extent they feel competent. Evaluation by the system staff will be sought in any area local personnel need assistance. System personnel may discover ways to improve services to local libraries in the normal course of providing such services. The cooperative system has a built-in evaluative organization in its member libraries. Because the local library staffs are in direct contact with the public, they can offer insights as to the effectiveness of system services that system personnel can never hope to have. In short, the member library should not hesitate to seek system assistance in evaluation of local services; the system cannot evaluate its own services without the thoughtful participation of its members.

Tools for Administration and Management

Administrative Manuals

An administrative manual is a convenience tool for the busy librarian. It brings together, usually in loose-leaf form, all essential documents, policy statements, and data records of current value in the administration of a library. The cooperative system may assemble model administrative manuals for reference and for loan to the member library. Through its workshops it may distribute guidelines for the content of manuals, which the local library may adapt for its own purposes. At outline on essential points in insurance coverage given in appendix D illustrates the type of material that is issued by a system workshop and includes pointers for data to be included in the local administrative manual. An administrative manual proves its value in the following ways:

1. It is a timesaver. Many problem situations and uncertainties about procedures in a library are repetitive. An administrative manual provides a quick reference to guidelines that might otherwise be buried in minute books or reports of committees.
2. It gathers together the entire range of established policies that may be reproduced in separate manuals to meet differing functional needs of departments and individuals.
3. It serves as a referral tool for infrequently used information available in other forms.

An administrative manual may advantageously include:
1. Legal description of library property
2. Objectives of the library
   a. Overall objectives
   b. Departmental objectives

3. Brief history of the library, or a listing of establishment and other commemorative dates
4. Statement of the responsibilities of the board
5. Statement of the duties of the librarian
6. Current lists of board members, with terms of appointment
7. Historic list of board members and service years
8. Organizational charts
9. Current salary schedules
10. Policy statements
    a. Personnel
    b. Materials selection
    c. Public use of the building
    d. Major gifts and memorials
11. Building regulations
    a. Emergency closing regulations
    b. List of holidays
    c. Rules on the display of flag
12. Records of major gifts
13. Contract information
14. Data on insurance policies
15. Departmental procedures
16. Data on system affiliation.

Procedure Manual

A procedure manual may be defined as an outline of a pre-scribed or standard method by which work is performed. A procedure manual is essential for training new staff or substitute help. It may also serve as a checklist for correcting oversights in operations. Procedure manuals are usually available in multiple copies in departments such as circulation where much of the basic activity centers around repeated routines.

A procedure manual is indispensable in a one-man department, such as a part-time business office, where only one person is familiar with payroll and other fiscal requirements and emergency help needs specific directives. A procedure manual for a small library's business function may include the following information and directives:

1. Statement on sources of income
    a. Tax funds: information on the local method of transferring taxes to the library account
    b. Nontax funds: data on sources of nontax income, such as daily revenue from fines, gifts, interest on endowments (where they are recorded, deposited, and controlled)

2. Brief description of business records
   a. Types of ledgers with sample entries
   b. Working budgets and expenditure forms
   c. Employee earnings records
   d. Duplicate payroll withholding transfer files
   e. Files of original invoices
   f. Other: such as accumulated monthly records of book expenditures by departments
3. Authorization for payment of accounts
   a. Information on the authority charged by law for approval of bills subject to payment
   b. Authority for check signatures
   c. Authority for use of type of check or voucher
4. Procedures for preparation of bills for payment
   a. Delivery to the business office of all invoices, with verification of receipt by check-off marks and initials of the receiver
   b. Audit of all bills, with a verification of total charges, credits, and discounts
   c. Referral of all incorrect invoices to vendor for corrected statements
   d. Gathering of all invoices from the same company for stapling, with monthly statement or adding machine tape
   e. Arrangement of bills for payment in order of budget classification for simplification in journal entries
   f. Totaling of bills and attaching adding machine tape for convenience at board meeting
   g. Coordination with payroll
   h. Preparation and distribution of checks
   i. Posting in appropriate ledgers
   j. Filing of invoices in accessible storage for referrals in payment claims and audits
5. Necessary information for payroll preparation
   a. Definition of a work week or month for full-time and part-time personnel
   b. W-4 forms for information on number of dependents, correct address, marital status, and social security number
   c. Pension and hospitalization deduction forms as required
   d. Base pay or hourly rates
   e. Annual increments when applicable
   f. Income tax and social security guides
   g. Employees' accumulated earnings records
   h. Day of distribution of salary checks
   i. Schedule for issuance of quarterly transfers of social security withholdings
   j. Accumulated records for yearly W-2 reports

6. Procedures for writing payroll checks
   a. Gathering time sheets for part-time employees and computing wages and deductions
   b. Verifying status of regular staff for compensation, changes in deductions, or placement in the salary classification plan
   c. Preparing checks and summaries of income and deductions for staff
   d. Entering payroll information in employees' earnings record book
   e. Preparing and forwarding checks covering employee withholdings

The business procedure manual may also include a listing of the length of time that business papers and records are to be retained by the library. The time of retention is often established by state law. The following is a sampling of the types of records that may be included in such a list:

Time Limit	Type of Record
Permanent	Employee records
	Annual reports
	Annual audits
	Ledgers
	Invoices
	Minutes
Until revised	Salary classification plans
Until superseded	Insurance policies
Statute of limitations	Business contracts

Essential Records

It is hard to break tradition in business habits and record keeping in any institution. However, many administrators have become aware of the hidden costs in all business operations. They have found, for example, that it may be less expensive to use a phone than to write a letter and maintain a correspondence file of accumulated carbon copies. They have found that many library records, such as accession books and shelf card files for withdrawn books, no longer serve their original function and should be eliminated. However, state laws on the disposition of public records should be consulted before disposing of official documents and business records.

The essential records in a library depend on the size of the library and the complexity of its operations. The test is actual use. Illustrations of the types of records, aside from financial papers and board minutes, that small and medium-sized libraries find essential are:

1. Statistics on number of borrowers, volume of circulation, amounts and kinds of material added and withdrawn, and number of reference questions—as needed for reports to the board and to state agencies
2. Inventory lists, which record supplies of items such as catalog cards, pencils, or mending supplies that are expendable in daily use (Sometimes called perpetual inventories because of their form and location, these lists usually are posted on supply cupboards to record quantities received. The quantity figures are changed as supplies are removed. Inventory lists are useful in a check on availability of current stock and in preparing requisitions for quantity discount orders)
3. Sick-leave and used-vacation reports (This personnel data tool records periods of absence for illness or vacation for each employee for verification of data as needed. It should include phone numbers for notification of relatives in case of emergencies)
4. Records of memorial books and other gifts
5. Pertinent material on special events or other data for library history.

Organization charts and position classifications are additional essential tools for library administration. They are not treated here because they have been so well covered elsewhere. Wheeler and Goldhor, for example, discuss organization charts in *Practical Administration of Public Libraries* with illustrative charts for libraries with four-person staffs to one-hundred-person staffs.[16] Position classifications are a part of the chapter on personnel in *Local Public Library Administration*.[17] The important point about both of these tools is that they are as valuable to small libraries as they are to large libraries. They may be used for orientation of trustees and staff, for training, and for performance appraisals.

The System and Administrative and Management Tools

The system is the member library's source for examples of organization charts, job descriptions, and other administrative aids—from personnel application forms to trustee manuals. A system makes use of administrative tools at appropriate workshops and institutes. The consulting staff demonstrates their value in working with individual libraries.

By assisting in analyzing and grouping tasks performed according to experience and training requirements, the system is able to aid the member library in the development of job descriptions, job classifications, and equitable pay plans. A questioning attitude in the process of task analysis can help identify unproductive tasks, leading to their elimination or replacement by new methods and to improved services. System consultants may offer guidance in techniques of evaluation of local library employees by providing evaluation forms and instruction in their use.

A well-planned series of systemwide training sessions provides the opportunity for the interpretation of the values of individualized manuals and handbooks and the way in which they may be developed by each library. Loose-leaf summaries of workshop presentations on budgeting, personnel administration, insurance, and other administrative topics may be prepared for the member libraries. Such summaries serve as follow-ups to training sessions and as referral documents for local librarians and trustees or other governing authorities.

5 Collection Building and Maintenance

The cooperative system recognizes three levels of collection building, which are essential if small and medium-sized libraries are to be able to provide access to the ever-widening variety of communications materials. This concept generally prevails for both the system that builds its own collection at a central headquarters and the system that contracts with a major library to strengthen an existing collection for system use.

The first is at the level of the community library. It is the target area at which other levels in the system structure are aimed. It is the point of initial confrontation with the conventional and the changing needs of library patrons from all walks of life. The collection at this level is conceived as basic and sufficient to meet the expected and repeated requirements of a unique community. The second is at the system level. The system collection reinforces the ability of the community library to meet citizen expectations of optimum access to ideas and information. It is an intermediate resource that complements the local collection with a range of materials beyond the scope of the community library. The third is at the level of the research center. It taps the exhaustive collections of metropolitan, state, federal, special, and university libraries which in their comprehensiveness go beyond the capabilities of either the independent library or the system.

An illustration of collection building at these levels is Shakespeareana. The local library, at the foundation level, maintains a representative collection of the plays of Shakespeare. The system collection, at the intermediate level, builds a comprehensive collection of both Shakespeare's plays and works of major criticism. The research centers, at an even more sophisticated level, are able to back up the other two with monographs and highly specialized studies of Shakespeare. The system concept of levels of collection

148

building eliminates costly and infrequently used duplications at the local level.

Local library collections are designed to: (1) meet the normal informational needs of people of all ages in the community, (2) encourage the growth of an informed citizenry and sustain community interests in continuing self-education, (3) assist the work of study groups, civic organizations, and local government, (4) provide materials for agencies serving individuals and families, and (5) offer vocational, avocational, and leisure resources to individuals. To achieve these and other aims, the basic collection at the community level is envisioned as a broad general collection of library materials that includes basic reference tools to answer frequent requests, subject material of general and local interest, current popular fiction and nonfiction, representative classic titles, material for children and young people, government documents, local history, selected periodicals, pamphlets, and records. The small library is book-oriented and is likely to remain so, with only token holdings in collections such as recordings or framed pictures. It will depend to a large extent on the system for the sophisticated aural and visual materials.

To assist in the fulfillment of the local library's objectives in collection building, the system designs its collection to serve not only the general reader but also the specialist in the community who turns occasionally to the member library for professional materials. The system collection, as a consequence, aims at breadth in subject fields and at quality in individual items. It includes books, reference tools, large periodical holdings for print-out and photocopying, films, recordings, and strong bibliographic resources for searching service and for referrals to the research library at the third level.

Collections at the research level are prepared to cover local requests with in-print and out-of-print materials on specific subjects, in all languages and formats, subject only to rarity or other conditions that may restrict loans to on-site use. The research library is at the pinnacle of collection building, but it is as close to the local community as the system's telephone or teletype machine. Some specific examples of the various levels of collection building are given in table 1.

The local library, as an independent unit and as a member of the system, is accountable for financing, policy-making, selection, and maintenance of the local collection. The cooperative system

Table 1   Levels of Collection Building Responsibility: Some Specific Examples*

	Local Library	Library System	Reference Centers
General Non-Fiction	Smith, Joni - How to Be a Flight Stewardess Chute, Marchette - Introduction to Shakespeare Dick-Read, Grantly - Childbirth without Fear Ginot, Hiam - Between Parent and Child Stillman, I - Doctor's Quick Weight Loss Diet	Davies, R.E.G. - History of World's Airlines Rosen, William - Shakespeare and the Craft of Tragedy Fielding, Waldo - The Childbirth Challenge; Commonsense Versus "Natural" Methods Miller, Daniel - The Changing American Parent Taylor, Clara - Foundations of Nutrition	Stratford, Alan - Air Transportation Economics Shakespeare Survey: An Annual Survey of Shakespearian Study and Production Richardson, Stephan - Childbearing: Its Social and Psychological Aspects Stolz, Lois - Influences on Parent Behavior Welsh, Ashton - Side Effects of Anti-Obesity Drugs
Medical Books	Killilea, Marie - Karen Lewis, Richard - The Other Child Dubos, Rene - Man, Medicine and Environment Rouche, Berton - Eleven Blue Men	Cruickshank, William - Cerebral Palsy: Its Individual and Community Problems Cruickshank, William - The Brain Damaged Child at Home and at School Baron, D. N. - Recent Advances in Medicine Stevenson, Lloyd - Nobel Prize Winners in Medicine and Physiology	Association of Bone and Joint Surgeons - Cerebral Palsy: Lower Extremity, 2 v. Luria, A.R. - The Restoration of Function after Brain Damage DeGroot, Leslie - Medical Care: Social and Organizational Aspects Atkinson, Wm. B. - Physicians and Surgeons of the U. S.
Fiction	Keyes, Frances - Dinner at Antoines MacInnes, Helen - Salzburg Connection Susann, Jacqueline - The Love Machine	Melville, Herman - Confidence Man Nabokov, Vladamir - Gift Le Clezio, J. M. - Flood	Scott, Walter - The Abbot (OP) Tolstoy, Leo - The Resurrection (OP) La Farge, Christopher - Sudden Guest (OP)
Juvenile	Cavanna, Betty - Arne of Norway Lambert, Janet - Confusion by Cupid	Cooper, Lee - Fun with Italian Lenski, Lois - Papa Petit	Aldrich, C. B. - Marjorie Daw (OP) Colum, Padriac - At the Gateways of the Day (OP)

*Prepared by Beverly Yacko, Suburban Library System, Western Springs, Illinois builds on the strength of the holdings of the member libraries. It is the system's responsibility to acquire additional strength and to keep improving the financing and the machinery for interloans within the library network for the benefit of all member libraries.

The factors in a local community that influence collection building include: (1) the characteristics of the community, (2) the budget, (3) the quality of the existing collection, (4) the realities of cooperative plans with other libraries in the community, (5) the depth of system and network collections, and (6) the book and library materials knowledge and the philosophy of collection building exemplified by the librarian and the staff.

Collection Building

Collection building is a term that has grown out of maturing concepts of a library responsibility known until recently as book selection. It came into usage in the mid-twentieth century to encompass all media of communication that contribute to the flow of information and to the preservation of the records of mankind. It does not diminish the image of the book. It simply recognizes that the products of technology in communications are as legitimate for library holdings as print.

The librarian as the builder of collections was once the keeper of collections, dedicated to the acquisition and control of shelves of books, preferably in hard covers. The contemporary librarian is a communications activist who looks to every media for creativity, for sound facts, and for many interpretations of life in order to fulfill the library's objectives. The hard-cover, the paperback, the microreproduction, the disc and tape recording, the art form, and the audio are recognized as equals among the tools that support each other in library service programs. "Collection building" is more than a change in vocabulary and more than a recognition of the existence of different kinds of information carriers. It is indicative of the profession's response to a changing world.

The basic philosophy of selection for public libraries has never been static. It has been subject to criticism and redesign by every generation. The redesign of the concepts of selection in the 1970s gives priority to people as actual consumers and potential users. It probes at the artificial distinctions and regulations that still keep public, school, and special libraries in separate categories—

each in ignorance of the others' aims and responsibilities in collection building. It recognizes that an overemphasis on self-reliance can never serve a tempestuous, ever-moving society whose members have not only urgent problems but also high expectations of solutions from tax-supported institutions.

The library's problems in meeting the needs of people were multiplied in the mid-twentieth century by a phenomenon that has been called the information, or media, explosion. The proliferation of new information, as the result of the constant redoubling of man's knowledge, has increased the rate of obsolescence. Recognition of the dangers of obsolescence became an insistent factor in the redesign of the concepts of collection building.

The need for redesign in collection building was furthered by the social revolution of the 1960s, which exposed gaps in holdings that made it difficult to assist the culturally unready. The so-called generation gap added still another thrust to professional rethinking of the purpose of collections in relation to people. Social upheavals and articulate youth brought the word "relevant" into the vocabulary of the collection builder.

"Relevant," as a word meaning pertinent, was dulled by repetition in the late 1960s, but it definitely carried a message to the alert collection builder. The search for relevance, when considered from the point of view of book selection, as one part of multimedia collection building, is not a new phenomenon. At various periods in the history of public libraries, the profession has made concerted efforts to be relevant in some phases of collection building. One example is the period between World Wars I and II, when both publishers and librarians sought material on current affairs, home management, and other practical subjects for adults with high interest quotients but limited reading skills. This was a search for relevance. Its relative unproductiveness was not the fault of a searching profession but of the failure to produce appropriate texts quickly and in enough subject fields.

Relevance in the 1970s is a fact of life for the collection builder, not just a professional project. It has been imposed on society, and therefore on librarians, by social and economic problems that demand answers. The relevant exists. It is to be found in every media of communication. The problem is not availability but decision-making. Prime questions center around the identification of audiences for whom the material is relevant. The problem has been further complicated by the fact that relevance is tied in with every facet of contemporary life: protests against the establishment, the demands of many minority groups, and changing mores and morals. It is expressed through innovations in art forms, experimentation in film-making, and the four-letter words and realism of contemporary writing.

Collection building in the last analysis is a service carried on by libraries and systems of libraries on behalf of the people who make up our society. Its broad function is to provide resources of knowledge, information, reflection, and inspiration that are modern tools for citizenship, for participation in the economy of the community, and for the fulfillment of an individual as a person. Collection building is more than selecting and purchasing standard materials. It is also the provision of costly information services that the average person cannot afford and the provision of materials that go beyond his expectations. Collection building is an act of faith in the power of ideas and knowledge and in the values of continuing education, which matches the life-styles of the organized and the unorganized individuals in the community.

Selection is the most satisfying part of the many-faceted job of a librarian. It is the justification for librarianship. It is a professional duty that has the unusual byproduct of continuing education for the librarian. Selection is a trust in which the factor of accountability has become more imperative as the world has become smaller and more frightening and the affairs of mankind have become more complex. The grave need for reliable collections and for expertise in their use points up the necessity for sharpening the book and materials knowledge of all individuals who work in libraries and for involving them in the collection building process.

The head librarian in the average library is charged by library practice and board policies with the authority for selection and the responsibility for the quality of a collection and for its usefulness. This authority is not a right. It is a delegated responsibility, which is further delegated to qualified staff. Involvement of the staff in selection does not mean that the chief administrator abdicates any responsibility. Final accounting for the degree of excellence of the collection rests with the administrator. The times in which we live, however, make it clear that no one person can be an expert on the literature of all fields of knowledge. No one person can handle all the demanding obligations of modern librarianship and keep up with the multiplicity of new materials in those fields, for example, in which growth of knowledge has been accelerated by scientific advances.

Viewpoints on Collection Building

Librarians of the 1970s are individualists with differing ideas and theories that influence collection building. Theories are a challenge to the individual collection builder and to the system. A theory is ultimately faced with a countertheory. The interchange of ideas and opinions about collection building and the interpretation of those theories that influence system policies are an important part of a continuing communications program within a system.

One theory that emerged with the establishment of systems relates to a source in the system for best sellers and light fiction. There are librarians who are not interested in using limited local funds on the ephemeral or the questionable. They are convinced that such books should be available through systems, in enough quantity to satisfy the requirements of reserve lists of all member libraries. This theory is subject to examination in the light of professional standards and overall system objectives. Some systems have dealt with the theory, in terms of types of books if not in quantity, by contracting for commercial lending services for all member libraries. Other systems, with the concurrence of the majority of their members, hold to the conviction that the provision of the popular is the province of the individual library.[1]

There are also opposing theories about the provision of quantity titles in subject fields. There are sponsors of the belief that every library should duplicate heavily the nonfiction titles or in subjects where there is marked public interest or a chance to promote lively interest.[2] Others take the stand that the library should limit duplication to provide a maximum number of unique titles. State and federal forms requiring a report on the number of titles added may have some influence on an excessive concern for unique titles. Either of these theories must find support in the objectives of the library and through enlightened interpretation of the needs of the populace the library serves.

The question of subject duplication spreads into deliberations on system collection policies. There are member librarians who insist that the system could serve best by purchase of multiple titles in subject fields in great demand by high school and college students. There are librarians who believe that system funds should be reserved for expensive, specialized materials, in recognition of the growing predominance of serious use of libraries by all kinds of individuals in a community. The answer can be found only in a system's objectives and plan of service.

The public demand theory is very much alive in small communities. It is based on the belief that the taxpayer has the right to ask and receive. Public demand, in actuality, is not the voice of the total population but the insistent clamor of an articulate minority. When it is directed at the local library, is usually takes the form of excitement over the best seller and other materials highlighted by the communications media. Supporters of the public demand theory point to the principle in the public library standards that states in no uncertain terms that the library must respond to the interests of the community. The problem for the public library, as for other tax-supported institutions, is to distinguish between loud voices and muted, but very real, needs.

The public demand theory is opposed by the value theory—sometimes called the usefulness theory. The value theory relates the philosophy of collection building to the objectives of a library. It is supported by the principles in the public library standards that point to the library's responsibility to take an in-depth view of basic community needs and to make vigorous use of library materials to meet those needs. The value theory has been challenged by critics who accuse libraries of being permeated with the cult of usefulness. The critics charge that book selectors choose a book for the extent of its usefulness rather than for its innate value. This criticism seems to overlook the fact that a volume that is utilitarian for one man may be a delight for another.

There is a fundamental distinction between the value theory and the public demand theory. The difference is not a mere quibbling over words. Selecting materials for their usefulness to help people is an act that supports the library's purpose. Responding to a demand in many cases may be yielding to a pressure. Understanding the difference between value and demand is tantamount to an understanding of the distinction between strength and weakness. Both theories should be examined by the policymakers of the small and medium-sized libraries. It is their right and their responsibility to determine whether the library is to be ruled by what has been called "the sovereignty of the unqualified" or whether the library is to take its place as an educational and cultural force in the community.

There is one theory that suggests that selection may be a dying art because of possible overreliance on regular system releases of suggested titles for purchase and because of dependence on such services as interlibrary loan and reciprocal borrowing.[3] This theory does not seem to have much substance in the light of published survey findings. There is evidence from such studies and field observations that book selection in small communities has been revitalized through system sponsorship of selection meetings, the routing of book selection tools where needed, and system advisory services.

The user-oriented theory of book selection emphasized in the late 1960s and early 1970s is, on analysis, a traditional concept. This theory has a corollary of interest to collection builders. The corollary relates to the arrangement of materials, which in turn has an effect on collection building. User-oriented arrangement discards the conventional division of adult and juvenile materials. It institutes a plan of arrangement that, for example, places juvenile and adult nonfiction together and makes the total nonfiction collection available to all readers regardless of age levels or reading skills. In this plan, adult and juvenile fiction and books for the very small child frequently remain separated at departmental levels.

User-oriented arrangement is based on the idea that both children and adults will benefit by exposure to a wide view of subject treatment. An introductory study to meteorology, for example, will appeal to both young readers and uninitiated adults. The gifted child and the informed adult will be challenged by advanced books on the same subject. The proponents of user-oriented arrangement point out the advantages for the adult with limited reading skills in finding in one location all of the materials written at different vocabulary levels. They emphasize the importance of removing artificial identification of age levels to attract the young adult. They claim that patrons of all ages become more self-reliant in finding materials that meet their own particular needs. A modification of user-oriented arrangement can be seen in the trend toward selecting nonfiction materials on both adult and juvenile levels for both departments to meet exceptional user needs.

Still another theory of collection building is a type-of-provision limitation to be undertaken by a local library. It has been suggested on the grounds that a library with a limited budget must perceive what it can and cannot do. The theory suggests that a library will be able to get the best returns from its book budget by concentrating on subject fields of maximum local importance and placing less emphasis on general materials. This practice may have value in a system collection development plan encouraging specialization in those areas where a library has a solid foundation and system grants could add strength for the benefit of the system.

Selection Purposes

A number of professional slogans have been attached to book selection in the past. They expressed the differing philosophies of different decades. The old ALA slogan was "The best reading for the largest number at the least cost."[4] This was modified by the 1940s to "The right book for even one reader at any cost."[5]

At one time the traditional book selector thought in terms of balanced collections. This concept stemmed from the belief that the library could be all things to all men. It was a difficult concept to define and implement. To some it meant keeping a proportional balance of holdings within each classification. To others it meant exact allocation of funds for each classification. In general, it meant a well-rounded collection, the goal of which was acquisition of material in as many branches of knowledge as possible. The literal interpretation of the balanced collection theory disappeared with the recognition that the needs of the people in each community take precedence over formulas in collection building.

This history of libraries shows that the spokesmen for each generation of librarians have been cognizant of the need for books to help individuals and groups of individuals. As far back as 1930, Francis K. W. Drury stated in his text on book selection that "the high purpose of book selection is to provide the right book for the right reader at the right time."[6] This high purpose got down to the grass roots by the mid-twentieth century because librarians assumed leadership responsibilities in adult education, in a sense creating the right time. If the profession had produced a book selection slogan in the post-World War II period, it would have been to the effect that the library had an obligation to see that no citizen within its sphere of influence was ignorant of the great issues of the day.

The profession in the 1960s did not lose sight of the goal of the previous decade to provide and promote materials to counter public apathy and ignorance of critical issues. It sharpened that goal with more specific objectives: to choose materials that would most effectively help people whose lives have been blighted by society's most crucial problems, and to break down traditions that would be barriers to the use of those materials. By the 1970s the needs of people and the issues of the community and the nation were firmly established at the center of collection planning by individual libraries and by systems.

Library programs for the disadvantaged have brought about a selection activity that might be called, for lack of a better name, participatory selection. In this area of collection building, the selector and representatives of neighborhoods to be served work together in building a collection that will attract and appeal to the potential user. It is the type of selection that lends itself to the experimental and to the nontraditional, offering an unusual challenge.

Selection for the disadvantaged involves children's, young adult, and adult services librarians. The audience is large. Librarians of all communities are aware that there are disadvantaged people to be found at every educational and all economic levels and in all age groups. However, selection for the disadvantaged in the 1970s is not selection for those who have chosen to stay out of libraries because of indifference or competing interests. It is to the disadvantaged in the decaying inner cities, in the camps of the migratory workers, on Indian reservations, in rehabilitation institutions, and in halfway houses that librarians are reaching out with special materials to open up opportunities and to provide hope. At the same time the profession is responsive to the needs of the physically handicapped. It has taken advantage of publishing developments in the field of large-print books for the visually handicapped and titles for use with ceiling projectors.

Special collections for businessmen, labor groups, hospital service, youth organizations, adult education projects, and community study and action task forces are common to many autonomous libraries. Special purpose selection has expanded in recent years to focus on needs for job training and rehabilitation, on the problems of the functionally illiterate, and on supportive materials of assistance to social agencies and others who work with the critical problems of people.

Anticipatory selection became an important facet of collection building in an age when city planners, conservationists, and citizens were concerned with the preservation of civilization itself. It is sparked and sustained by staff participation in adult services activities, by their alertness to trends in local government, by their receptiveness to the interests of the organized and unorganized members of society, and by their initiative in exploring the needs of the unserved. It is an area of selection that builds public confidence. It offers evidence that the library assumes a role of leadership in the acquisition of materials which are essential to the solution of problems that threaten the well-being of future generations and the planet they will inhabit.

Audience-creator selection is a type of collection building that recognizes the library has a responsibility for the encouragement of new talent. It must provide beginning writers, illustrators, artists, and musicians with a public. The most neglected field in library selection is reported to be that of modern poetry.[7] Ignoring any form of expression verges on censorship even though it may be simply a form of disinterest on the part of the selector or an assumption of disinterest on the part of the community. The obligation to create a reading public calls for joint action by the system and its member libraries.

Retrospective selection is a traditional but important part of modern collection building. It is the deliberate analysis of holdings and the purposeful study of choices that will add depth or change the emphasis in a particular collection. It involves replacement of good titles that have been lost or worn out as well as the weighing of the value of the old against the new. It is subject to budget allocations. It is a spark for staff discussion of books that are "worth their keep," to borrow a phrase from the working vocabulary of many children's librarians.

System Approaches

A goal of many cooperative systems is to provide community exposure to new publications and subject fields at a rate and with a diversity that often is not possible at the local level. The "instant package" plan is an example of this type of system service. This plan takes many forms. The system, for example, may respond immediately to the announcement of a release of a report by a President's Commission on crime or some other problem of intense and universal concern. Rush orders for multiple copies of such a report are placed by the system and the copies distributed as quickly as possible to member libraries. Reserve stock is frequently made available at system headquarters for replacements at the local library when the initial shipment is exhausted. The system may follow up with reading lists or suggestions for possible purchase on the subject of the "instant package."

This type of service shows how the system can help its member libraries mobilize resources for public information in crisis situations. The system has facilities for quickly acquiring materials that may not be handled by a regular jobber but that are particularly suitable to meet inquiries arising from community anxieties. The system is also in a position to find "the resources for research to alleviate the public crisis," which Margaret Monroe indicated must be available for the effective use of collections in a time of crisis.[8]

Package collections are also used by systems to provide related materials on a specific subject, such as civil rights or poverty, for the use of individuals and agency personnel working with the disadvantaged. In the Monroe County Library System in New York state these compact, portable collections came to be known as capsule collections. They are small packets of books supplemented by magazine articles, filmstrips, films, records, and reading lists. They are kept together for quick loans to help with immediate and pressing needs for background reading and program material. The Monroe County plan involved the system membership through a special introductory meeting and the inclusion in each capsule of suggestions of additional material available in the member libraries.[9]

Exposure to new materials is provided by many cooperative systems through book pools and rotation collections. The book pool has different names throughout the country. It may be called a book bank, a resources center, or even a mini-library on wheels. Essentially a book pool is a collection held apart from the collection at the central library. It is a stock from which member librarians personally select material to be loaned to their patrons through their own library facilities. The location point for the actual selection may be at the system headquarters or in the system mobile unit traveling on a regular schedule to the local community, or both. A rotation collection is one in which the titles are selected by the headquarters staff and rotated among members on an established schedule.

Many cooperative systems maintain examination centers to bring new materials to the attention of the member libraries and to provide an opportunity for firsthand pre-selection review. These centers ordinarily do not loan items from their holdings. It is expected that the member collection builders will visit the center—whether it is in a permanent building or in a mobile unit—to handle books, compare editions or subject treatment, and check published or locally written reviews. A permanent center is likely to have more comprehensive displays of both books and nonprint materials. The mobile examination unit, although smaller, has the advantage of moving to the home site to exhibit revolving collections in subject fields, recommended basic collections, or special purpose materials to use, for example, with children of low-income families or for other programs given priority emphasis in a particular section of the system area.

The programs of examination centers vary from system to system. In some the program consists of visitations at the convenience of the member librarians, with guidance consultation on request. Other systems combine this opportunity with regular book and/or film discussion meetings led by the materials consultant, knowledgeable member librarians, or by nonlibrary subject specialists in the region. A number of centers actively involve the membership through voluntary reviewing assignments. The reports of the local reviewers are attached to the individual books reviewed or gathered together as reviewing aids. Many centers provide annotated lists, prepared by member librarians and/or the system staff, to be used as a guide at the examination center or as a refresher at the time of actual selection. In many systems the facilities of the examination center are open to the area school and special librarians as a step toward expanding cooperation between types of libraries and in the interest of effective collection building for all purposes.

Paperbacks have become a reliable item in system efforts to move quickly in collection building. They have been utilized in many ways. Paperbacks are purchased to fill gaps in headquarters or membership resources and to build sufficient stock for quantity use. They lend themselves to the publicizing of system services through such devices as depositories of portable and replaceable paperback collections in the reception rooms of hospitals and government or social agency offices. Paperbacks have been the backbone of outreach programs in reading centers and in demonstrations because of their acceptability to a public not interested in the traditional hard-cover book.

Systems have been able to demonstrate to their members the value of paperbacks as supplementary material requiring minimum processing. They have been able to alert librarians to publications, such as material for the beginning reader, that are often available only in paperback. The system example has helped to dissipate some of the residual tendency to reject paperbacks as legitimate library items. Exhibits of paperbacks in system examination centers give member librarians an opportunity to learn that content and use is more important than format. System book discussion meetings can produce guidelines for membership acquisition and circulation of paperbacks as reprints, original titles, or as publications released simultaneously in hard-cover and soft-cover editions. System policy may make paperbacks quickly available through coordinated ordering and distribution for all members.

Other exposure techniques and materials information devices used by systems include union lists of magazine holdings in member libraries; purchase and distribution of printed booklets, such as *Notable Books* and *Growing Up with Science;* rotating of advance reviewing services to member libraries; and providing bibliographies and published information in the headquarter's center for telephone or in-person referrals. An introduction to the reviewing and location aids through the system frequently leads the individual library to assume the responsibility for subscriptions to the reviewing media for professional and public use.

The informational or exposure approach of cooperative systems is not confined to new publications or the latest audiovisual production. There is also a focus on basic collections, which may take the form of suggestions through distribution of recommended lists of minimum essential reference tools. It may mean the actual purchase of new editions of encyclopedias and other reference books for financially handicapped libraries.

The cooperative system approach to collection building also encourages the exchange of information on local or area history.

A system may take the responsibility of preparing, with membership help, a master card file or a printed catalog on the local history holdings of member libraries. A more ambitious proposal is
a system-subsidized, but eventually self-supporting, reprint project to make out-of-print local and regional histories available at
a reasonable cost to all interested libraries, schools, and collectors.[10]

Collection building at the system level includes a responsibility
for gathering professional literature. The professional collections
of member libraries are naturally limited, when they are available
at all, to material dealing with the public library and possibly a
few school library publications. The literature originating in
university and special libraries covers subjects of value to public
libraries, but a limited local library budget precludes their purchase. The cooperative system has an opportunity for service to
its professional membership in providing a centralized collection
of the publications of state library associations and books of the
library publication houses, which cover many aspects of library
science. A professional collection is of special value when library
extension courses are scheduled at one or more locations in the
system area.

The system recognizes a responsibility to help member libraries
in their service to the visually handicapped and the blind. Many
systems are building up such service collections in coordination
with state and regional specialists in materials for the handicapped.
The collections include comprehensive resources in large-type
publications, reference material in braille, periodicals on tape,
children's stories on records, general materials in braille and audio
forms, optical magnifying devices, talking book catalogs and
machines. This type of collection building provides an opportunity to interpret to the member librarians the *Standards for Library Service to the Blind and Visually Handicapped,* adopted in
1966. It further provides the opportunity to take browsing collections for the visually handicapped into the local library and to
open channels for meeting the scholarly and sophisticated interests
of the visually handicapped in every community.

The system approach to collection building reflects an alertness
to widespread economic problems which may prevail in the system
area. A single example is job information. The system brings to
the attention of the small library the best in programmed instruction books designed for self-teaching. It helps the local library

reach and serve citizens who are looking for information on retraining or vocational opportunities. The system collections on vocations and job information provide a basic service through both permanent and rotating collections, which may be correlated with special events in local communities ranging from career days to the county fair.

Collection building at the system level takes on an information-gathering function with the establishment of bibliographic files of the acquisitions of member libraries. This requires the cooperation of member libraries in the preparation of a main entry card to be sent to system headquarters for interfiling in a union catalog or for incorporation into a computerized bibliographic bank. A bibliographic center is essential for locating titles for interlibrary loans and for expediting access through reciprocal borrowing. By quick location of a needed item, time may be saved (perhaps enough to make the difference between use and nonuse), and user satisfaction commensurately improved.

All system approaches to collection building involve educational experiences. An example is to be found in magazine resources for reference and copying services. The system's approach is to match periodical strength with a corresponding strength in indexes. The system encourages the acquisition of basic indexes in member libraries and, where necessary, provides such indexes and instruction in their use. In addition, the system points the way to most effective use of the specialized indexes housed at the system center. The system can respond quickly to patron needs at the local level only if accurate information is forthcoming from the local library. This situation underscores the fact that the system approach to collection building involves more than just materials. System responsibility for collection building does not rest with the headquarters staff alone. The strength of a system's collection building philosophy and practice depends on the insight of every individual involved in the use of system resources.

Administrative Aspects of Collection Building

Ideally, every library should have a person on its staff whose prime time is devoted to the identification of community requirements for the particular, the general, the highly specialized, and the sophisticated in library materials. Acquiring practical knowledge of the kinds and levels of communication materials of greatest help to people necessitates studies of the needs of the served and the unserved. It requires more than a casual perception of individual differences. Classifying needs by age groups, vocations, broad avocational interests, or some other generality does not satisfy the responsibility for excellence in an understanding of collection potentials.

Through necessity the librarian in the small community must use simple methods for the identification of individual interests and community concerns. There is no time or money for scientific studies. Clues to existing or emerging needs arising from contacts inside a library building provide only partial answers. There is, however, the time-tested practice of moving the librarian and key staff members out into various neighborhoods and meeting houses for purposeful and frequent communication with people. This is person-to-person and person-to-organization library activity. It means participation in civic and cultural affairs. It means that library personnel become resource people for community leaders and for individual members of organizations. It means that librarians are on the front line to discover at first hand the current problems, interests, and plans of all segments of the local population. However, it means frequent absences from the library, too. Community analysis to be effective must have continuity. Without proper interpretation, library work out in the community may symbolize nonwork to the library clerk and even dereliction of duty from the standpoint of a trustee. The purpose of involvement of library staff in activities outside the library must be understood as a legitimate part of the evaluation and planning functions of library administration.

There are a number of ways for the small library to identify needs. The librarian may persuade study and action groups to join the library staff in studies designed to reveal community developments that will require new types of knowledge and information in library holdings. Ordinarily, the techniques used by the librarian in a small community are more likely to be correlated with existing services that support organized society or with planned fact-finding projects. Recognition of a need may come through analysis of the questions following a program presented by a library staff member. Insight into requirements for materials is a natural adjunct of the library's cosponsorship of adult education projects and its association with representatives of social agencies. Identification of collection needs often involves planned information-gathering. An example is an interview with a personnel director of a local industry to determine ways in which the library may build resources to help prepare workers for promotion or retirement.

The real purpose of a conscious plan to identify the community's needs for library materials is to get behind population statistics and circulation figures to test professional assumptions about men, women, and children and the materials that can best meet their needs. It is to develop an awareness with which to perceive at the outset the shifts in overall community interests—from ecumenicity to ecology and on to some other social concern. To identify needs from a position outside the library is to listen to people as individuals on their own grounds and under the influence of their own environment. The librarian who makes use of the identification function finds that it makes a difference in collection building and in the services stemming from collection building. It is community awareness in action.

It is equally imperative for the system to engage in studies leading to the identification of present and future collection needs of people in the entire system area. The system has many sources of information: trends in interlibrary loans, field trips and observations of consultants, regional planning reports, and user and socio-economic surveys initiated by the system.

Selection Policy Statement

One of the major administrative responsibilities in collection building is the local library's selection policy statement. In 1962 James F. Fixx observed:

> Although all libraries, from the very best to the very worst, have their share of failings and misjudgments, each of them tries, sometimes clumsily, sometimes with a skill approximating art, to provide its public with a reliable and useful collection of books. In this task they are ordinarily guided by formal statements of policy that have been thoughtfully worked out to explain to themselves, to their readers, and to potential book-banners why they choose the books they do.[11]

The pertinent words in this quotation are "to explain to themselves, to their readers . . . why they choose the books they do."

This is the prime purpose of a book and library materials policy statement. It is an instrument of communication. It gives evidence that the policy planners are able to answer basic questions: Where will the library concentrate its strength? What does it expect to be able to offer its patrons in ten years? What redirections in collection building may be taken on the basis of system development? A materials selection policy statement indicates an awareness of necessary steps to move into a world that, as Robert Oppenheimer said, "alters as we walk in it."[12]

System affiliation changes neither the character nor the content of a local library's selection policy statement. System encouragement to develop local selection policy statements is based on the wisdom derived from years of experience within the profession and documented in library literature. The responsibility for the preparation of a selection policy statement in a local library is a joint responsibility of the librarian, the staff, and the board. It may begin with background readings suggested by the librarian and frequently obtained from the system's professional collection. These readings will bring out a number of important points helpful in understanding the need for such statements.

One basic point brought out by the literature is that the right to read or to listen is not one which can be passively accepted; it is one which is subject to constant vigorous defense. A materials selection policy statement in the local library will not solve all problems connected with intellectual freedom for all time. It will, however, help to solve problems more intelligently. Another frequently repeated professional observation is that the average American citizen has the capacity to judge library materials without the help of labels or warning signs. Many social commentators have noted that the nation has made remarkable progress on the assumption that there are extraordinary possibilities in ordinary people. The intelligence of the average library patron must not be underestimated. The literature continuously restates the obligation of modern libraries to make certain that citizens are given a chance to become aware of the pros and cons of the issues in their communities, the nation, and the world. One of the most vital assignments undertaken by the public library is to provide attractive factual material on all sides of contemporary problems so that citizens may get their mental exercise not by jumping at conclusions but through the process of thinking about information, ideas, and opinions.

The selection statement must fit the specific needs of the library and the community concerned. There is little value in merely adopting the policy of another library, although the statement of another library may well serve as an index to the subject areas to be covered. The process of developing a sound selection policy for any library involves analysis of existing resources, sensitivity to continually shifting trends and interests, and alertness to the types of materials required by current conditions and foreseeable changes.

The materials policy statement must be built on established objectives of the library. It may bring out supporting objectives such as the planned guidance of purposeful individual readers or the long-term strengthening of a specific part of the collection. Whatever the goals, they must be the library's own. They must have significance for a particular library at a particular time.

A materials policy statement should recognize the distinction between the use of books by children and the use of books by adults. It has been said that children want a good book and adults want the latest book. There frequently is a difference. The policy statement should indicate an awareness of suitability without limiting book opportunities for any age group. The policy should serve as a reminder of the importance of equity in the allocation of funds to meet the book or nonbook needs of skilled and unskilled library users of every generation. It also must acknowledge the importance of objectivity in the choice of materials in order to save the collection from the unconscious personal prejudices or the ungoverned bibliographical enthusiasms of the librarian and staff.

The statement should give evidence of high standards of selection, with particular concern that a library item be judged as a whole rather than by sections to which there may be objections. It should reflect the library's appreciation of one of the fundamental American traits, that of fairness in judgment. A book or a film must be assessed by what it is rather than by physical appearance or the racial, political, or religious affiliations of the author or producer.

The materials policy statement should cover the disposition of free material that comes unsolicited from many sources and is outright propaganda. The basis for decision is use. The best use may be to add weight for a wastepaper sale. The material may, on the other hand, be a good example of its kind and thus be valuable for students or citizens interested in the methods of practitioners of the art of propaganda. Directions should be given for proper identification of the source of propaganda as a gift to the library so that there is no possibility of inferences that tax funds have been used for its purchase. The materials statement must further point to local decisions on the acquisition of pseudoscience, textbooks, duplicate copies, withdrawals, or any other problem area.

The selection policy statement may be used in many ways. It is most useful for clarification and guidance and for the stimulation of those who are actually engaged in the practice of book selection. It is designed as a tool for information and interpretation. Librarians work in a communications field, and it behooves them to become experts in interpreting in words their objectives and concepts of standards and service. The University of Wisconsin Library School once had an instructor who said that no one should accept the responsibility for book selection unless he were willing to speak up as an expert. Selection of books and related communications materials is the librarian's specialty. No one else in the community has the opportunity or the desire to apply positive criteria to the evaluation of materials or has the awareness of possible choices related to fulfillment of the objectives of the library.

For many librarians the book selection policy statement is a tool in the defense of intellectual freedom. Granted, this is a more critical issue in some types of libraries than in others and in some parts of the country than in others. However, a selection policy provides a positive approach to the acquisition of controversial materials. It puts the focus on selection rather than on censorship. It is a tool that reminds librarians that "freedom of book selection and fears for book selection"[13] cannot operate simultaneously in a climate productive of intelligent collection building for a well-defined purpose.

The selection policy statement is also a device for in-service training. It can give direction to the handling of situations which occur and recur in collection problem areas. Public libraries are besieged with problems, sometimes called pressures; the consequences can sometimes be circumvented by well-considered and well-expressed principles. Many times librarians tend to think their most distressing problems are related to books with four-letter words and realistic bedroom scenes, but there are others. To take just one example, the field of popular medicine all too often offers half-baked theories about diet, arthritis, or the use of hypnosis. What does the library's policy statement have to say about this type of material? Then, too, there is the question of student use of library resources under the impetus of highly accelerated educational programs. What does the selection statement indicate about the responsibility of the library to adults in a youth-oriented society?

A materials policy statement, like the library itself, is never finished. It is subject to frequent revision. Without continued vigilance, policies become outdated. They lose their power to stimulate. To be of real value, a materials selection policy statement must be revised often, and constant attention paid to the rate of change in technological advances, social attitudes, patron interests, and expanding system services.

Every library has complete autonomy in the development of its book and library materials policy statement. The points recommended for inclusion are:

1. Simple explanation of the way in which selection relates to objectives
2. Description of the library's clientele: a statement that reflects sensitivity to the materials needed by the served and the unserved in the total population
3. Statement of accountability: who in the last analysis is responsible for the materials chosen?
4. Interpretation of the scope of the collection: what it is to include and what it will exclude, not in the sense of self-censorship, but on the basis of a planned program of local collection building that recognizes other collections in the community and wider access through system resources
5. Short commentary of the principles of evaluation, indicating an alertness to criteria that will maintain high standards of acquisition and control of obsolescence
6. General policies on subjects such as gift books and magazine subscriptions, textbooks, and duplications
7. And last, but perhaps most important of all, the library's stand on intellectual freedom.

Supplements to the local library's materials policy statement may include the Library Bill of Rights, the Freedom to Read Statement, and other pertinent releases from the American Library Association, which may have been studied and adopted by the local library board. These statements are of great value as supporting documents for the local library, but they are not substitutes for the library's own statement.

A system may participate in discussions on the development of a member's materials policy statement, but only on request. The system may collect policy statements from many libraries, in and outside the system, for reference by local policy planners. It may help the local library in fact-finding as a basis for policy-making. It will provide professional literature on policy-making and stand by to give advice through its consultant service. The local materials policy statement, however, is not the system's responsibility.

System Materials Policy Statement

The cooperative system's policy statement on the selection of library materials should explain to member library administrators and trustees the responsibility the system assumes in collection development. The statement should also indicate what the system collection is not designed to provide, thereby defining the distinct responsibilities of the system and the local library in collection building. The responsibility for definition of roles rests with the member libraries. The responsibility for developing collections in accordance with the definitions rests with the system administrator, for the system collection, and with the local administrator, for the local collection.

Obviously, membership understanding of the cooperative system's policy is essential. This seems to be particularly true in systems that have been unable to contract with strong existing libraries and have been required to build and house separate collections to fulfill their function. The system policy statement should be discussed in open forum meetings and reinterpreted with reasonable frequency so that old and new members of the system know exactly what to expect from the implementation of system selection and collection building policies. The local librarian who is familiar with the system's selection policy will be better able to tailor the local library's collection to the community's more frequent demands and will know what less frequent local needs can be satisfied from the system collection.

The system materials policy statement should be based on the system's unique objectives, as outlined in its plan of service, and on its role in developing a collection of communications materials as the second-level resource for the library patron. Included will be recognition of the broad geographical area and the wider, more diversified clientele than that of the local library. The system's intention of avoiding unnecessary duplication of local holdings will be included. The role of the system in developing and maintaining an up-to-date professional library will be clearly stated. Standards and quality, the importance of bibliographies and indexes as selection tools, and selection in accordance with the Library Bill of Rights should be emphasized in the system statement, a model to be emulated by member libraries. A sample cooperative system Materials Selection Policy Statement is given in appendix E.

Intellectual Freedom

Intellectual freedom cannot be divorced from selection policies. Safeguarding a climate of intellectual freedom is an obligation shared by the local library with all types of libraries and all kinds of systems and information networks. The library by its very nature is hospitable to continual change in ideas and opinions. Librarians as professionals are advocates of mankind's right to create, to write, to read, to listen, to look, to accept or reject ideas and opinions. The library as an institution has been a symbol of intellectual freedom through the ages. The librarian's and the trustee's acceptance of this heritage involves responsibilities.

The local library is on the firing line where professional theories and the courage of librarians and trustees are tested by community standards and customs. The exploration of once-taboo subjects in creative literature and the arts arouses the protesters in the average community. Worries about taxes, street gangs, dissenters, national defense, poverty, and hunger practically disappear with the news that the library is circulating a novel filled with four-letter words and vivid bedroom scenes.

The frustrated middle-class adult, usually the parent of a teenage daughter, needs a target. There is little he can do about the overall state of morals in American society. The closest target, and the easiest to attack, is the local library, which is allegedly packed with realistic novels, frank social studies, and sex instruction books for children. The Supreme Court has not been able to define pornography, but the citizen thinks he can. The librarian in the small community often is caught between the commitment to the principle of freedom to read and community outrage. The adult revolt against vulgarity and other forms of expression that diminish the dignity of the human being is understandable. A deliberate citizen hunt for offensive words and scenes to safeguard the morals of others may be explainable even though it is not acceptable in a free society.

To many librarians, there is more of a challenge in fighting attempted censorship of opinions and ideologies than in defending four-letter words. Arguing over vulgarity becomes as boring as the words are. There is some incongruity when a library with an avowed educational objective and a concern for excellence must become overly concerned with the defense of the cheap and the tawdry in popular publications. Nevertheless, the basic right of the adult to choose his own reading remains a constant in the philosophy of librarians.

The librarian in the small community comes closer to the disaster area in censorship conflicts than does the librarian in metropolitan centers. The large library with adequate funding is justified in claiming its responsibility to collect highly controversial materials for the use of specialists and for the historical record. The larger library can justify the collection of the near-pornographic, which according to some librarians must have social significance because there is so much of it. The departmentalization of large libraries is a shield against the censor's most persuasive piece of ammunition: that the offending item will fall into the hands of a child.

Recognition of the vulnerable position of the librarian in the small library does not imply less need for dedication to the principles of intellectual freedom. It simply acknowledges that the individual librarian can be helped by system exploration of problems, techniques, and experiences. One of the benefits of the system is that the librarians and trustees of the small library no longer have to stand alone in resolving censorship problems unless they choose to do so.

The cooperative system has a stake in maintaining an environment of intellectual freedom in the communities within its jurisdiction. The maintenance of such an environment requires more than a universal adoption of the Library Bill of Rights by member libraries, helpful as that is. It involves more than making available a collection of material on intellectual freedom for the use of member libraries. The system must actively assist member libraries to develop the skills necessary for the defense of intellectual freedom.

The system has the capacity for direct assistance to its member libraries troubled by problems in intellectual freedom. One avenue for this assistance is the establishment and training of an intellectual freedom committee composed of member librarians, trustees, a representative of the system staff, or any combination of interested system people. The first assignment for the committee might be to define intellectual freedom as it applies to the circumstances and interests of the members of the system. "Intellectual freedom" in libraries is a phrase that stands for freedom of the press and the right to read. Interpretations of intellectual freedom in the early 1970s introduced other concepts involving elements such as civil rights and the insistence on strong institutional positions on social problems of national concern.

Intellectual freedom, regardless of interpretations, relates selection and collection building to the Library Bill of Rights, which focuses on the rights and needs of the user. At the same time the personal convictions and professional zeal of the book selector may overemphasize some aspects of collection building, and trouble may arise in the name of intellectual freedom. A system committee must be prepared to establish policies that determine the conditions under which it is proper for a system committee to engage in membership controversies involving the rights of the library, the rights of the librarian, or both.

Specific charges to a system's intellectual freedom committee will naturally vary from system to system. There may be a charge to determine what types of educational programs the system will sponsor. There may be a directive to examine the degree of need for system action in critical cases, in view of the specialized assistance available through the American Library Association. It may be the committee's responsibility to monitor and disseminate information on legislation affecting intellectual freedom being proposed on both state and federal levels. A system's intellectual freedom committee would be a logical liaison between the system and the professional associations, the state library, and the other systems active in the defense of intellectual freedom.

A prime function of a system's intellectual freedom committee is education. The framework of the system lends itself to the establishment of a forum through which librarians and trustees may become familiar with the literature, the case studies, and the defense techniques of the 1970s. An intellectual freedom forum offered by the system and its committee to member libraries can do more than channel information and build up a background of strategies. It can help the individual clarify his own convictions, which influence selection. The librarian, after all, is as human as the censor. The librarian as a person is not always free of qualms about strange political opinions or free of prejudice against extreme realism in literary forms. There is a certain amount of ambivalence in practice even among some of the staunchest defenders of intellectual freedom. This is not necessarily a form of self-censorship. It is more often a failure to think through the human elements in matching philosophy and practice.

The system forum can serve as a continuing reminder that freedom to read cannot be taken for granted as a gift from the authors of the federal constitution. The profession rightly assumes responsibility to protect this basic right of a free people. It is a freedom that each generation of librarians must defend anew. To paraphrase Somerset Maugham: If the library values anything more than its freedom, it will lose that freedom; and the irony is that if it is security and peace of mind that the library values more than freedom, it will lose that, too.

The advisory function of an intellectual freedom committee or of the system itself requires carefully developed policies. Advice may be requested by a member library to prevent trouble. An appeal for help may follow an attack on a book or a film. The problem may originate with the leadership of an irate community organization. It may rise because of philosophic differences between the librarian and the trustees. The system must differentiate between types of problems related to intellectual freedom. There are community-generated problems, for which system fact-finding and the counsel of experienced librarians and system consultants will provide the answers. There are internal problems, in which the system may best assist the local library through counsel on the best use of the services of specialists in library organizations or legal firms. There are also occasions when the local library and its system advisers may be asked to participate in the formulation of policies for academic freedom in area schools and colleges.

Problem Areas

When librarians talk about collection building problems, they are usually concerned about local trouble spots. These are the

difficult and sensitive areas in selection that relate to public reaction and to appropriateness in use. Any selection activity that
relates to trouble falls into the category of a problem area. The
term "problem area," unfortunately, is a panic phrase. It implies
a need for caution on the local level that borders on rejection.

Problem areas need thoughtful book selection. However, selec-
tions involving deliberation do not necessarily generate crises. The
selection of a controversial title is not tantamount to flirting with
patron disapproval. Selection in problem areas means the assumption of a responsible position by fostering community awareness
of political and social ideas, by providing reliable materials, and
by responding to contemporary modes of expression that will attract and hold the "library dropouts" of all generations and from
all segments of society. Some problem materials are selected with
the awareness that their most effective use depends on the reader
guidance skills of librarians.

The problem areas in collection building are in flux. They
come and go, depending on variables such as the dominant themes
of the news media, the impact of advertising on public demands,
community prejudices and fears, and the differing individual
levels of readiness to understand new forms of creativity in a
changing society. The following are representative of problem
areas common to many small and medium-sized libraries:

Political and Social Opinion

Political and social opinion is a perpetually sensitive area. It
is dominated by viewpoints, theories, and ideas that widen the
horizons of some readers and raise the blood pressures of others.
The contents of volumes interpreting political action or the findings of sociological studies do not lend themselves to universal
acceptance. The vital issues of the day are always controversial,
but the inflammatory ones do not become less so by being ignored.
The library's justification for collection building in the area of
opinion rests squarely on its objective to provide resources broad
enough to help people become informed citizens. It is a positive
and defensible position.

A new facet to collection building in this area appeared in the
1960s, with the publications of the so-called underground, or
alternative, press. These newspapers provide an outlet for spokesmen of the under-thirty generation. Their columns and illustrations present social and political viewpoints together with calls

to action that are not available in any other form in exactly the same way. The contents of these papers are of interest to many young people regardless of their place of residence or their occupation. They are of interest to older generations that seek to understand new voices. Judith Krug has pointed out that "there may be only a few people in a community who adhere to their philosophy, but everyone in the community should be aware of what the vocal minority is saying, thinking, and doing."[14] There is no question about the eventual research value of these publications. The deterrent to their selection in small libraries centers more on their vocabularies than on their ideas. Publications of the underground press are reviewed by library publications, in recognition of their contribution to analysis of contemporary social and political movements. The small library, with limited funds and only occasional inquiries for the material, may find it necessary to depend on the system for access to the alternative press.

Problems arise in selection in the area of opinion because some citizens are inclined to measure the worth of a publication, and even its place in a public library, by judging the author's private life. Some small-town citizens check reports on the author's or publisher's reputed associations with organizations against the *Attorney General's List of Subversive Organizations,* published by the Superintendent of Documents. They search the newspapers, hoping to discredit a young author for reported participation in a campus revolt.

The selector knows that an author's political affiliations, past or present membership in any organization, and personal or public activities cannot serve as the starting point for the evaluation of a book. The cardinal principle for all book selection—that it is the book to be judged and not the author—is never more in evidence than in areas of opinion. The book selector may believe the author completely wrong in his theories, but the book selector, of all people, must recognize the author's right to interpret his opinions, as long as they are presented with honest intent.

In social and political studies, as in all other fields, the library stands on neutral ground. The library is not pro-Republican or pro-Democratic, pro-white or pro-black, pro-Israeli or pro-Arab. Its collections must demonstrate the profession's conviction of the importance of keeping open the channels of inquiry and its faith in the public to make the right decisions when it understands the issues. The danger for the American public lies, as Anne

Carroll Moore said in another connection, not in knowing too much but rather in not knowing enough to think things through.

It is sometimes contended that library materials in the area of opinion should not be purchased if the ideas expressed do not meet with the approval of the majority of citizens in the community. There is not a single community in the United States in which the majority approves of communism, but if the libraries in those communities ignored books on communism, their citizens would be handicapped by ignorance of one of the dominant forces in the modern world.

The idea has been advanced with surprising frequency by laymen and trustees that libraries should label material that is controversial. Experienced librarians and system specialists know that labeling, like book-banning, only excites curiosity and creates an attraction that is just the opposite of what the proponents of labeling intended. There is also the question of what subjects should be labeled. Some very sincere citizens are convinced that fluoridation is a communist plot. Others are certain that student uprisings, protests from the ghetto, integrated education, and other current issues are subversive and should be so identified to protect the public. The possibilities of labeling and mislabeling are endless. The impossibility of the task in a world of continuing publication explosions is obvious.

Behind-the-Iron-Curtain Materials

A small minority of citizens in some small communities have contended that the library should not provide stories or personal narratives describing life in Russia or in any other nondemocratic country with sympathy for the customs or understanding of the people. The basis for this theory is that such materials may indoctrinate the young. Proponents of this theory forget that the American young will soon assume responsible roles in a world in which they must be prepared to face the fact that democracy is only one form of government. The theory implies that adult Americans have not done a good job in selling their way of life to themselves or their offspring. Banning of books that interpret other nations not only leaves young America in a vulnerable state of ignorance but also tarnishes the image of the United States and all it has stood for since the days of the Founding Fathers.

The professional problem for the selector in this area is finding reliable, up-to-date factual material on nations in the communist world. Current travel guides and United Nations publications are sometimes the only nonreference book sources for background data on such nations as Albania, for example. Judging the authority of a reporter to speak about current conditions in countries where travel is permissible takes more than passing examination. Critics have pointed out that there are few experts on foreign nations. This statement epitomizes the librarian's quandary about reliability of observation and interpretation of facts. The selector must assess from a number of reviewing sources the background, training, and experience that make an author a trustworthy transmitter of information about lands where free inquiry is at a premium. Selection tools available through the system increase the opportunity to determine authenticity of such materials.

Contemporary Illustrations

Advances in publishing technology have given the illustrator a chance to steal the show in promoting the book as a colorful, appealing, and even exciting form of communication. The treatment of subjects through illustrations has changed, just as the treatment of subjects in writing has changed. There were, for example, the decades when illustrators used only white children as models for illustrations in children's books. There were few artistic representations with which the contemporary child of Oriental, Spanish, Negro, or American Indian descent could identify. This was followed by the self-conscious period when illustrators put them all together. The day finally came when illustrators found the freedom to use models and backgrounds specifically appropriate for illustrating a text or making a picture book.

A slight, but growing, number of illustrations in children's books fall into sensitive areas, not for lack of artistry but because children are not ready for them. The indigenous illustrators, members of ethnic or national groups, speak through their illustrations with relevance to their contemporaries who "understand it as it is." An example is the black artist who develops a fine picture book on the ghetto struggles of a black pioneer leader with such skill that it is immediately appreciated by an adult. It is beautiful art. However, in some communities there is evidence that it does violence to the black child's image of himself in a different age and a more sophisticated environment. To the black child the drawings seem to be a new kind of stereotype. He resents them and fears the reactions of his white friends. Until the day comes that there is understanding, even at an early age, of the tragedies of black history, this type of book should be used with discrimination by perceptive children's librarians and system specialists.

Racial Slurs

Derogatory names for minority groups appear in many types of books. When the derogatory becomes inflammatory, it does not have a chance to belong in a library collection. Nevertheless, the selector becomes a little confused when an outstanding author from a minority group uses offensive words and phrases to describe his own people. This may be explained as a form of catharsis, but it remains a sensitive problem. Racial slurs in print are akin to religious slurs in print. The problem in judging good books marred by derogatory words must be resolved in terms of selection policies and the skilled use of criteria.

Health-Fad Books

The sheer volume of well-publicized health food books gives the book selector a headache. Physical well-being is a major concern of the nation. It is also a preoccupation, particularly of the overweight citizen. Every new diet book excites the curiosity of a large proportion of men and women with middle-age spread. All of these books aim in their way to keep people slim, youthful, attractive to the opposite sex, and free of premature coronaries. There are books advocating the eating of fat and books recommending the elimination of fat. Shelves of diet books hold wide varieties of recommendations for potions ranging from molasses to safflower oil. Like all popular self-help books, these volumes have their peaks of popularity and are soon replaced by a new scheme, for the simple reason that the weight-conscious citizen is eternally shopping around for the most painless combination of weight control and gourmet eating. Many health-fad patrons are also devoted to the cookbook section of the library.

The usual criteria for selection are difficult to apply to health-fad books. Take, for example, the criterion of the authority of the author. In some instances the authors are medical men, who are members of professional associations and successful in their own practices. They have good reputations in their specialties. Advance reviews usually refer to the professional standing of the authors but do not always indicate their competence in the field of nutrition.

The criterion of soundness of information in popular health books is difficult to apply without the help of competent reviewers. The book selector who is untrained in biochemistry has no way of making a judgment from personal knowledge. Authoritative reviews written by specialists frequently are not timed to coincide with heavy public interest. A further question arises as to the extent of soundness "for whom." It is obvious that variables in physical condition mean that a special diet may be relatively safe for one individual but dangerous for another.

A library selects a health book because it is recommended in dependable pre-publication reviews. Later the book may be challenged in court as dangerous. It would seem that a library has two choices in such a situation. One is to withdraw the book in the interest of public safety. The second is to hold it for limited use through the discretionary channels of reader guidance. For example, after the news of the Food and Drug Administration action against specific health books in the 1960s, a public health nurse asked to see those titles at the public library in order to counsel her clients who had heard or read about the claims of the books. This is an illustration of the legitimate use of such books.

Another health-related area in which difficult decisions must be made centers on medical texts recommended by teachers of exceptional children for use by parents. A case in point is a text on care of the brain-damaged child that includes drug dosages. The librarian's reluctance to stock this type of manual for the open shelves is related not only to the possibilities of erroneous self-diagnosis but also to the dangers of misinterpretation by laymen of the chapters on medication. It is based on the same principle that restricts public library collections in medicine to first aid, patient-doctor relationships, history, public health, and medical dictionaries.

An informal survey of the attitudes of the medical profession toward one small library's acquisition of controversial books about diseases and their cures was made during the 1960s. One general physician pointed out that the individual seeking a means of self-diagnosis and treatment in print was going to find it whether it was in the library or not. Still another stated very positively that the public library should stay out of the medical field entirely. Others reported that they recommended the library to patients as a source for both specialized and popular medical books as a basis for understanding a particular illness or the demands of a recuperative period. All offered advice and counseling in their own specialties, a service that may be tapped by all communities and systems.

Sex Education

Sex education falls into a unique hypersensitive category. It is a subject of public panic rather than of reason, and one that divides parents, clergy, teachers, school boards, and organized groups in many small communities. Selection of sex education material necessitates particular attention to authoritative reviews such as those in *Science Books,* published by the American Association for the Advancement of Science. The materials require special handling through reading guidance techniques for both children and adults. Special handling does not restrict open access for adults. It means controlled access for children in terms of their reading and understanding readiness. Advisory service in the acquisition and use of sex education materials is a part of the function of the system materials specialist.

Reprints

Still another problem for the small library is the product of the reprint publishing business. An example is the massive attack made by some reprint houses on the gaps in the literature of black culture. The reprints were largely titles in the public domain. Many libraries at that time had greater need for contemporary material. The telephone brought direct high-pressure calls from the publisher to the small library implying that the library would fail its constituency if it did not confirm an immediate reprint order. The outpourings in black culture reprints were followed by reprints of titles related to the Women's Liberation Movement. The librarians' friends, the out-of-print dealers, pointed out that a number of reprints in both fields are available in trade editions and at a lower cost. The source of advice on reprints for the small library once again was the system's materials consultant.

Restrictions

Most librarians believe in open stacks for maximum public convenience. Increasing incidents of theft and mutilation have forced the reintroduction of locked cases for rare and expensive materials and of restricted shelves for subjects such as automotive repair and karate, and even for complete reference collections. This is a protective measure, not a form of quasi-censorship. The hazard in using restricted areas is the temptation to include all items that might be suspected to be vulnerable. Restricted collections are resented by many adults as a curtailment of the confidentiality of their browsing rights. One answer that has been suggested is to warn the public and the teaching staff of the local schools about the rising cost of book thefts. This is a slow and discouraging method. Some communities have installed security devices available through commercial firms. Certainly the use of copying machines has cut down on mutilation. Providing information on the experiences of libraries in the handling of theft and mutilation problems is a service of the system headquarters.

Other areas challenging the small library include books that "have something to say" to teen-agers, foreign language books for both children and adults, technical materials in which the terminology is new and strange to librarians in small communities, frequently overlooked government documents, and the search for books that fairly and objectively present the accomplishments of representatives of minority groups. These problems and challenges in materials selection, and others like them, frequently evoke the liveliest sessions at system book and materials discussion meetings.

Selection Process

In general, books are selected for reasons relating to the library's objectives. In small libraries these reasons may include:

1. Usefulness in form, content, and reading levels for individuals in the community
2. Importance in strengthening existing collections
3. Significance in interpretation of social change
4. Appeal to the reluctant reader
5. Vitality and originality of treatment
6. Recency and accuracy
7. Authority of a bibliographic listing
8. Best book of its kind
9. Public interest.

Time is an important corollary to good collection building. Virginia Haviland once quoted a children's librarian as saying, "The less time I have, the more titles I buy. It is so easy to be taken in by a title that sounds as if it would fill a need."[15] Others have forecast that the library staff of the future will need to spend more hours on materials selection than they did in the past.[16] It is almost certain that, with system help in so many areas of service, the staffs of small libraries will be able to spend more time with library materials and people.

The collection builder makes use of criteria. The traditional criteria for the selection of library materials are explained in many texts found in individual libraries and system professional collections. The significance of a criterion is something the collection builder learns through experience and applies subconsciously. For example, he does not use a rigid scheme in the evaluation of a novel—with a given number of points for unity, so many for plot development, a percentage for characterization, and points off for each four-letter word. Selection cannot be reduced to a mathematical formula. It is a high-level intellectual activity in which the selector constantly utilizes the elements of criteria and the benefits of his prior reading as they relate to a knowledge and understanding of the community.

The first criterion for builders of collections is quality. The librarian seeks the best materials available for the consumer at his level of receptiveness. Excellence is a goal for collection building in both traditional and innovative library programs. The dream of excellence is sometimes diminished by the lack of good materials to meet a specific objective, by subservience to public demand, or by misleading reviews. Nevertheless, it remains a constant in the philosophy of the librarian whose goal is to build a collection that rises above the mediocre.

The basic criteria for the selection of books are shared by book selection people at all levels. They include quality of content and format, distinctive literary values or craftsmanship, authoritativeness, recency, and local significance. Criteria as guidelines for the selection of multimedia materials are akin to specifications for a furniture bid or a checklist for the purchase of a bookmobile. They are reminders of objectives, of standards, and of suitability to match the known and anticipated needs of the ultimate consumer. The vocabulary of contemporary criteria has been reshaped by the response of librarians to current issues, by the ideologies of a changing society, and by the brushfires of censorship. Terms that have new meaning for the collection builder in the last decades of the twentieth century are represented by the following:

Authenticity. Is the book or the product of any other media acceptable to a person who has lived in the environment interpreted by the author or producer? Is it the authentic voice of an ethnic group?

Communication. Does a book, recording, film, or picture say something to the generation for which it was written or created? Is it relevant?

Contribution. Does the work contribute to man's understanding of changes in the world, which he must accept? Is it stimulating or innocuous?

Defensibility. Is the work defendable in a court of law?

Sincerity. Is the writer or the artist honest in his presentation? Is the presentation patronizing or devious? Does the work become insincere through lack of documentation or deliberate omissions?

Selection aids are designed to provide bibliographic information and/or evaluations. There are selection aids for every type and size of library and for all media. Each has a well-defined purpose and scope, which are carefully stated in the introduction or preface of each new species or each new edition. It is the responsibility of the user to discover independently or with system help what a selection aid can or cannot contribute to his type of library or to the selection process. The value of any selection tool is dependent upon knowledgeable exploitation of those serviceable factors that make it a unique item among bibliographic resources.

The selector in a small or medium-sized library needs background knowledge of a number of factors in the acquisition and use of identification or evaluation aids: (1) the competence of the individuals who are responsible for the content of the aid, (2) the publisher: whether professional or commercial, (3) the price, (4) method of acquisition: whether sold on a service basis determined by budgets or size of library, by subscription, or as a single purchase, (5) provisions for updating: supplements or new editions, (6) suitability to library: intended for small or large libraries, public or college libraries, booksellers or librarians, or combined interests, (7) scope and limitations, (8) arrangement, (9) subject fields: current and/or retrospective, (10) kind of data and evaluation included or excluded, (11) priority value in relation to other aids, and (12) availability for referral or consultation within the system.

Selection tools are not decision-makers in collection building or collection maintenance. The librarian is not expected to abdicate responsibility to a buckram or paperbound assistant despite its authority. The selector becomes "the authority on authorities," with full recognition of the hazards of dependence on reviewing and bibliographic tools. Selection aids make excellent recommendations, but they omit equally good recommendations due to space limitations, publishing schedules, or human oversights. Someone said years ago that the saddest words spoken behind the scenes in a library could be, "It is not in *Children's Catalog;* discard it."

Systems serving very small libraries are resource centers for identification and evaluation tools for their member libraries. In some systems, aids such as the *Booklist, Library Journal,* and *Kirkus Reviewing Service* are circulated on a rotation basis for use by the member libraries. The system helps when necessary with justifications for local acquisition of such tools.

Book reviews in newspapers or magazines are of particular interest to the librarian because they frequently are the stimulators of public interest. The term "book review" is used loosely to cover several types of commentary and evaluation. Reviews vary from subjective newspaper columns to critical evaluations in the literary and professional publications of many disciplines. They appear in time sequences ranging from pre-publication recommendations to post-publication analysis by the quarterly journals.

Reviews are handled in many ways. Some reviewers take up their allotted space with a rambling commentary on the subject treated by a book and never get around to a substantial evaluation of the book itself. The librarian may appreciate the literary value of the essay-review but deplore the lack of specific information and judgment. The useful review for the librarian states clearly what the book is about and predicts an audience. It gives a judgment on the contribution the book makes to its field and the values it has for the individual reader.

Authors, too, are treated in different ways in the general reviewing press. The ordinary author may be given great credit for effort, and a talented, experienced author may be torn to pieces in a querulous review concerned with minor defects. There is a theory that this happens because the professional reviewer may want to encourage the ordinary to become extraordinary, whereas the experienced writer who has something to say offers the reviewer a challenge to reveal sins of commission or omission. It is interesting to watch the treatment of books of well-known authors. There are some who always have a warm and appreciative reception. For example, Dan Herr once pointed out that "books by E. B. White, James Thurber, S. J. Perelman, and Frank Sullivan are never reviewed—they are eulogized."[17]

Signed reviews, such as those found in library periodicals, have professional significance. The selector soon learns the bias and personal enthusiasms of an identified reviewer who frequently appears in print. Librarians are generous in their contributions to the reviewing field. The majority are adept at pinpointing the value of a book and its usefulness for a small or medium-sized library. Some forget that the small library exists. The librarian learns to be a judge of reviewers and to assess their judgment of books through recall of their past reliability. A review is one man's opinion, and for this reason the selector may turn to several sources including the system before his decisions are final.

Some phrases used by book reviewers are suspect because of indiscriminate applications. An old one is "a must book." The word "must" has become a shorthand symbol for "indispensable." It implies that a book is an obligatory item for purchase, without always indicating to whom the word "must" refers. What is a "must" for one person or one library is not necessarily a "must" for another. Frequently the book selector needs more than the word "must" for sound decision-making. Another loosely used phrase is "definitive edition." Its use by some reviewers indicates a high personal enthusiasm. Its use by other reviewers seems to indicate that the author has said more about the subject than they are interested in knowing. The book selector needs to know if "definitive edition" is used as a form of praise or if it means "final, conclusive, and authoritative." There are times when the phrase "authorized edition" is used without giving any idea of who did the authorizing. Single words also have become synonymous with types of writing. "Honest" has come to stand for "sordid."

The citizen reader of book reviews usually wants the answers to three questions: What is the book about? Is it worth reading? Who wrote it? The librarian has more questions. The librarian should be able to expect certain information from reviews, particularly those written specifically for librarians. This includes not only judgments on content, style, or authenticity but also information on format and some comparison with earlier material on the same subject. The helpful review indicates the depth of realism and whether or not the treatment is appropriate. It reveals how violence is handled. It suggests the type of reader who might be interested. The basic principle of judging a book in its entirety is not violated by watching for these or similar kinds of detail any more than being alert to a statement on the size of print used in the book's design is a violation of basic principles. It is a matter of acquiring background for selection purposes.

The reputation and stature of a publisher is an important factor in book selection. The history of the publisher, the type of publications associated with his imprint, the longevity of his backlist, and his association with individual authors are all a part of a useful body of knowledge for the selector. Purchases of long-established publishing houses by nonpublishing industries and mergers of various publishing groups are watched by librarians for insight into changing publishing emphases, standards, and advertising methods. Publishers of interest to the small and medium-sized libraries include the trade book publishers whose lists are general in nature, the specialists who concentrate on specific subject fields, the reprint houses, the foundation and university presses, the library press, and federal and state governments.

Cooperative action between librarians and publishers has resulted in benefits to both professions and to the general public. It produced such outstanding documents as the Freedom to Read statement. Among the many other achievements of cooperation between publishers and librarians has been the joint search for materials to fill gaps in areas of information and knowledge. Small libraries, too, are able to contribute to the awareness of needed materials. For example, about a decade ago there was no suitable material to use with a small child to explain the sudden death of a grandparent. A children's librarian in a small library pointed out the gap to a number of children's book editors. This stimulated lively correspondence about possible authors, age levels, and other aspects of the problem and involved librarians in larger libraries in a useful project that still engenders lively discussions among authors and writing groups.

The role of the cooperative system in the member library book selection process is educational and informational. A collection building workshop or a continuing in-service training program provides the opportunity to interpret the contemporary factors that influence criteria, to alert member librarians to changing characteristics in reviewing tools, and to introduce new or little known sources for reliable reviews. System specialists may stimulate cooperative projects among the membership in a search for appraisals of materials not covered adequately by standard aids. Most important, the cooperative system may bring together the member librarians and specialists in subject fields to learn the significance of selection criteria from the specialists' point of view and to discuss with them the problems of apparent lack of coverage in reviews or in actual publications from the librarian's point of view.

Purchase of Library Materials

Many trustees turn to the system consultant staff for information on how much of the book budget should be allocated for different kinds of books in a small library. They are aware that usually only 18 to 23 percent of the general budget is available for books, periodicals, pamphlets, and other library materials. The profession in the past has attempted to estimate percentages that should be reserved for children's books, general adult collections, young adult materials, and reference. These formulas proved to be unrealistic. The determinants in any division of the book budget are the library's objectives and its priorities, which are established on the basis of self-knowledge and analysis of critical need.

The allocations that the local library has established as a part of the working budget are reflected in its financial records. These records may be kept in such a way as to show how much has been spent for each department. They also serve another interest of the trustee—the cost of books of different kinds. The national averages are available in the *Bowker Annual,* in the cost-analysis estimates released by the Public Library Association of the American Library Association, and in the research files of the system. The individual library may determine its own average costs in different categories for any one year by dividing the total expenditure for adult nonfiction, for example, by the number of nonfiction books purchased. This will give the library its own per-book cost and in a faster time than published figures.

Discounts sometimes disturb trustees and administrators of small libraries, particularly when they make comparisons with other libraries. Discounts, however, are affected by the size of the library and the volume of its business. Discounts also vary with types of materials. Prebound books for children may not be subject to discount unless annual purchases exceed a stipulated amount. Larger discounts are allowed for trade books with heavy printings than for technical books with limited printings. There are other publications, such as periodical indexes, for which there is no discount. The processing centers that handle the orders for many small libraries frequently request that the individual library refrain from specifying a particular jobber so that they may negotiate for the best available discounts on behalf of all of their clients.

Most libraries that order and process their own books use a single jobber for economy in bookkeeping and for effective jobber-librarian relationships, which expedite the handling of orders.

The publishing industry has developed a plan whereby an individual library may contract for examination privilege of the entire line of a publisher. The disadvantages for the small libraries in the examination and purchase of the products of individual publishers are many. There are the added burdens of bookkeeping for separate accounts. There is the human tendency to catalog an entire shipment—even though it includes nonessentials for a particular library. There is also the possibility of using a disproportionate share of the budget of a very small library on the output of a few publishers without being aware of the availability of other materials from other sources. A major value of selection aids for small and medium-sized libraries is the sifting of possible choices and essentials from the tremendous publishing volume that overwhelms the profession.

Traveling salesmen for publishing houses sometimes provide useful news of forthcoming titles and new editions of standard works, but also they may be a menace to the librarian in a small community, whose limited funds are vulnerable to the zeal of a voluble salesman. Now and then, stories circulate about the sad state of a small library whose entire book budget was spent by the book salesman, not by the librarian. Few librarians get caught in these circumstances. It is important for the newcomer to book selection to remember that the list of a single publisher does not represent the current wealth in materials. It must also be remembered that the fact that a neighboring library bought a certain set of books is no criterion for selection.

A limited number of publishers do not cooperate with jobbers and require direct orders. Standing orders for the automatic shipment of materials required annually are time-savers and also cancel out the chance that such essentials might be overlooked in the rapid passage of time. Arrangements may be made with jobbers and processing centers for standing orders on an annual or biennial basis.

Convenient in the buying process for libraries that contract with processing centers are the lists of current books predetermined as possible purchase items of widespread interest or popularity. These lists are prepared and distributed by the centers to facilitate centralized purchasing. They are a convenience to the small library. They are not selection aids nor are they used to judge the collection building philosophy or practices of any library.

The small library selects materials other than books for its collection. Annual periodical and newspaper lists selected by the local library are handled by jobbers known as subscription agents. In some states libraries are required by law to obtain bids on such lists. A trend among subscription agents to reject opportunities to handle an account on a bid basis may add to the local library's difficulties in placing subscription orders. General advice to those who are not under obligation to obtain bids is to stay with an agent who has proved that he can give good service.

The small and medium-sized library's collection of metropolitan papers often is limited to a few major papers of national importance. The local newspaper is frequently a gift from the publisher to the library. The preservation of local papers is important to the library and to the community. In many instances the files of local papers are being microfilmed, with the costs being shared by the publisher and the library. In some areas duplicate film of local newspapers is being purchased by systems and other units in the library network as supplements to microfilmed holdings of metropolitan papers at the central library or serials center.

Pamphlets and government documents are direct order responsibilities of the local library although some systems make such materials available for special projects and urgent informational needs. In many systems the central library is a designated depository for documents.

Nonprint Materials

In the interest of developing a more comprehensive collection than any one library can supply, nonprint materials such as records, tape recordings, films, paintings, sculptures, and slides should be a part of a system's services. System selection policy will reflect joint decisions about centralized or rotating collections of audiovisual items. The policy for selection will relate to the objectives of the program and will, for the most part, include evaluative factors similar to those of the book selection policy. Additional factors will be those related to the specific media. For instance, when is it necessary for a film to be in color? Does the subject of a film control the length of the film, or the length control the subject? Is the story in a talking book authentic, abridged, or distorted? Is the performance in a musical recording outstanding, abridged, or adapted for a particular rendering by voice or instrument? Is the recording well produced or are there technical problems of noise or fidelity?

Selection of audiovisual materials should be made by an experienced professional or a person who knows the value of the materials as communications media and as art. A thorough background in audiovisual sources is necessary. Although film reviews are helpful, it is customary to preview films prior to purchase to assure conformity to the selection policy. Because of the time involved in previewing, selection of films by committee is not to be encouraged. In the selection of recordings, it is usually necessary to depend on reputable reviewers.

Maintenance of a Collection

The maintenance of a collection means keeping a collection alive, attractive, and useful. It is much more than adding new materials through the selection, acquisition, and cataloging process. It involves the elimination of the deadwood that does not move, the obsolete that misleads, the worn, weary volumes that repel rather than attract, and the planning for necessary replacements. The quick obsolescence resulting from an unprecedented rate of technological progress and from research in all disciplines necessitates constant control in collection building. An obsolete book is a dangerous tool in today's world. A sound principle is that it is better for a small library to have no book on a particular subject than a book that presents out-of-date material. The system is the backstop for the library that has the good sense to remove the obsolescent despite the possibility of a slow recovery through new acquisitions.

Books in the field of science become obsolete most rapidly. Many are out of date in some details by the time they leave the printing press. At best, the valuable life of a volume in the pure and applied sciences, exclusive of the classics in the field, is five years. Encyclopedias have a useful five-year life that is extended temporarily, and with some inconvenience, by yearbooks. A planned replacement schedule for encyclopedias is particularly advantageous to the small library with a limited supporting collection. The factual, nonhistorical classifications in the general collection, such as business, food products, government, etc., are superseded within eight or ten years of their copyright dates.

Obsolescence undermines the philosophy of sound collection building. A reverence for statistics can wreck it. An increase in total holdings far too often is equated with progress. Mere numbers that represent book stock in a report are meaningless. Statistics can never reflect quality. An up-to-date small library can be an asset to its community and to the total system complex. A small library that is a near-permanent storehouse buries the significant in its collection in an accumulation of the past, whose only value is numerical. Antiquity in its holdings is a deterrent to public confidence. The reports on its total collection distort inventories of systemwide resources. There are very human reasons behind an obeisance to mathematics as opposed to a concern for quality in small communities. There is local pride in statistical evidence of growth. There are trustees who, alert to obsolescence in materials in the literature of their own occupations, forget that withdrawals are as important as additions in collection building.

The librarian is not in the collection maintenance business to make excuses but to carry out policies. The policies of maintaining a collection cannot be divorced from the policies of selection. The principles and standards that serve as guidelines for decision-making in the purchase of materials carry over into decision-making in the control of the collection. They are subject to interpretations but not to apologies.

Public library standards suggest annual withdrawals of approximately 5 percent of the total book stock.[18] This suggestion brings mathematics back into collection maintenance. However, this percentage is not meant to be an obligatory rate for all libraries. In fact, the annual percentage of withdrawals in the average library varies from year to year and frequently exceeds the recommended average. The major value of the recommendation is the reminder that withdrawals are a responsibility of all libraries. This process of making withdrawals is commonly called "weeding" —a descriptive term raising idle speculations about the avocations of pioneer librarians, who so firmly fixed the term in professional parlance. The act of weeding is the physical removal of materials from the working collection. Most discards are headed for an incinerator or for sale as bulk paper or comparable small income-raising measures, depending on state laws or local ordinances determining the disposal of public property.

A plan for the maintenance of collections in addition to current selection may include: a schedule of replacement for encyclopedias; the placement of standing orders for annuals and irregular publications needed in reference and other service departments; systematic checking of bibliographies and selection aids for new editions, replacement titles, and subject area expansion; bindery shipments; and a continuous program of weeding. Responsibility for the control of collections may be divided among the staff even in small libraries, where there are few people. Some libraries assign this responsibility on a rotating basis, so that over a period of time each person acquires first-hand knowledge of the strengths and weaknesses of the collection. Such assignments involve overall responsibility for alertness to obsolescence and to gaps in the collection as well as the handling of designated jobs in the maintenance plan.

Taking inventory is a periodic job in collection maintenance. It is the process of determining the actual existence of an item and its current location. Some libraries take inventory at five-year intervals or on some other fixed schedule. Still others take frequent spot inventories of material in heavy demand, particularly at the end of a school year. The theft of library materials diminishes the overall effectiveness of a collection. It is never the dust-catcher that disappears. A spot inventory is the only sure way to ascertain that a book is still available for an essential service or that it needs immediate replacement.

The preparation of materials for the bindery is a regular maintenance operation. It is lifted above the routine level by the observance of selection criteria, which help to determine whether a book is worth binding. Particular attention is given to the date of the copyright; whether the book is in or out of print; its value to the collection; its physical condition, including adequacy of margins and condition of the paper; the replacement cost, as compared to bindery cost; and the title's availability in paperback.

The role of the system in the maintenance of the member library's collection is consultative. System specialists give advice on weeding and replacements, arrange for contract services for the local library in emergency situations, and underwrite through the education program those conditions which encourage excellence in collection maintenance throughout the system.

Special System Action in Collection Building

Some systems are able, through their plans of service and budgeting programs, to initiate coordinated acquisition programs. In this type of collection building a library is assigned the responsibility for selection in a subject field in which there is evidence that a good foundation in that field exists in the local collection. The aim of this program is to build on existing strength, to improve collections for local need, and to provide greater access for the benefit of all members. The system subsidizes the collection and the costs related to selection, acquisition, and processing. The local library contributes in kind through the administration of the collection from the point of selection to the intershelving with the local collection and the providing of loans to its own patrons and to the other member libraries.

Every library has in its holdings many books whose contents continue to hold all or some of their original value but are no longer of interest to the local community. These may be once-popular books. They may be titles that are out of print and subject to a search by other libraries on behalf of students, researchers, or even retrospective readers. The small library ordinarily is not able to store idle books. The system solution to this problem is a central storage warehouse operated by a single system or by several systems on a shared-cost basis. The warehouse relieves the local library of the burden of caring for unused materials and opens up access for possibly greater frequency of use. The controls for such service include pre-transfer selection plans, which eliminate heavy duplication and the handling of absolutely dead titles. Guidelines in the warehouse policy in turn may indicate directions for the small library in its weeding and discarding program.

The system staff is prepared, through its consultant service, to evaluate local collections at the request of the local library. An evaluation may be focused on sections of the library's holdings, such as reference, or may deal with the total collection. It may be an independent study made at the time of a change of administrators, for example, or it may be correlated with in-service training for the staff who will serve as collection builders in the future. Such evaluations are concluded with recommendations and counseling to stimulate renewed interest in a quality of collection building that will lead libraries more quickly to a realization of their objectives.

The system's great opportunity in collection building in support of member libraries and their separate goals is sevenfold: (1) continuous improvement of the policies and procedures for bibliographic control and accessibility to resource networks, (2) resource planning and building with and for member libraries, (3) programming for continuing education in selection and knowledge of subject fields, (4) maintaining and disseminating information on professional materials of help to member libraries, (5) supporting a climate of intellectual freedom, (6) providing materials consultant services, and (7) research into reader interests and changing area needs.

6 Administering Services for People

The local library in a cooperative system is responsible for direct service to library users. Therefore, each member of the staff has an obligation to learn how to take maximum advantage of the system plan of service. The local librarian also is responsible for the quality of the library's environment so that services may flourish. The responsibility means supervision of innumerable details, from the maintenance of physical properties to the techniques of communicating with the library's many publics. The local librarian is so close to his own operation that he often has difficulty identifying the means to achieve overall effectiveness. Deliberate, periodic self-examination is helpful in revealing the oversights that lessen public confidence in the library's capacity to provide service. This self-scrutiny may include the following types of questions:

1. Library building and grounds
   a. Is the exterior library sign legible and well lighted? Are the entryway notices up to date?
   b. Does the landscaping need attention? Do the plantings take advantage of the site? Are the sidewalks in good repair?
   c. Are the curbside book depositories well painted and marked?
   d. Has a minor repair problem become an unsightly hazard?
   e. Has everything been done that can be done to make the interior colorful, warm, and inviting?
   f. Has the technical literature been checked for estimates of time required for washing windows, sweeping, and dusting to help ascertain adequacy of custodial help?
   g. Is an inventory of furniture and equipment and its condition maintained for the library's own information and to provide data for occasional inventory audits by local government?

197

2. Communication
   a. Is the library listed in the telephone book only under a **me-morial** name? Is it listed in the Yellow Pages?
   b. Has the library stationery been redesigned in recent years? Does it include zip code and telephone number?
   c. Are the police and fire departments regularly notified of any change in emergency numbers?
   d. Does the library communicate through well-planned directional and location signs throughout the building?
   e. Is the bulletin board eye-catching, or is it overloaded with outdated material?
   f. Do library reading lists and other releases include the library address, telephone number, and date?
   g. Are posters and displays amateurish or attractive?
   h. Has the staff had the benefit of talks and demonstrations by telephone company specialists on how to use the phone as a public relations tool?
   i. Are there advance public notices of library board meetings?
   j. Have all of the staff heard about system services and how they work?
   k. Does the community know the library belongs to a system and what system services are available?
   l. Does the library effectively display or distribute informational brochures coming from the system?
   m. Does the community know about the Library Bill of Rights and what it means to them?
   n. Does the staff have an opportunity to see and talk about the new materials?
   o. Has the community ever been told about the library's specific objectives and how it plans to meet them?
   p. Is the librarian acquainted with the local newspaper editor and local government officials?

3. Services
   a. Does any one segment of the community receive predominant attention in materials and staff time—to the neglect of others?
   b. Have service procedures been analyzed to help eliminate unproductive steps?
   c. Is the staff alert to the comments of newcomers for an assessment of their expectations?
   d. Does the staff feel free to transmit service ideas for program changes to the administrator and board?
   e. Is there adequate delegation of responsibility to qualified personnel?

f. Has the library considered a review of its routines by a system consultant to confirm effectiveness or to analyze procedures for increased effectiveness?

g. Does the staff have an opportunity to take annual visiting days to observe the service programs of other libraries?

h. Does the staff have an opportunity to attend system in-service training sessions related to library and system services?

Local Library Services

The small library's organization by age levels has not changed through decades of library history, and yet it is now different. The nature of the informational requests directed at a small library by both children and adults has changed from the simple and uncomplicated to the sophisticated and the demanding. Modern devices, such as automatic charging machines or microfilm readers, have reshaped the routines for handling some services. The library public, which was once surveyed as the middle-class intellectual elite, promises to become an exciting mixture of the total population. State legislatures have enacted laws that provide the framework and the funds for accessibility to a wide range of resources. The small library is involved in a change of pace. Trustees and librarians in small communities have been stimulated by statewide planning, changing emphases in laws, and the needs of their fellow citizens to take a close look at their resources and at the people they are expected to serve.

Self-analysis of the range and depth of local services may reveal that there are the half-served as well as the unserved in every community. A small library, for example, is vulnerable to the pressures resulting from overserving students to the partial or the complete neglect of the businessman or the worker in the community. Statistics prove that adults are the minority users of public library services, particularly in smaller libraries. The profession has never taken the time to unearth the real reasons for widespread adult disinterest, or even unawareness, of library services that will help them as individuals. There are indications, however, as witnessed by the periodic revisions of standards, the professional support for sound library laws, the call for innovative techniques in identifying needs, and the spread of systems, that the profession intends to do something about its objective to provide services to meet the needs of all the people. The system provides help in meeting this objective through its consultant services.

Consultative Responsibility of the System

A standard item in the plan of service of a cooperative system is the provision of consultative assistance to member libraries. The aim of the advisory program is to help the independent library help itself. Consultative services are available in all fields from staff training to joint conferences with government officials. Access to advisory services is augmented, when necessary, by referrals to outside experts such as insurance counselors, regional planners, or consultants in unique specialties from other systems. The scope of a system's consultative service may be said to be unlimited. It can be restricted only by the failure of the independent library to recognize such a service as a resource for professional information and as an aid to in-depth problem-solving.

The values in the concept of system consultative service have been responsible for the assumption by systems of many duties and activities handled in the past by the extension departments of state libraries. This has been a logical and beneficial step, which has moved the source of advice out of a governmental complex into a more accessible and familiar setting. At the same time a system advisory program frees the state library personnel for a major concentration of effort on high-level consultant relationships with urban and rural systems, and for research and long-range planning of value to all types of libraries in the state.

System consultants may be classified as (1) generalists, who know a great deal about many aspects of library work and who know where to turn when they do not, and (2) specialists, whose expertise is limited to one or several related fields such as film service and audiovisual programming. System consultants do not operate in isolation. There is collaboration between consultants at the system level, and they often work together as a team on complex problems facing a single member library or a group of member libraries.

There are two types of consultant services. One consists of establishing an understanding of the need for consultation, examining the elements of the problem, determining solutions, and making recommendations. This is an advisory service. The second, a consultant-trainer service, extends the advisory function into an educational program designed to help the member library become a self-reliant unit in the system. This is a training-on-the-job service.

The requests for advisory service from the field are comparable in a way to the inquiries that flow over a reference desk. Some requests leave no doubt about what is needed. Others require considerable probing to assess what is hidden behind the words of the request. It is as imperative for the system consultant staff to determine what is not serious as to learn what is critical. The consultant must exercise sensitivity in ascertaining the motivations behind a request, assume neutrality in conflict situations, and maintain a high degree of self-control to resist the impulse to take over as a shortcut in helping the local library.

The general guidelines that have evolved from cooperative system consultative experience suggest that: (1) the use of an advisory service and the acceptance of its results must be recognized as voluntary on the part of the member library; (2) such service must be available on an equitable basis to all member libraries; (3) the participation of the consultant in the affairs of the local library must be temporary; (4) the consultant's contribution must be fact-finding, counseling, or training and not actual performance (except when performance serves as a demonstration in training situations or as explicitly determined by contract arrangements); and (5) the consultant should encourage the feedback of results from the local level and the building up of system case files to be used for referral in comparable situations or for planned evaluation of the consultative services.

Types of Local Library Services

Children's Services

Children's services have been singled out as the outstanding achievement in public library service. Children's librarians have developed their strength through single-minded pursuit of objectives to reach each child as an individual They have supported their objectives by an unusual dedication to the literature and supporting materials in their field. Children's librarians aim to provide an opportunity for the unrequired reading among the young, which counts not only in their happy association with books but also in developing their confidence in the use of a library as a personal tool. Children's librarians seem blessed with a rare skill in communicating a real enthusiasm for books. Robert Leigh's conclusion that "children's rooms and children's librarians have been the classic success of the public library,"[1] made in 1950, was substantiated by reports during the next two decades. The New York system survey, for example, found that "a great deal more enthusiasm, ingenuity, and imagination was demonstrated by local staff in handling the questions relating to materials for children than in handling those relating to adult resources."[2]

This enthusiasm seems to carry over into activities on the system level. Children's librarians as individuals and in groups urge the establishment of media reviewing centers to help them become even more skilled in book selection. They look to film previewing sessions to find book-related film productions to further their objectives. The literature also indicates that even though a large proportion of children's librarians are experts, they welcome the ideas, studies, advice, and programs of system consultants in work with children. The system children's consultant has many duties. Perhaps the most important are to help the small library maintain a balance between service to the child as an individual and service to the child as a member of a student body, to keep alive the story hour as one of the great heritages of childhood, to open up opportunities for children's librarians from isolated communities to share experiences and book knowledge, and to provide in-service training in the administration of children's departments and in techniques of working with administrators and with other departments in a library.

Young Adult Service

It is difficult to determine exactly what small libraries mean by "young adult service." To some it is a focus on the high school crowd; in others the age range is from junior high school to the college student. The span of years does not seem to make much difference, in view of the fact that young people have access to aural and visual media that, in many instances, put them on alertness and vocabulary levels beyond those of their elders.

The small public library can be an idea communications center for young adults. It stocks the ideas they are interested in; and with system help, it may supply the forms, such as records, paperbacks, and films, to which many young adults will respond if they know of their availability. The public library becomes a stronghold of resources for the young who want to make something out of rare moments of solitude or who are looking for something to add to the spectator or activist roles of youth in a highly organized society. The open stacks of a library are an invitation for leisurely browsing and for independence in selection.

The young adult, like the adult, has user rights in a library: a right to be regarded as an individual, a right to expect that collection builders in libraries will recognize that his interests are as complex as contemporary man's social problems and as fast-paced as technological change itself, and a right to expect to find materials in his library that say something to his generation even though they may say nothing to another generation.

Young adult librarians have goals well covered by library literature. The underlying philosophy of young adult service may be summed up by the observation that, if young adults are to understand the problems of society, they must be introduced to the best resources accumulated from the minds and the experience of all generations. If young adults are to succeed in the world they are trying to remake, they must know how to use those resources. For this purpose young adult librarians in small libraries and their co-workers, the young adult consultants in systems, exist.

The responsibilities of a young adult consultant may include: (1) helping the local library develop a selection policy statement on materials for the young adult; (2) recommending paperbacks, periodicals, and films that attract and hold young adult interest; (3) defending (on request) intellectual freedom for the young adult; (4) counseling on innovative programs to involve young people; (5) assisting with publicity; (6) planning workshops on the psychology of the young adult, new materials, and related topics of interest to young adult librarians in the system; (7) stimulating effective communication and cooperation with school libraries; (8) coordinating activities with young adult consultants of other systems in planning in-service training programs, bibliographies, or demonstration projects; and (9) serving as liaison with agencies and state and national associations serving youth.

Adult Services

"Adult services" is a phrase applied to the functions and activities of the public library designed to meet the interests and needs of an adult population as individuals and as members of groups. It is the part of the library program that mobilizes all of the library's resources and resourcefulness to help produce and sustain a truly alert and capable citizenry and to enrich the years of adulthood. Adult services means much more than filling shelves with books and files with pamphlets for the casual use of men and women who have reached the generally accepted age of maturity. Adult services is a correlation of judicious selection of materials and the promotion of the imaginative use of those materials.

The phrase in itself implies a creative approach to meeting the actual and potential needs of men and women who must exercise their responsibilities as informed voters, knowledgeable community leaders, and skilled participants in the economic, cultural, and social life of their communities and the nation. Adult services is adult education in action. Adult services provides the materials for lifelong process of self-education for adults from all kinds of backgrounds and with all levels of schooling and experience.

Adult services is covered in the official objectives of most public libraries, but frequently a conscious plan is required to assure the neglected adult a meaningful place in a balanced library program. A conscious plan is the result of deliberately and conscientiously examining a library program, independently or with system help, to determine the original causes for neglect of the adult. The independent library at one time in its history may have been forced to establish a priority for service to children. The priority may have become a habit. It may have encouraged patterns in collection building that discouraged the adult. It may never have offered an opportunity to think of the continuing educational needs of every generation.

A conscious plan for the development of adult services recognizes that its implementation needs constant attention and active promotion. The system consultant staff is able to provide help in the development of a plan for adult services possibly by recommending improvements in the use of space, by counseling on the separation or combination of services to adults and young adults, and by giving advice on the most expedient way to strengthen resources in materials for adult services.

Attention to the quality of adult services is important to a small library for many reasons. The adults of a community are the taxpayers. They are the voters, whose decisions are of vital importance to democracy. They are the people whose opinions and actions raise or lower the tone of community life. The adult population includes some who think of a library as a place for their children to attend story hours or complete school assignments. Others consider the library only as a source for recreational reading or a storehouse of best sellers. Thoughtful community leaders, however, recognize the importance of increasing community awareness of the library as an educational institution that can provide information, stimulation, and knowledge for personal and corporate use through local collections, the resources of the system, and the expanding network of libraries. Adult services is often overlooked as an area which could have wider patronage through skillful interpretation and promotion.

Some small community librarians assume that their fellow citizens want only to be entertained in their free hours. They also assume that an adult reader knows what he wants to read or that he can take care of himself in a library. Many small libraries challenge these assumptions. It is admittedly difficult to redirect patterns of book use among adults. However, librarians who have used even the simplest form of reader guidance in person-to-person conversations about books and ideas know that individual reading interests can be broadened. These librarians know that a reluctant reader can become an enthusiastic idea-explorer through informal introductions to materials that widen personal horizons or revive latent interests. On the surface, it seems adult services do not have the natural appeal of a children's department constantly enlivened by contagious curiosities and the enthusiasms of boys and girls. The truth is that adult services have equal satisfactions for the perceptive librarian who, through experience in recommending books, has watched people open closed minds or become articulate about important local or national issues.

The activities that are part of adult services may be as varied as thoughtful planning, time, and talent permit. The small library cannot be all things to all people. It can spark many an idea. It can tap the brainpower and enlist the unique competencies in the community at large to plan and produce library-sponsored programs. It can initiate book-focused projects to be carried out in cooperation with or by education groups and social agencies. It can concentrate on those activities that meet the most pressing informational needs of the hour. Librarians and trustees, by virtue of their positions, are committed to an appraisal of their own attitudes towards adult services and to a concentration on plans to strengthen those services.

The working tools for adult services are up-to-date reference and general collections, pamphlets, public documents, indexes, periodicals, recordings, and films. A small library may not own all these tools, but it can have access to them through a system. Quality of service depends not so much on the size of the local collection as on the suitability of its contents and the resourcefulness of all members of the staff in using that collection and augmenting it with system resources. The smaller the library, the more important this element of resourcefulness becomes.

In 1970 the Adult Services Division of the American Library Association adopted a statement on the Library Rights of Adults in which it was positively declared:

> Every adult has the right to a library which seeks to understand both his needs and his wants and which uses every possible means to satisfy them. His library offers:
>
> *Wide resources*
>
> Full and prompt access to all recorded fact, opinion, and creative effort in whatever physical form he feels is most useful to him
>
> The books, films, works of art, and music he wants to see and hear; an opportunity to encounter new material and creative works of which he may be unaware
>
> A conveniently located library through which he can tap the resources of all libraries through its participation in regional and national information networks.
>
> *Skilled staff*
>
> Personal assistance from a librarian who creates a welcoming atmosphere, who seeks to understand his needs (either expressed or unexpressed), and who has the knowledge and skills to select, locate, evaluate, and interpret materials for him
>
> Equal respect and the same high quality of service whether he is skilled or unskilled, sophisticated or naive, conservative

or radical, serious or casual, knowledgeable or ignorant, practical or visionary

Guidance from a librarian who seeks to help him use the library and who focuses attention on those materials which relate to current issues of vital concern.

Efficient service

A library organized for his benefit with up-to-date methods and technology and an effective publicity program whose messages reach him.[3]

The system consultant in adult services has a responsibility to the member library to encourage the strengthening of adult services at a pace the local staff can accommodate. The adult service consultant working with the local library is a stimulator, an analyst of the local collection in terms of its capacity to be of value to existing or new adult services, and an advisor on the development of an outstanding adult services program.

The advisory function of the system adult services consultant involves direct counseling on services, the dissemination of information on new materials, and in-service training. The adult services specialist may assume all or some of the following responsibilities: (1) interpretation of the standards of adult services to librarians and trustees, (2) guidance for the member library in the strengthening of objectives, policies and programs, (3) assistance in building collections and using system resources to meet changing adult needs, (4) planning for in-service training to instill a commitment to the concept of adult services and skill in its implementation, (5) interpretation of legislation applicable to adult services, (6) liaison with other systems, state and national library groups, and adult education associations, and (7) planning pilot projects and demonstrations for the unserved and the partially served adults in the area.

Services to Older Citizens

Library service to older citizens has engaged the attention of the profession for many years and has led to many guidelines and recommendations for action at the local level, including:

1. Provision of large-print materials for general reading and reference from local and system collections
2. Publicizing of information about access to system resources

for materials of unusual and exacting personal post-retirement interests
3. Maintenance of informational files on community service activities, recreational opportunities, and organizations of interest to older citizens
4. Provision of access to library materials of value to social agencies serving the elderly
5. Planning for library-sponsored programs and the preparation of reading lists and displays to attract retired citizens
6. Selection of materials and delivery service to the homebound.

In some communities there is a barrier to the development of separate service to senior citizens. It is the very understandable attitude of the older citizen who resists institutional attempts to set him apart in an isolated class requiring special handling. A person does not automatically become a lesser member of society at the age of sixty-five. The nation needs the accumulated wisdom of its older citizens and their continued participation in community life. Libraries can help keep this national asset alive, responsive, and unresentful through planning services to senior citizens compatible with their personal and community interests. The physical problems of the aging can be recognized in libraries in simple, unobtrusive ways: by making books easily accessible on floor areas without steps, by stocking displays with books in large type, and by planning renovations and new buildings with the problems of the elderly and the handicapped in mind. However, a person's interests and tastes do not deteriorate with his body, and the programs for senior citizens often require depth and sophistication to match unusual intellectual pursuits and avocations that have become realities only through the increase of leisure time.

The library has an obligation to the older citizen of today. It has an equal obligation to the older citizen of the immediate future. Librarians must use all of their ingenuity to help that citizen look ahead and prepare for retirement. The library is not a social agency. Nevertheless, as an educational institution, it has the tools to do the job of helping people find those inner resources that will make the years of retirement more fruitful and satisfying. Libraries must work long in advance of retirement dates to help people develop meaningful outlets that will carry over as part of their successful adjustment to eventual retirement.

This obligation cuts across all age levels in the person-to-person and group relationships librarians can handle so successfully. It is fundamental to the profession's goal of reinforcing lifelong educational opportunities for all citizens.

Libraries also have an obligation to cooperate with agencies responsible for recreation, housing, and medical care for the aging population by providing the best of unbiased, factual information on their needs. Service to shut-ins is an adult service that can be handled cooperatively on the local level. There are retired men and women in every community who do an indispensable job of visiting the elderly, the infirm, and the hospitalized on behalf of churches and clubs, or just on their own. In many localities they also have taken on the assignment of delivering and picking up books for shut-ins. These volunteers and visiting nurses can be enlisted as emissaries of the public library to find out just what the shut-ins want to read. Doctors who are alerted to the availability of the service provide still another source for the cooperative information pool to help a local library staff select materials that will bring the greatest satisfaction to the immobilized individual.

Service to the Functional Illiterate

The library profession has assumed a major role in the national effort to end functional illiteracy. It has been engaged in testing appropriate material. It has initiated cooperative planning among agencies and voluntary groups concerned with community development, employment, education, and welfare. Some libraries have sponsored literacy classes or have provided instructional materials suitable for self-study. Still others have employed librarian-specialists to work on functional illiteracy projects involving individuals and groups. The small library, too, has been able to participate in this program in the following ways:

1. Providing access to interesting materials written at various reading levels
2. Supplying through the system films, slides, recordings, and other audiovisual materials for local use
3. Keeping informed and disseminating information to community leaders on regional, state, or national literacy programs of value to local efforts
4. Cooperating with all local groups working with the beginning adult reader and the functional illiterate

5. Providing space for adult classes conducted by schools or other qualified groups
6. Preparing and distributing reading lists of books of adult interest written in simple language
7. Orienting the beginning reader to the services of the library
8. Providing reading guidance in subject fields of interest to the adult beginning reader
9. Presenting library programs such as book talks, films, and discussions of local issues involving the adult beginning reader
10. Participating in system or professional association workshops designed for librarians involved with literacy programs
11. Correlating local literacy programs with library publicity
12. Consulting with the system specialists on planning for literacy programs.

Group Services

The small library has built-in resources for working with adult groups in the community. It has materials and access to additional materials through the system. It often is the community clearinghouse for local events and local program files. Some systems have assembled data on area speakers, with subject specialities, fees, and other background information provided by system members, as an informational service to everyone in the system and in neighboring systems. Others have given help to small libraries in conducting program planners' institutes in collaboration with area newspapers or adult education divisions in school districts. Some systems have prepared traveling exhibits on system services, to be displayed at meetings where a member library may have the opportunity to promote local and system services. Many systems provide packaged materials to support the library's work in counseling officers and program chairmen of local organizations. Work with community groups is a form of reader guidance in which the member library and the system are able to collaborate effectively.

The library-sponsored discussion group is one of the most rewarding of all adult services to groups. It has taken many forms in libraries throughout the United States and Canada. One of the best known is the Great Books discussion, which has been carried on by many libraries with the help of community leaders. The film is an effective device for the library-sponsored discussion program. Films offer the advantages of visual impact in documentation and group sharing of an on-the-spot experience. The minimum criteria for selection relate to content in terms of discussible issues, suitability for the background or age levels of the participants, the quality of the production, the length of the film in relation to discussion requirements, and its relationship to books and other library materials. The criteria are used in advance viewing—an indispensable step in film discussion programming. The establishment of preview centers and film collections at a system headquarters offers broad selection opportunities. System film workshops provide refresher or training courses in the art of introducing the film, methods of directing attention to features pertinent to discussion, suggestions for supplementary reading lists, and the techniques of follow-up discussion.

A grass-roots type of discussion group that has an appeal to librarians and citizens alike is one dealing with current affairs. This sort of group has the advantage of adaptability to the headlines of the day, to pressing local problems, or to an important international issue and is at the same time grounded in books. Many librarians enlist the help of citizens as co-leaders in this type of program. The core books for current affairs are the fundamental documents of the United States: the Declaration of Independence; the U.S. Constitution; the Bills of Rights; and the state constitution. Many men and women have never read these documents and find a new understanding of past history and history in the making through joint study and discussion. Current events are correlated with these documents and with books interpreting them. Any number of interesting and informative classifications of books can be tied in with current affairs. It should be pointed out that the discussion group should establish its own simple ground rules, such as a limitation on membership so that everyone can participate, an agreement that all participants must read the basic documents, and an understanding that all discussion be directed to the group as a whole.

The importance of the discussion group as promoted by the public library is that it usually attracts a cross-section of the population who ordinarily have no other common meeting ground. It has the benefit of offering viewpoints from varying backgrounds of faith, education, and life experiences. The friendly atmosphere of books and the interchange of facts and reasoned opinions takes these people out of the contemporary crowd culture, which seems to make some people opinionated and others inarticulate. The returns to the library from the discussion group are to be seen in increased use of library materials, in the natural spread of informed opinion, and in the effects of group interaction on the personal development and the reading habits of individuals —full compensation for the expenditure of time.

The most successful community forums sponsored or cosponsored by libraries are those relating to everyday practical problems and to library materials pertinent to those problems. Examples of library forums that have been presented throughout the country include: "Investments for Women," "What the Wise Widow Should Know," "How to Start an Investment Club," and "The Art of Rapid Reading." The leaders for such forums are lawyers, bankers, insurance men, teachers, and other specialists in the area who are pleased to cooperate with the library on a strictly noncommercial level in presenting knowledge of help to people. The film center as a system resource provides many subject ideas for the planning of community forums.

Service to Business

Library service to local business is not a new idea. It has been promoted by the small library in many ways, from channeling information about new materials through the local Chamber of Commerce office to simply calling the businessman down the street. The factor that has complicated this service for the small library is the widening diversity of businessmen's interests, which necessitates access to an increasing spread of informational data. The businessman has come to expect instant reports on the stock market and the latest source material on the economy. The problem for the small library in meeting these expectations is usually a budget that will not allow for the acquisition of all the business information services that would be useful.

The role of the cooperative system in strengthening service to business is: (1) to help the local library establish practical priorities in its selection of expensive informational tools and to provide a backstop in supplementary aids through its reference and interlibrary loan programs; (2) to help the local library promote public awareness of the availability of extra resources through the system; and (3) to initiate studies of trends in economic growth in the system area, through which it may anticipate the changing needs of the local library in serving the businessman.

System services designed to help the local library serve occupational needs are not limited to business interests. They support the local library's traditional services to labor groups, to farm organizations, and to any other dominant economic units in the community. Alertness to the needs of economic groupings within a system area is a responsibility of the adult services specialist at system headquarters.

Supportive System Services

The services developed by cooperative systems throughout the country are many and are constantly being changed as the needs of the members dictate. A service provided by one system does not necessarily have the same priority in another. The quality of local resources, the degree of sophistication among librarians, the size of the system area, the sufficiency of system funding, and the known needs of the area are dominant influences in the number and character of system services. The literature indicates that each step taken by any system substantiates the frequently expressed opinion that the public library does not know enough about its patrons or their changing needs.

As one observer, Eleanor Smith, has pointed out:

> Public librarians know segments of their communities quite well. They know children and students and they know the small group of adults who demand best sellers and other popular books and the very few who are dedicated and discriminating readers. But what do they know about all the people who never or almost never use the library? They know almost nothing about them. I believe it is important before any pattern of library development becomes set, to find out about these people and the needs they have which the library may be able to provide.[4]

Research into the needs of people, the elements that motivate an individual to use a library, the barriers that keep adults out of bookstores and libraries, the skills that must be developed among librarians to identify local needs is a challenge to the system of tomorrow. It is an area of common concern to publishers, with whom a system or group of systems may collaborate on definitive studies that may be advantageous to publishers, librarians, and the people they try to attract and to serve. Systems have not been able to wait for comprehensive studies of people and their needs. They have turned to their member libraries for direction. A newly established system may poll its members to identify priorities in services. It may re-poll its members at intervals to determine shifts in priority needs. A system evaluation study may indicate that some services may be dropped in the interest of more demanding services. A system may take advantage of the element of flexibility at any point in its program development. Basic to most cooperative public library systems are interlibrary loan, central reference, audiovisual, consultant and delivery services, and a systemwide reciprocal borrowing program.

Supporting Services for Access

A service that has been implemented by all types of systems to open up access is the interlibrary loan. Institutional loans have had a long but uneven history in libraries. They have always been considered an acceptable practice but were not pursued with any vigor or organization until the advent of the system. As Jean Connor says, "Interlibrary loan is not new. What is new is a service that is publicized regionally as a reader's right. It is not just a special courtesy."[5]

The principle behind the interlibrary loan program is to provide materials not available in the community library or to meet an emergency request for a title that cannot be recovered quickly on the local level. Interlibrary loan programs are not designed to substitute for local initiative in providing material in constant demand. A prime asset of the interlibrary loan service is that it not only opens up access to the breadth of a supplementary collection but also provides essential materials for unusual situations.

Different organizational patterns and operating policies characterize the interlibrary loan program from system to system. Some restrict the service to adult books only, with further limitations on fiction or types of fiction. Many have specific rulings on best sellers. Other systems have no restrictions on types of material and no reservations about age levels. Interlibrary loan centers frequently make use of photocopying to provide essential material from normally noncirculating collections. It is highly probable that as systems expand their own resources and undergo periodic evaluations of their services, arbitrary restrictions on circulating materials will be unnecessary.

The most critical point in the interlibrary loan program is the local level, where the first indication of need for material originates. This is the point at which perceptiveness is essential in judging when a patron's needs go beyond the scope of the local collection. It is the time to interpret to the patron the many advantages in the resources of the system network. It is primarily the point at which professional skills come into play in identifying titles or subject materials that may be borrowed from the system. The local staff makes the first contribution to public satisfaction with system service through their ability to communicate exact needs to the interlibrary loan center. The system has a responsibility to aid in the development of this kind of communications skill through training and informational sessions.

The local library is inclined to think of interlibrary loans as a free service. It is not free. It is a costly service involving special personnel, equipment, bibliographic resources, search and referral costs, delivery charges, and contracts for administration, supervision, and/or materials in the library or office performing the function on behalf of the system. It also can be expensive in terms of lost effort if the procedures of the local library and the interlibrary loan center are not coordinated. The time between a patron's request and his receipt of the material may be costly from the standpoint of the patron's deadlines. Actual costs of interlibrary loan services in different systems are not easily compared because of the variances in factors involved in arriving at reported costs. The literature indicates that most local libraries would agree that the service is worth whatever it takes of the system budget to make it effective.

Reciprocal Borrowing

Reciprocal borrowing or direct access, may be defined as an arrangement making it possible for a person registered at one library to borrow materials in person from any other library in the system upon presentation of a library card or other identification validated by the home library. Systemwide access borrowing provides the opportunity to examine and to borrow materials from a number of collections that may be comparable but richer in different ways. Reciprocal borrowing is personal access, as distinguished from institutional access which is handled through the mechanics of interlibrary loan.

A literature search made by a cooperative system committee in 1968 revealed that British librarians were the first to engage actively in reciprocal borrowing or "interavailability of library tickets," as it is called in England.[6] In the early 1930s, librarians in many English towns were accepting "tickets" issued by librarians in other towns. A few American librarians of that decade were publicly noting the desirability of working toward a universal plan for direct access. The literature search pointed out that only six articles on reciprocal borrowing appeared in the indexes from 1876 through 1956. Within the next decade, the number of articles began to pick up, with presentations for and against reciprocal borrowing. By the middle of the 1960s, the active participation of American librarians in programs of reciprocal borrowing became manifest, with published reports of successful trial periods and permanent inauguration of reciprocal borrowing in various systems.

Reciprocal borrowing is probably the most sensitive area of library cooperation. The term itself implies reciprocity. However, in most systems, loans made on systemwide borrowers' cards by member libraries cannot be considered to be in balance. In rural systems with widely scattered libraries, the problems are minimized. In thickly populated metropolitan systems with libraries in close proximity to each other, the problems are magnified by the easy flow of borrowers from one library to another. This very ease of intra-use in areas where residents shop in one community, work in a second, and reside in a third compels systems to develop direct access programs.

In both rural and metropolitan systems the libraries strongest in depth of collections and with the most skilled staffs are the magnets drawing the holders of the systemwide borrower's card. The principle of reimbursement to libraries providing services on behalf of the system applies here, and some method of compensation is usually a part of the system's reciprocal borrowing program. An example of one type of compensation plan is as follows: Records are kept of all loans made to reciprocal borrowers at each library. The total of all loans made to out-of-town patrons, less all transactions made by the local library's own patrons in all other participating libraries, gives a plus or minus figure. The plus transactions, less an arbitrary figure for cooperation, are subject to reimbursement at a per-item amount set by the system. Some systems also assume responsibility for materials lost in reciprocal borrowing transactions by reimbursing the lending libraries for the cost of the materials and their processing.

The approaches and the features of reciprocal borrowing programs differ from system to system because of the differences in conditions and requirements affecting member libraries. All systemwide borrowing programs, however, are based on one important principle: the maximum benefit to the user. It is doubtful that any system would initiate reciprocal borrowing as one of its first programs, but a systemwide borrowing program is an indispensable part of providing convenient access to system resources. There is general acknowledgement of a professional obligation to match system-funded programs with a corresponding local effort to break down arbitrary barriers for convenience in library service to more people.

The reciprocal borrowing, or direct access, program is the natural result of professional emphasis on the needs of people. This emphasis implies corresponding advantages to both the library and the patron in the establishment of a minimum code of procedures to be accepted and followed by all member libraries. Studies have shown that patron dissatisfaction centers largely on borrowing rules, which differ from library to library. The establishment of a uniform code of procedure on the surface seems to cancel out the principle of local autonomy. However, it is doubtful that the code, which deals primarily with the mechanics of loans, would touch on matters of major significance to the local library. A code of common procedures is, in actuality, a timesaver for the local library in its routine procedures and in interpreting the program to the public. The importance of a code of procedure is underscored by the standards, which state that "each library system should design lending and intra-agency loan practices which make for uniform, coordinated service over the whole area served."[7]

The uniform code usually covers items such as: rules for the validation of cards for resident and nonresident borrowers; agreements on the types of materials that may be loaned (such as all printed material loaned by a local library to its own patrons); loan limitations (such as for audiovisual equipment); the handling of fines and overdue notices; responsibility for payment for lost material; a definition of delinquency and provision for distribution of delinquency lists; arrangements for return of materials to the home library; and procedures for reporting circulation statistics.

System policies for a reciprocal borrowing program are easier to establish than are uniform practices among member libraries. A system policy may be viewed more objectively than a local practice reflecting the philosophy or the inclinations of an individual librarian. An example of a necessary policy, for which justifications are obvious, is that of a minimum fee for nonresidents who wish to use system services in addition to those provided by the local library. The minimum fee is an equalizer to prevent the patron from shopping from library to library to find the cheapest fee card permitting him to use the most expensive collection in the system. Ordinarily the system regards local practice such as renewals or nonrenewals as a local library decision. Differences in practice result in confusion for the reciprocal borrower. The confusion may be resolved by membership agreement on uniform practices in the interest of well organized service to all borrowers.

It must be recognized that there are some disabilities in the reciprocal borrowing program still to be resolved by the systems and their member libraries, with the help of the state libraries. A single example is the perennial student problem. The reciprocal borrowing program has opened the door to student and parental pilgrimages from member library to member library in search of materials frequently needed by all schools at the same time. This has raised the specter of heavy duplication in some areas. In others it has reinforced the effort to seek improved coordination with school libraries and officials. It also points to the need for statewide surveys that will lead to the establishment of effective policies and guidelines for cooperative practices to accommodate the needs of students of all ages.

Nevertheless, the reciprocal borrowing, or direct access, program has not resulted in problems which are insoluble. In fact, living up to its name, the Pioneer System—a multisystem cooperative—led the way to a broader base for direct access by introducing intrasystem reciprocal borrowing. This is a development that without question will be a pattern for wider access in the future.

Reference Services

System reference service is comparable to system collection building as a part of the system structure designed to give that extra support a local library must have in reaching excellence. The system reference service goes into action after the local library has expended its ingenuity on the resources it has available. The main function of the system reference service is to handle the in-depth reference work beyond the capabilities of the local collection. In many cases, it has proved also to be a stimulus to local librarians in making better use of their collections.

The common means of transmitting reference requests from the local library to the system reference center are the telephone, teletype, the U.S. mails, or the system delivery vans. The system reference center expedites the referrals through the provision of request forms, which include data such as the name, address and phone of the patron, the specific question or topic for a general subject search, the scope of material needed (whether it is introductory, intermediate, or advanced), required deadline dates, and information on the sources checked by the local library prior to the transmittal of the request. As may be seen from the sample reference request in appendix F, the form may include a section recording the action taken at the system level. The reports on the source or sources used in answering the request by the reference center may serve as documents in in-service training on both the local and system levels.

Cooperative system reference centers have been organized in various ways by the systems of the nation. The service may be handled from a headquarters or central library. It may be located by contract arrangements in a large metropolitan library, with the administering of the service by system staff. System reference services may be shared by more than one strong library in the system, with a division of responsibility based on specialization or on the geographic requirements or other needs within the system. An illustration of divided responsibility is found in those systems covering large areas dominated by agricultural interests in one section and business and industry in another.

The specific aims of a reference center may be general or specialized, depending on the resources of its member libraries. The aims reference centers have in common are: the creation and maintenance of strong informational and reference resources to meet the needs of their particular clientele; the expediting of referrals to other levels in the network; and the provision of continuous educational experiences for member libraries by precept, informational bulletins, and in-service training. System reference centers have a legitimate concern for the strengthening of basic reference collections in local libraries and for their most effective use by local staffs.

An essential part of system reference service is serials service, which provides copies of needed periodical articles (usually in microform with print-out equipment) for patron use at the local level. This is a popular service organized like that of interlibrary loans to tap resources at all levels of the network. One of the

problems in serials work at the system level is to define a reasonable request. Should the serials center, for example, honor requests for copies of every article on a particular subject listed
in an index? Does it have the right in terms of the goals of access
to ask for screening of requests at the local level? These are
questions that have to be answered in analysis of available manpower, equity in service to all member libraries, and the system's
own objectives. Some cooperative systems have found it expedient
to prepare in advance packages of articles on subjects forming
the bulk of repeated requests. The subject package preparation
involves knowledge of the content of each article and the application of criteria, as in the selection of all other library materials.

Audiovisual Services

As Lowell Martin has said, "It must be as possible to *hear* or
to *view* in the library as it is to open a book and read. . . ."[8] The
importance of audiovisual materials in the library is seldom de-
bated. Some medium-sized and small libraries have been able to
provide audiovisual materials in their collections. Others have
been slow to add even disc recordings because of budgetary and
staff limitations or an unwillingness to depart from the exclusive
provision of printed materials. If communications materials in
nonprinted form are important, they should be available to the
patrons of the smaller as well as the larger or more sophisticated
libraries.

The 16mm film, as one form of audiovisual resources, has distinct advantages over printed materials as a communications
medium. Reading is a one-to-one experience between reader and
author; a film showing provides the opportunity for a group experience when followed immediately by a discussion of reactions
of the viewers. Reality can be intensified for the viewer by the
film's treatment of time factors, such as showing the growth of a
plant or the movement of a hummingbird's wings. History comes
to life through reconstruction of events that convey visually the
mood and appearance of the past. Worlds that are invisible to
many, such as undersea or microscopic life, can become visible
to all through films.

Most nonreaders find the film an acceptable medium. The film
is an art form requiring different but no less demanding talents
than those involved in writing. The disadvantages of films as
contrasted with books are obvious. They do not offer quick

referral to an important point or description. Viewing a film requires equipment and a power source. Films are more expensive and more easily subject to damage. Because of changes in fashion, some films are more subject to becoming outdated than books. The film, therefore, is an expensive type of library material. To be continually useful, a public library film collection must cover a wide variety of subject matter. Consequently, a film collection is usually beyond the financial capabilities of the small and medium-sized autonomous library. Film services have become a recognized obligation on the part of many cooperative systems. (A system film evaluation form is to be found in appendix G.)

One direction a cooperative system may take in fulfilling the responsibility for audiovisual services is the establishment of a film center. This requires space for housing, previewing, and maintaining the collection and handling the mechanics of loans to member libraries. It requires the employment of experts in the identification of film needs of member libraries, in the selection of appropriate films, and in skills to work with local library personnel in previewing sessions, film workshops, and procedures for quality service.

To keep the collection in excellent physical condition requires expensive inspecting, cleaning, and repairing equipment as well as qualified equipment operators. For these reasons, the system may consider the centralized housing of films to be advantageous. One disadvantage of centralized collections is the inability to make spot bookings, necessitating advance planning by the user, particularly in requesting topical or seasonal films. Scheduling procedures must recognize the time needed to inspect films after use and to deliver them to the local library.

Purchase of 8mm films in reel form may be recommended for member libraries; the films are inexpensive, and providing them locally makes them easily accessible. The cooperative system should consider the purchase of the more expensive 8mm sound films in cartridge form for rotating collections for member use. Decisions will need to be made as to whether the collection of cartridge films will be optical or magnetic sound.

The audiovisual services of some cooperative systems include phonograph and tape recordings as useful media for supplying language instruction, oral history, and literature as well as popular, classical, and folk music. The tape cassette is growing in popularity, as is the tape cartridge for home and portable players and automobile tape decks. All types of recordings should be considered as a part of the library's locally owned services.

Framed art prints, in actual size and in reduced size for children, and reproductions of works of sculpture are materials that add a new dimension to both library and system collections. Sets of 2″ x 2″ slide pictures have a place in public library audiovisual collections. A camera may be added to the local library's equipment to take pictures of community buildings, historical sites, and events that will be of historic value in future years. In addition, the member library may acquire slide sets of antiques, paintings, or garden and wild flowers through purchase or with the assistance of a local amateur camera club. Slide projectors are more easily operated than movie projectors, and maintenance of slides requires no particular skill.

The leadership of the cooperative system in the audiovisual field is needed to keep abreast of the latest technology, to measure a new media's adaptability to library use, and to determine the most efficient way to provide all library patrons with a variety of audiovisual experiences. In some cases it may be feasible to share the cost of audiovisual materials among the system and the member libraries, with the system providing the incentive of a nucleus collection for each member library willing to build on the starter collection from its own funds.

Automation

Each library in a cooperative system has autonomy of decision on methods and equipment used in carrying out the services of the library. As a consequence, various types of charging methods may exist within a single system. Some of these methods are carryovers from the nineteenth century. Even the most recent automatic devices have not moved circulation departments totally into the age of technology. However, some systems have been able to help their member libraries take a first step toward greater efficiency in circulation by providing automatic charging machines. Others have engaged in studies of advanced charging devices that may be recommended to their members for economy in local operation, minimal delays for patrons, elimination of the time-consuming carding process, and adaptability to the requirements of reciprocal borrowing, interlibrary loans, and delivery services.

If library systems aim to provide services beyond the capacity of each member library to provide for itself, then electronic data processing should be considered seriously as a system responsibility. Traditional methods of acquisition, technical processing, card catalog maintenance, and circulation control are expensive, cumbersome, and out of date. Library systems add an additional complication—the need to locate shared but widely scattered materials. A union card catalog of members' holdings becomes formidably expensive when the size of the files to be maintained is projected into the future. A computerized systemization of all bibliographic functions, from purchasing and cataloging through location of materials, holds great promise for library systems. The whole spectrum of traditional library procedures eventually will undergo a transition since it is doubtful that automation will be adapted to existing methods.

In the distant future magnetic tape editions of books may be developed and computers used for storing entire "books." But present equipment is too primitive. The direction for the immediate future lies in a centralized bibliographic bank of resources of member libraries providing the means of remote control, query, and alteration from each member library. This use of the computer implies the survival of the book as still the handiest and most economical device for information storage.

Only by a combination of many functions does computer use become economically feasible. Some functions will be more practical to carry out by computer than others, but the automation of these reduces the cost of the less appropriate ones, which become byproducts of the computerized system. Automated centralized technical processing has been described as economically feasible if the volume of work is large enough. With every local library ordering all its materials through the center and receiving them fully processed, standardization of bibliographic records becomes a necessity. An automated processing facility lends itself naturally and with relatively little additional cost to the creation of a bibliographic bank. Once the bank is a reality, catalogs of the cooperative system's collection become a possibility. Remote connections of the computer to each library would permit local query of the bank for location of desired materials. With remote connections circulation control may prove feasible, with the computer automatically fed charges and discharges of materials at the local library. Centralized and automated overdue procedures then become possible.

Such an automated system is accomplished in phases, one phase leading automatically to the next. However, the equipment will be correctly designed only if each phase has been planned in the beginning and its place in the overall pattern has been predetermined. The total system concept must be designed before the first phase is implemented. A computerized system is neither easily designed nor inexpensive to maintain. Considerable research and planning are required for a workable program. Adaptation and standardization of traditional library procedures are necessary. Even then, as some libraries have discovered, successful automation is not guaranteed. The library system is responsible for planning, coordinating, and implementing automated services for its members. The member libraries are responsible for agreement on standardized procedures and policies.

Communication as a Service

Communication, as was pointed out in other chapters, is the most fragile element in the system-member library relationship. There seems to be a system law: the greater the volume of communiques, memos, and news releases, the lesser the chance they will be read. This, however, is a risk that the system headquarters must take if the vital flow of information and feedback is to be sustained. The system is just another agency if it operates in a noncommunicative vacuum. The member libraries cannot move in a noncommunicative environment. Written communication is supplemented by verbal communication at system meetings. At this point the system has to reconcile the impatience of those who read communiques with the needs of those who are new to the system, who have not read the system messages, or who do not understand.

A useful form of communication originating in a system office is a monthly or quarterly newsletter. This may seem unnecessary to some member librarians, particularly to those who have access to many professional publications. However, there are member libraries where such material is limited. As a consequence, a system newsletter is of value to trustees and staff who do not have ready access to many publications, who do not attend system board meetings, or are not continuously involved in planning or decision-making functions related to system development. A typical newsletter may include system progress reports, statistics on the use of system services, system board action, news of significant happenings within the system membership, summaries of workshops, research findings, and references to articles and books available on loan from the system's professional collection.

A system's communications program may also include the preparation, constant revision, and distribution of membership directories covering essential information on librarians and on trustee representatives to the system. It also includes the preparation and distribution of manuals on each of the system services. These manuals emphasize the objectives of the service and outline those minimum rules and regulations that must be imposed to guarantee fair usage by all participants. An audiovisual manual, for example, may cover the purpose of the service, eligibility for use, showing restrictions, procedures for telephone or mail bookings, rules on booking fees, responsibility for film damage, and suggestions for handling films at the local library.

To be effective, system communication must involve more than the system staff. The experienced, the well-trained, and the committed have the right and the obligation to take a professional position of planned participation in system communications. The typical system staff is not large. Their field visits may be restricted at times by special assignments. The system staff needs help in communication with the membership at large, just as the staff of a small library needs the help of trustees, a Friends organization, and a responsive press to communicate with the local public.

There are various ways to involve membership in a system communications program. One is to follow up a system staff visit to a new librarian at a member library by visits from experienced system members, who will be able to sense those areas in which system help or system staff interpretation is needed. Another plan is for the members of the executive committee of the librarian advisory councils to make visits to all member libraries during their term of office. The purpose of these visits is to obtain informal evaluations of the effectiveness of the system's program from the viewpoint of practicing librarians who are also in an authorized position to report back to the committee and the system staff. Many systems involve trustee representatives in communications programs for their fellow trustees, either on a system-wide or area basis. This involvement ranges from public meetings to attendance at the board meetings of neighboring libraries.

One very valuable form of system communication is an inter-system directors' program. The system directors go "on circuit" for this type of communication to explain the distinctive features of their plans of service, to interpret their goals, and to give system members in different areas a fresh view of system plans and developments. Another form is an annual program meeting arranged by the system to accommodate, as well as possible, the work schedules of members of the staff, board members, city officials, and the interested public. This type of program may be system-oriented, or it may present an outstanding speaker and a subject of major concern to trustees and librarians. A program meeting has the double function of communication and education.

One area of communications deserves more than casual study by system planners—direct communication between a library patron and a system specialist. The roadblocks to system involvement in this kind of communication are many. The objectives of a system place on the member library the initial responsibility to take full advantage of existing resources. A system is not interested in bypassing the local library. Moreover, the special service offices at system headquarters, such as reference or interlibrary loan, would not be able to complete their normal work loads if unlimited patron communications were added. For direct public communications these offices would have to employ highly skilled inquiry receptionists. Experience has shown, for example, with the highly specialized reader guidance services of the 1920s and 1930s, that this type of development is costly and not as effective as training an entire staff to serve in the same capacity. On the other hand, there are occasions when a patron knows what he wants but does not know how to ask for it. The local librarian may not have the background even to try to interpret what he says. This is the type of situation that cries out for a specialist. It is a system responsibility to work out guidelines for patron interviews on the local level and for handling exceptional patron interviews at the headquarters level.

Another vitally important form of system communications is a public relations program. Many systems employ talented people who can produce exciting publicity ideas, model displays, and topical posters for delivery to member libraries. An even greater essential is public relations as a unified, continuous program of communication with the public at large on the subject of the system, what it is, where it is, and what it can do for men, women, and children wherever they are. Public relations—systemwide—is a day-after-day production on a professional level that sells the system as an advantage to the individual citizen. It should be factual but attractive. It should never promise more than the local library and the system can deliver. It should, however, challenge any sluggish local library staff to live up to their responsibility in making system services meaningful to their community. Public relations for a system is not a hunt for free advertising or "selling hot air before it cools off."[9] It is a job for experts who can see the total program and translate it into communications that will make a lasting impression on the public. Consequently, it is wise to consider placing all public relations responsibilities in the hands of one individual or firm professionally engaged in public relations functions. Regardless of the size of the firm, the public relations planning and implementing almost invariably rest with one individual in that firm. Therefore, the system should carefully evaluate the individual whom it trusts to perform public relations functions and related advisory services to the member libraries.

Evaluation as a Service

Evaluation of a tax-supported institution is both proper and helpful. It is surprising that citizen insistence on periodic evaluations of all publicly supported institutions has been so long in coming. There are signs that such evaluations will be required in the future. Many large and small libraries have contracted over the years for some type of evaluation. Surveys by ALA-recommended surveyors or library school faculties were extremely popular in the pre-World War II period. Many gathered dust. Others, such as the succeeding comprehensive studies of the Chicago Public Library, made a permanent contribution to library literature.

Evaluation services covering the entire administrative operation of a library, or any of its parts—the book collection, the management functions, or the individual services—are now available through the system. Evaluations by a system staff have advantages over evaluations made by surveyors from outside the area. The system plan is based on systemwide studies. The system staff knows the state law as it applies to varying governmental and taxing units. They know the problems of their member libraries. They have an equal stake with the library to be evaluated in a sound analysis and practical recommendations. It is not necessary for the system staff to establish reputations as surveyors. Evaluation is part of their business, but they make it their business only at the request of a librarian or the board of trustees of a member library.

Techniques for evaluation differ from system to system. In a book collection evaluation, an experienced system specialist may survey the collection by Dewey section and suggest to the local staff where the needs for weeding, updating, and strengthening are apparent. In personnel evaluations, the system staff may make recommendations, following a review of personnel policies, job descriptions, and organization charts supplemented by interviews. In an administrative services evaluation, a system specialist may actually work in the library for a number of weeks to study conditions preparatory to an evaluative report to the library board.

From these evaluations a library may expect judgments based on public library standards, recommendations based on sound library management practice, and counseling in redirection. The evaluation will be developed as a learning experience and not as a criticism. A major benefit in system evaluation is that a system can afford, and is interested in, a follow-up to help in the implementation of any recommendation. This is a feature that usually does not prevail in evaluations by outside consultants.

The system itself is not exempt from the need for periodic evaluation. Although the alert state library will make periodic evaluations, self-evaluation of the system by all involved is a profitable exercise for all who participate. Evaluation sheets may be provided to those attending system workshops and training sessions. Questionnaires may be mailed periodically to member libraries asking for opinion ratings on various services. A series of evaluation workshops every three or four years provide an opportunity to review system services and procedures and to chart new directions. Such workshops include local library boards, administrators, and staffs as well as system headquarters personnel. Possible new services, the elimination or upgrading of current services, and the streamlining of procedures are major agenda items for analysis and discussion. The candid exchange of opinions in membership sessions, where all who are present are given the opportunity and encouragement to express themselves, is an important factor in keeping the cooperative library system a vital and viable service agency.

Types of System Services

The major services developed by cooperative systems in their relatively short history are: access services (interlibrary loan, reciprocal borrowing, reference and serials), centralized purchasing and cataloging, administrative and consultative service, in-service training, and public relations. There are many variations on these major services. In addition, there are secondary services (such as delivery service) that support the major services, and special services that have been devised to meet the needs of a particular area. The wide range of services developed in various parts of the country may be seen from the following selective list.

TYPES OF SYSTEM SERVICES

1. Access services
   a. Audiovisual centers
   b. Book catalogs
   c. Book pool collections
   d. Book selection examination centers
   e. Bookmobile service
   f. Central headquarters library
   g. Central storage of little-used materials
   h. Film catalogs
   i. Interlibrary loans
   j. Location tools and indexes
   k. Periodicals copying service
   l. Professional collections
   m. Reciprocal borrowing
   n. Reference service
   o. Rotating collections: books, records, framed prints
   p. Selection tools
   q. Specialization in member libraries
   r. Subject package collections
   s. Teletype for referrals to networks
   t. Union catalogs: books and periodicals
2. Administrative services
   a. Advisory and/or referral services on budget planning, referendums, building planning, legal questions, insurance, personnel problems, security devices, local administrative organization, and expansion of taxing units
   b. Circulation controls

    c. Collection and distribution of policy statements and other administrative aids to members
    d. Contractual arrangements for short-term executive assistance
    e. Fact-finding on economic, cultural, and social trends for the system at large
    f. Gathering and interpretation of statistics
    g. Information on prevailing salary schedules, implementation of standards, and/or current library practices
    h. Orientation of new administrators into the system
    i. Payroll processing
    j. Recruiting and placement assistance

3. Central processing
    a. Ordering
    b. Cataloging
    c. Processing
    d. Binding
    e. Provision of cards for union catalogs

4. Central purchasing
    a. Audiovisual and other equipment for convenience in membership purchase
    b. Centralized ordering of magazines
    c. Equipment for placement in member libraries
    d. Supplies

5. Communications
    a. Brochures for system services for public distribution
    b. Informational releases to member libraries
    c. Intersystem informational program meetings
    d. Legislative information networks
    e. Membership meetings
    f. Newspaper, radio, and TV releases
    g. System newsletters
    h. System reports on use of system services
    i. Traveling exhibits of system services

6. Consultative services
    a. Audiovisual specialists
    b. Consultants on adult services
    c. Consultants on collection building
    d. Consultants on library building planning
    e. Consultants on library administration
    f. Consultants on work with children
    g. Consultants on work with young adults
    h. Information specialists
    i. Public relations consultants

    j. Referral services on library law, library construction, protection of library facilities, and insurance

7. Delivery services
    a. Bookmobile service
    b. Delivery by station wagons or vans
    c. Direct mail service
    d. Transportation pools for meetings

8. In-service training
    a. Audiovisual previews and training sessions
    b. Book selection discussion meetings
    c. Refresher courses for professionals
    d. Special sessions for clerical, middle management, and professional staff and for trustees
    e. Training and informational sessions on system services

9. Publicity
    a. Artwork for system distribution: posters, signs, bookmarks
    b. Central printing of library publicity materials
    c. Exhibits
    d. Publicity releases: newspapers, radio, TV
    e. System brochures

10. Reference services
    a. Backstop for local reference work
    b. Central serials and copying service

11. Research

12. Special projects and demonstrations.

System Services and the State Library

The standards for library functions at the state level emphasize the need for vigorous leadership on the part of the state library to maintain a legal and professional climate in which system services may achieve their objectives. High-qualified performance and enthusiasm at the state level have visible influences on attitudes at both the system and the local levels toward the development of services.

A fundamental responsibility of the state library is library law. It has the responsibility for a legal plan of system service with sound state financial support. The legal structure must include safeguards for preserving maximum financial strength at the local level. A system plan, for example, is weakened by loopholes that give a local library board the impression that it can reduce local financing because the library is receiving superior system services. The state library also has the responsibility to take the initiative in the clarification of ambiguities in the law, which lead to membership misunderstandings about local library acceptance or rejection of system services. It has a further obligation to incorporate library standards into the law and into the state plan.

The state library has a responsibility to provide a channel for the continuous revision and upgrading of the state plan in order that systems may be challenged to avoid institutional ruts or rigid patterns of service. It has an opportunity as a partner of the federal government to select and provide grants for experimental system projects to test new ways of improving services.

The state library is in a position to establish guidelines for system services to unserved areas. It has concern, with the systems, for a statewide public relations program that will interpret the advantages of a network of libraries to the people of the state. The state library should encourage systems to serve as examples to the member libraries in office administration, in preparing job classifications, in salary ranges and employee benefits, and in conducting stimulating board meetings.

An important activity for the state library is sponsorship of research to close the gaps in professional knowledge. This may range from studies of the total library needs of the state to examination of the impact of system services on the people of the state. The state library has a joint responsibility with the systems to analyze the costs of current services and to determine the values of technological developments in speeding up services.

Perhaps the most important state library responsibility related to system services is the periodic evaluation of those services. The purpose of system evaluation is not to compare one system with another but to help each system achieve its own potential.

The channeling of system services through the local library has lessened or eliminated direct patron access to state libraries. This emphasis on the local library as the center of action and access is viewed by many as the element that will revitalize the community library. It has been viewed by others as "a decline in access and quality service."[10] Proponents of multiple outlets for access and distribution of materials believe that the public should be given options in direct access.

There are those who believe that system services will reach a point of excellence when systems mature and fulfill all that is expected of them. There are others who feel that the key to excellence is the quality of response from the member librarian. History will probably record the fact that it took the combined efforts of all of the systems, their member libraries, and the state library to fulfill a dream of superior service to all of the people.

7 Continuing Education for Librarianship

Continuing education is one of the elements that distinguishes a profession from a skilled occupation. The library profession has had a long history of interest in continuing education, reflecting a widespread understanding that "the future is too important to be left to tomorrow."[1] Continuing education for librarianship may be defined as planned career development. It takes many forms. It may be on-the-job training. It may involve sophisticated techniques, the use of varying communications media, and the expertise of outstanding specialists from many fields of knowledge. It is more, however, than a structured educational plan. It is a process that must search for, and respond to, the motivations and values that sustain the enthusiasm of the participant. It requires a conviction that the profession must provide channels for growth among trustees or other officials who give direction to the development of library services and among the staff who carry out those services.

There are three possible levels of continuing education in a cooperative system. All are essential and valid. The first is the in-service training program at the local level. The second is an in-depth training and/or refresher type of educational opportunity at the system level. The third is a research-based "new knowledge" educational program at the state level. Each level makes a unique contribution to continuing education in terms of its own objectives, its own resources, and its special competencies. The goal all levels have in common is the creation of an environment in which each individual associated with a library may gain new perceptions for problem-solving and for public service.

The general principles for programs in continuing library education that are applicable at all three levels include the following:

1. The goals must be practical but mind-stretching. The planners must know what they want to accomplish within the framework of the challenge of the subject field and the limitations of time schedules.
2. The needs of participants must be clearly identified and must take precedence over the assumptions, motives, or interests of the librarian at the local level or the joint planners at the system or state levels.
3. The methods of presentation must be appropriate for the purpose and content of each unit of the program and suitable for the particular capabilities of the participants.
4. The program must involve the participants through planning, discussion, reacting, and evaluating.
5. The program must use the most effective media to accomplish its purposes. The planners must be willing to experiment with innovative techniques that may be suitable for subject presentation.
6. Resource people and education specialists should be chosen for their potential contribution rather than their reputation.
7. The program must allow for a follow-up, such as personal counseling, group demonstrations, or additional educational courses.
8. The program should be cumulative in building a body of knowledge and experience.
9. The program should be planned for periodic evaluation for the purpose of improving future programming.
10. The program must include provisions to bring newcomers up-to-date through consultative services, repeat programs, or access to taped program reproductions.

The factors influencing a productive training program include:

1. The objectives
   a. Single-purpose programs
   b. Cumulative training programs
2. Relationship of the training program to the local, the system, or the state plan of service
3. Characteristics of the participants
   a. Background in education and training
   b. Extent of prior exposure to in-service training opportunities
   c. On-the-job experience backgrounds

    d. Length of tenure in present position
4. Number of participants to be accommodated
5. Levels of complexity in program content: elementary, pre-professional, or post-professional
6. Availability of outstanding in-service training leaders and/or instructors
7. Rate of technological and societal change
8. Budget allocations.

Continuing Education at the Local Level

Libraries were established for the benefit of society, rather than for the benefit of the people who direct or staff them. Nevertheless, it is axiomatic that the provision of opportunities for professional growth advances the objectives of the library. Sound, carefully planned training programs on the local level are concomitant with effective management.

In a sense, when libraries employ an individual they lease a service. The basic charge is, of course, the salary and its annual increments. Most services, however, involve some additional costs. An air-conditioning service contract, which represents a preventive maintenance cost, does not include the cost of replacement of a burned-out motor. The same principle applies to personnel. The investment in the "preventive maintenance" of continuing education will postpone the "additional maintenance cost" of turnover due to "burned-out" personnel. As a consequence, an essential cost, and one infrequently listed as a budget item, is in-service training. As a general rule, employees are selected for their potential. It is the library's responsibility to make the added investment needed to provide continuing education to develop that potential.

As was noted earlier, there is a current trend in library administration toward staff involvement in the examination and improvement of library policies, programs, and methods. A staff with this responsibility must have exposure to many educational opportunities and experiences. In short, a participating staff must be trained differently than a staff limited to executing the directives of a board or the decisions of an administrator.

Another professional trend is the intensified examination of the meaning of quality in library collections and library services.

This trend frequently is identified by concern and the random checking of standard lists at the local level. It indicates an educational opportunity for the system to develop programs to integrate library objectives and standards with expertise in the use of library materials. In-service training at the local level is a means of preparing a staff with understanding, background, and techniques needed for the fulfillment of the library objectives. Library personnel must be literate, not just in the use of materials, but in understanding the ever-changing human condition.

The basic type of in-service training at the local level is on-the-job training, which consists of instruction in the routines and methods employed by the local library correlated with an interpretation of the library's objectives and its service policies. However, a local in-service training program must consist of more than instruction and supervision of performance. It must be based on a careful appraisal of what the librarian and the staff need to know to carry out their individual and collective responsibilities. It must offer a challenge to the staff. It must also give the staff an appreciation of the interdependence that exists within all libraries and between libraries.

Community libraries make use of many in-service training combinations. Some place major emphasis on departmental training as developed by the coordinators of service or subject departments. Others schedule frequent meetings for the entire staff. These may be informational and interpretative from the standpoint of local library developments. They may focus on community developments by featuring speakers from public service agencies. Some libraries establish planning committees, made up of new and experienced staff members, to study existing service patterns in the light of changing community needs. The findings and recommendations of such committees are shared with the staff, through the in-service training channels, as an educational experience. Other libraries use the in-service training program to explore the feasibility of innovative ideas and to test methods for bringing people and materials together. As Marie Davis has said:

> With the increasing emphasis of library education on the "why" of librarianship rather than the "how," and the pressures of the knowledge and population explosions reflected in library use, it becomes more and more necessary to give professional staff members special direction in developing skills to bring books and

readers together and to reach out to non-users who include those who cannot read easily as well as those who can but do not.[2]

This training may be a system responsibility in some areas. In some libraries it may follow the basic in-service training, which includes:

1. Orienting new personnel to provide background needed for understanding the community, the overall objectives of the library, and the specific goals of their positions
2. Training or retraining in skills for job operations, such as circulation procedures or the use of tools for verification of bibliographic data for interlibrary loans
3. Training in ways to use the total collection in the local library and the supplementary collection at the system to meet reference, informational, and general needs
4. Continuing exposure to problem analysis to increase capacity for employee judgment in job performance
5. Providing an environment conducive to the defense of intellectual freedom.

A superior local in-service training program looks for potential strength in individuals and builds on that strength. It requires insight into the ways in which a continuing education program may help a particular person. In a very small library such needs may be identified by close association. In larger libraries they may be noted in periodic performance appraisals. The purpose of a staff appraisal is to ascertain ways in which performance may be improved through direct guidance or additional education. An appraisal is of major value in determining the type of in-service training that will foster growth in capabilities.

Continuing Education at the System Level

The acceleration in library education activities that has accompanied the spread of systems has been due to the requests of librarians and trustees for educational opportunities, the evidence of need as observed by system consultants, and the deepening sensitivity of system personnel to the importance of quality and high level content to attract and hold the interest of their co-workers at the local level. Continuing education programs on the system level derive their vitality from helping member librarians and trustees gain new knowledge or insights in fields with direct bearing on their individual responsibilities and interests. The system is able to provide specialized educational experiences of a depth not usually possible at the local level. However, continuing education at the system level is not mandatory for the member libraries. Consequently, the system is challenged to plan and to execute, with the advice of the membership, educational and training opportunities of such quality that they will come to be viewed by the membership as essential.

Incentive for Participation

The incentive for participation in continuing education at the system level begins in the local library. The administrator and the trustees of a member library must have the vision to see the cumulative values of an educational program in relation to the advancement of their own purposes. They must recognize that perfecting an educational program to meet the precise needs of all member libraries takes time. It may require some years of experimentation with formats and program ideas. It certainly requires the help of every member library through active participation and constructive evaluation. The incentives for staff participation in continuing education must be supported by the librarian and the trustees. The staff must be convinced that their administrator and the board have an appreciation of the impact learning experiences may have on their analytical and reflective attitudes toward policies and the local service program. They must be assured that the board recognizes that growth in staff knowledge is as important as growth in collections.

The trustees' appreciation of staff involvement in system training may be expressed in several ways. It may be visible through a provision on the board agenda for the librarian and/or members of the staff to report on training programs directly to the board as a whole. It may become evident in a board policy allowing added compensation for cumulative educational experiences. The system also may arrange for incentives, which may take the form of scholarships for special training. A system may award scholarships on a merit formula for attendance at a non-system educational institute, such as those conducted by graduate library schools.

The basic goal of a system's educational program is the same as the goal of every other system service: to help the member library help itself. There may be some corollary goals, depending on the nature of the system. They may include: the continuing interpretation of emerging viewpoints of library responsibilities; the rekindling of a fire of enthusiasm in tired administrators and bored trustees; the development of new styles of dialogue between member librarians; or the alleviation of the blight of dullness in library programming. The outstanding potential is the renewal of vision through the effect of a far-reaching overall program of continuing education.

The general goals of continuing library education at the system level may be:

1. To assist librarians and trustees in determining the institutional role of the library and the functions of librarians in a changing society
2. To help develop capacity among member libraries for current and emerging leadership roles in the community and in the profession
3. To aid librarians and trustees in keeping up with new knowledge, professional trends, and improved techniques
4. To provide learning opportunities for all ranks of personnel
5. To inform and to share with professional librarians the essentials in new developments in library school curricula
6. To provide library personnel with appropriate sociological awareness and education in a new body of skills for reaching the unserved
7. To assist librarians and trustees in developing executive skills related to policy-making, planning, and fiscal responsibilities
8. To provide learning situations for training in specific skills
9. To provide colloquies on issues involving differing opinions
10. To correlate training programs with continuing research into the needs for continuing education: the organizational structure, types of programs to be offered, levels of presentation
11. To evaluate the effect of continuing education in attitudes, performance, and achievement of objectives.

Involvement of member libraries in planning specific programs is a common practice among systems. One method is the distribution of a questionnaire, which gives member libraries an opportunity to rate subject fields in order of priorities. The establishment of priorities is usually difficult because it means making choices among attractive alternatives. A plan of priorities, however, seems essential to provide those programs in the order the membership indicates will be of the greatest value.

Some systems have established rotating planning committees, representing the membership, to work with the system staff in developing programs within the framework of membership priorities. The rotating principle limits terms on such a committee, spreads responsibility, and brings in new viewpoints. Such planning teams attempt to identify those aspects of a study topic that will meet the interests of actual and potential participants, and to determine the best means to ensure membership interaction in an educational situation. This group is responsible for judgments related to very practical questions: Is the proposed plan compatible with the needs of the member libraries? Is the program one that the system is uniquely equipped to handle? Will the program result in the strengthening of each member library? Experience, reflection, the results of studies, and new information must be included in continuing educational experiences.

The system not only assumes the responsibility for providing in-service training opportunities, it also takes the responsibility, with membership or program committee help, for finding teaching talent. The conventional method of finding continuing education instructors is to employ the services of those who have outstanding reputations in some particular field or to enlist the help of older, more experienced librarians or trustees who are known to be particularly effective in working with groups. It has been suggested in recent years that greater recognition be given to the teaching capabilities of persons at both ends of the age spectrum. Systems should also recognize that the reservoir of potential educators in their areas may be augmented through the mobility of librarians and that systems may exchange information on talent as it moves from one section of the country to another.

A system remote from educational or library centers may find itself in the position of having to provide the guidelines and the training ground for area leaders with little experience but high potential. Some systems have drafted help from library schools in the region. Others have borrowed skilled leaders from other systems. The use of skilled librarians and trustees as instructors and leaders in continuing education has a valuable byproduct in the recognition of their ability and in the possibility of their continued advice and counsel as supplementary aides to the system consultant staff.

The system consultants and the program planning committee have a difficult but challenging assignment. It is difficult because of the dissimilarities in background, attitudes, and receptivity among the trustees and librarians, who are no longer accustomed to the student role but are active practitioners. It is challenging, however, because it requires ingenuity to discover, not the lowest common denominator, but what constitutes the "take-home quotient" that makes a participant feel that continuing education can make a difference. Systems can achieve success in training by giving the training program the same careful attention that other services receive and by assigning the task to system consultants who have the ability to bring life to the program.

One of the essentials for sustaining a productive continuing education program is a knowledge of the levels of experience or training of the participants. Who wants what, when, and why? What are the differences and the similarities in the training and job experience backgrounds of participants? There are critics of system planning who feel that this is an unnecessary step since it is obvious to any knowledgeable observer. However, as Whitehead pointed out, "It requires a very unusual mind to undertake the analysis of the obvious."[3] As a consequence, the system may need to take a systemwide personnel inventory to determine the best grouping of participants for maximum benefits.

Continuing education at the system level is considered by some system directors to be a part of the consultative function of the system. It is only one phase of system responsibilities. It is intermeshed tightly with other programs in the plan of service. There is a strong possibility that a single system may not be able to cover in a reasonable time all the subject fields that would be of value to the membership. This suggests that a group of systems might consider a plan of long-range specialization. One system, for example, might take complete responsibility for high-grade programs for trustees. A neighboring system might take over the refresher course for administrators. Still another system might assume the responsibility for training middle management or clerks. The training personnel from all systems cooperating in a specialization plan would be interchangeable and would be available to individual systems as needs arose. A specialization plan would make use of the basic system concept of building on existing strengths.

Another form of specialization is to be seen in subject field concentrations. A system, with the concurrence of its membership, may elect to focus its entire attention on a single subject during a one-year period. An example of a subject area is communication as a tool in serving the community. Various aspects of this subject might be presented in different forms to all training groups: trustees, clerks, middle management, subject coordinators, and administrators. The approach to this single subject might be interdisciplinary, with different aspects being presented by different outside experts such as an anthropologist, a linguist, a social psychologist, a newspaper editor, and a public relations expert. This type of program planning has the advantage of providing a unified learning experience for trustees, administrators, and staff. It enhances the possibility of integrated application of what is learned to the local situation. The participant in such a cumulative learning experience becomes not only an independent learner but also an interdependent learner who may more successfully apply the learning experience through group interaction at the local level.

Program Formats

The cooperative system has an opportunity in its continuing education activities to experiment with different program formats and program materials. For example, the system may depart from the standard teaching format to try out simulation devices from role playing to scenario presentations. It may use films, tapes, charts, and graphs. It may use video-tape recorders and computer-assisted instruction aids such as the electronic blackboard. It may tie in with closed circuit facilities of universities.

The system also makes use of traditional formats, the most familiar of which is the lecture used in the presentation of a single subject or a series of related subjects. The lecture accommodates itself to single-purpose meetings, such as the system's annual meeting, or to those occasions when the purpose of a lecture series is to inform or to provide an overview of a particular subject in the shortest period of time. The lecture may be followed by a commentary by a second individual, known as a reactor. This plan is effective in program situations in which the reactor has an opportunity to see an advance copy of the lecture. The lecture type of program can involve the audience by planning for sufficient time for a question or discussion period.

The demonstration-lecture program focuses primarily on the skilled performance of an activity before an audience. It combines the features of a lecture with the elements of a demonstration. Its purpose is to demonstrate an analysis of a process and a pattern for such a process. An example is a demonstration on budget-making which may utilize blackboards, graphs, slide projections, and paper aids together with a verbal interpretation of the principles, the terms, and the elements that go into a budget.

The panel is another familiar program format. It consists of presentations on a single subject by several people. The advantage of the panel program is the opportunity it provides to stimulate reactions through presentations of aspects or differing viewpoints on the same topic. Its value to a system is that it may involve several member librarians or more than one system staff member. Because of its informality, the panel generally lends itself to spontaneous audience participation.

The "in-basket" format, or case-study conference, has an appeal to the system membership because it gives everyone an opportunity to participate in discussion. In this type of program a live problem of common interest is selected for analysis and discussion. The participants are divided into groups, each with a discussion leader, a resource person, and a reporter. The main points from the discussions of each group are presented to the reassembled audience at the close of the discussion periods. The "in-basket" format takes advantage of the average librarian's desire to talk about his problems with his peers. It provides an opportunity for an interchange of ideas and experiences. It also points to areas in which concentrated continuing education is needed and to subjects of sufficient interest to large groups for continued attention.

The practice laboratory is an educational format used successfully by system consultants. It frequently takes the educational experience into an actual working setting. A consultant may select a member library in a convenient location for training sessions in special fields. All member libraries are invited to send staff representatives to such sessions, where they will have an opportunity to see demonstrations and to try out a particular technique under expert guidance. The practice laboratory idea is promoted by some individual libraries and systems when they offer open invitations to members of a system to participate for a limited period of time in an innovative program for the disadvantaged. The intent of these sessions is not observation but actual involvement in the work of the project.

Informal study groups have been suggested as an approach to professional growth. Their major purpose is information and opinion exchange. Voluntary study groups arise spontaneously within many system areas, with and without system sponsorship. The more sophisticated groups "collaborate in research, hold meetings, correspond with each other, read papers to each other, circulate pre-prints and reprints—all designed to keep each member informed in the latest developments in a given field of learning."[4] A system may make use of existing study groups in its continuing education program, or it may encourage the establishment of such groups within zones of the system area.

A part of the responsibility of the system in its educational program is the preparation of special lists for advance or post-session study. Many systems also make a practice of preparing and distributing special bulletins with summaries of important conclusions from the training sessions to be used on the local level.

The most effective programs in continuing education are those that have continuity. These are the programs that build on the content of each preceding program to achieve the goal of comprehensive knowledge. The results of continuity may be manifold. They may range from specialization in book knowledge to insights that will "keep us from doing efficiently what doesn't need to be done at all."[5]

Library literature and numerous system reports indicate that the cooperative systems have covered many subjects in their efforts to meet membership needs for continuing education. A selective list indicates the following topics are typical of continuing education efforts at the system level:

1. Administration
   a. Building and equipment
   b. Effective use of manpower
   c. General management theory and practice
   d. Library finance and governmental controls
   e. Library standards
   f. Local library cooperative techniques
   g. Organization of library resources

    h. Personnel administration
    i. Public administration
    j. Public relations
    k. Security measures
    l. System relationships
    m. Techniques in evaluation
    n. Work simplification
2. Building collections
    a. Administrative problems in collection building
    b. Audiovisual materials
    c. Cooperative acquisition holdings and their use
    d. Local history collections
    e. Selection tools and their use
    f. Sources of materials
    g. Subject fields, such as science
    h. Use of paperbacks
    i. Values of government documents
3. The community
    a. Community self-survey techniques
    b. Identifying the needs of the unserved
    c. Library involvement in social change
    d. Programming for changing community needs
4. Finances
    a. Bookkeeping methods
    b. Principles in budget development
    c. Reporting
    d. Techniques in presenting and justifying budgets
5. Intellectual freedom
    a. Community censorship problems
    b. Self-censorship problems
    c. The system and intellectual freedom
6. Services
    a. Changing objectives of traditional services
    b. Effective use of system services
    c. Interpretation of library services
    d. Local service to the handicapped
    e. Problems in reference and information
7. Staff
    a. Interpersonal relationships
    b. The responsibilities of middle management
    c. Techniques for library assistants
8. Trustees
    a. Buildings

b. Growth planning
c. Library law
d. Library standards
e. Municipality-corporate relations
f. Personnel
g. Principles of policy-making
h. Role of the trustee in legislation
i. Standards for public libraries and for systems
j. Trustee-administrator relationships
k. Trustee liabilities and legal responsibilities
l. Trustee responsibility to system development
m. Trustees' fiscal responsibilities.

Continuing education is subject to evaluation, as are all other system activities. Usually the evaluation takes the form of a reaction questionnaire, which seeks to determine if the participants liked the speaker, the physical arrangements, the food, and the program content and if they derived anything from the training session. Some reaction questionnaires attempt to explore the participants' ideas about how they will make use of the learning experience. A true evaluation would involve pre-testing the participants before the course starts to determine attitudes or levels of their knowledge and a post-session test to determine how successful the program actually was.

Continuing Education at the State Level

The responsibility of the state library, at the third level of continuing education, is to expand the horizons of every librarian and trustee in the state by sharing the results of sound library research, professionwide planning, or special projects. The emphasis at the state level should be on new developments with long-range implications for library development.

A state library sometimes is associated with a permanent center for library research. The products of such research centers ordinarily take some time to reach the grass roots. A vigorous continuing education program at the state level, with occasional meetings and a good communications program, would result in a well-informed professional body throughout the state. If the research center also had teaching responsibilities, it might provide a particularly stimulating environment for the state's contribution to continuing library education. The state might also establish satellite research centers, operated by a cluster of systems, where practicing librarians might not only attend educational meetings but also participate in some type of research. The specific goals for continuing education at the state level may be:

1. To provide programs of continuing education with major emphasis on fields where new knowledge has accumulated at an accelerated rate

2. To plan programs based on state-initiated research to provide background knowledge for essential change in focus or direction at the local library or system level

3. To provide for new patterns of library education to demonstrate the interdependence of types of libraries and the values of interdisciplinary approaches

4. To provide programs of continuing education for system administrators and consultant staffs.

The suggestion has been made that state agencies establish a library reserve corps as a means of maintaining the preparedness of inactive, but potentially active, librarians.[6] The reserve corps would consist of professionals who had interrupted their careers for marriage, those who took early retirements, and others who may eventually return to the profession on a temporary or permanent basis. These individuals might be invited to participate in continuing education at the state level and to general meetings at the system level so that they can keep abreast of developments in the library field. The advantage in the proposal for a library reserve corps is not only preparedness but also the creation of a supportive group of informed laymen in various localities in the state.

Jacques Barzun emphasized the need for more "roving, reading" librarians to maintain a responsive "intelligence agency" for society.[7] Maintaining such a body of professionals is a major charge for continuing education in librarianship. It is imperative for our institutions to maintain currency and relevance in a society undergoing accelerated change. Only by staffing our public libraries with individuals who are constantly stimulated to achieve excellence will our libraries remain in the mainstream of society and be able to fulfill their roles in their communities. The responsibility for stimulation is shared by the local library, the system, and the state library.

8 A Pattern for Public Library Service – A Summary

The concept of independent public libraries joining together in the planned partnership of a cooperative system offers the opportunity for each library to reach for excellence and to relate its services to the needs of people in an era of rapid change and technological innovation. The cooperative system is a flexible design adaptable to rural or populous areas. By the combining of talents and resources it provides the means to:

1. Create a greater depth and range of resources
2. Open avenues for the use of the resources
3. Equalize library service
4. Raise the level of personnel expertise
5. Offer the newer types of communications media
6. Take advantage of the new technology
7. Experiment and innovate.

The cooperative public library system *is* its member libraries acting in concert through the system headquarters to attain desired objectives. Member libraries plan together. To the local library, therefore, the only threat inherent in the system is the threat of change. The system offers the opportunity and the flexibility to enable the library to change from an institution unable to meet the needs of the present to one equal to meeting the potential needs of the future. The independence of the local library will be threatened only if it allows the system to become a crutch for its own underachievement. By fulfilling its obligation to improve its own condition by its own efforts, the member library will maintain its independence while contributing to the strength of the partnership.

249

Cooperation is not a philanthropic donation of resources and services from the stronger library to the weaker system member; it is the genuine sharing of services, resources, and responsibilities by all library members. The system has a responsibility to stimulate the underachieving member library to contribute, by greater local effort, to the overall strength of the system. By assembling statistical data related to its members, tabulating them in comparative form, relating them to standards, and interpreting their meaning and use, the system will assist the local library in establishing specific goals. By determining realistic cost figures and interpreting them to the members, the system will stimulate the local library to reexamine procedures and to develop more efficient methods. By refusing to be a crutch and requiring local effort at every opportunity, the system will prevent itself from being reduced to the lowest common denominator. All member libraries cannot contribute in the same way or to the same degree to system excellence. But each library can contribute through self-strengthening. Systems reaching for excellence will be composed of libraries that insist on striving for self-improvement and expect the same effort from their fellow members.

Cooperation, even though subsidized, cannot thrive without communications, participation, and compromise. To reach the potential inherent in a cooperative system requires a high level of personal involvement on the part of all participants. System personnel will remain alert to the possibilities of improving services to patrons through the local libraries. To remain alert to such possibilities the consultant staff will avoid the natural tendency to become desk-bound. Through personal visits to the member libraries, system personnel will become familiar with each library's problems, weaknesses, and strengths. Local library personnel will maintain constant communication with system headquarters. They will attend system meetings and training sessions, thus benefiting from self-improvement and contributing to the improvement of their institutions, other members, and the system as a whole. Much is asked of the librarian of a library that is a system member. The trite expression, "You only get out of it what you put into it," can be rephrased: a library's patrons will reap the benefits of the system to the same degree that the library contributes to the system in terms of involvement.

If the member library is obligated to be involved in the system, the system staff is obligated to provide opportunities for member participation. Regularly scheduled meetings of all local library administrators on at least a semiannual basis will offer the opportunity for productive communications. At least every five years, system personnel should review the plan of service, not only for the purpose of evaluating ongoing services but also to consider the addition of services new technological developments may have made possible. The revision of the system's plan of service offers an ideal framework for member librarian and trustee participation. A closely scheduled series of workshops with opportunities for "brainstorming" on the part of the membership has proved rewarding in at least one system. Innovative membership ideas from the series for possible inclusion in the system plan of service included: (1) one library in each zone to be open twenty-four hours a day, (2) round-the-clock central reference service, (3) a policy of system personnel visiting member libraries without invitation or specific purpose, (4) a system pool of infrequently used building maintenance equipment, and (5) a systemwide overdue collection agency.

There is no phase of library operation in which the system does not have the potential to be of assistance. The library that benefits from the full potential of system membership is the one that makes full use of the system's consultant services. By seeking system help in problem-solving, the members will stimulate the system headquarters to assemble up-to-date materials, to hire superior staff and to bring the combination to bear in suggesting solutions. To be of value to its members in assisting them in the efficient use of library buildings, in planning capital improvements and referendums, in collection development, in policy-making, in budgeting, in organizing personnel, in evaluation, and in research, the system is obligated to have personnel with a greater expertise than the member libraries have. The libraries help maintain strong system personnel by challenging them with problems. The initiative in seeking system assistance, however, rests with the local library. The system desiring to maintain local independence does not foist its advice and counsel on a library that has not asked for it.

In addition to consultation, services basic to most cooperative systems are: central reference, interlibrary loan, some audiovisual services, systemwide borrowing privileges, and delivery of materials. These basic services create the avenues for patron use of the area's resources. The system will also build a collection of materials that is more sophisticated than the collections of the member libraries and that will enable a high percentage of the informational needs of the area to be satisfied within the system itself. For those still unanswered needs, the system provides additional avenues of access to materials. By working with other types of area libraries to establish equitable and reciprocal use of materials and through the adaptation of technological means of communication, unfilled requests at the system level will be referred rapidly to the other available resources within and beyond the system's boundaries.

In fulfilling its responsibilities to areas within the system with no library service, the system will assist in the formation of new libraries. Where justified, the system will act as the catalyst in stimulating the creation of larger, more viable, special taxing districts which may include existing member libraries. The system of the not-too-distant future will have no unserved persons within its area. Every resident will be supporting local library service, and each library will have a realistic tax base on which local library support will rest.

The system must keep abreast of developments that offer opportunities for new services. The potential of cassette and cartridge tapes, 8mm cartridge films, and electronic video recordings as library materials has yet to be tapped. The use of computers for public library bibliographic and circulation control, and for central processing of materials and central bookkeeping is still in the pioneering stage. In cooperation with other library systems, jointly operated public library services computer centers can become a reality. The local library of the future will not be burdened with routine. Charging and discharging locally loaned materials, preparing overdue notices, ordering and cataloging of materials, and inventory of local holdings can be performed by the center. The local library staff will finally catch up to the housewife in being freed from the drudgery that has interfered with full-time service to people.

Systems in metropolitan areas with propinquant libraries are fortunate in having additional opportunities for the budget-stretching allocation of services and responsibilities. Libraries can be grouped in logical service zones, with each library in a zone specializing not only in subject areas of printed material but also in other forms of communication such as framed prints, tape cassettes, cartridge tapes or films, and audiovisual playback devices. Using his systemwide borrower's card, the patron will find within a convenient distance the form of material to suit his needs. By allocation of responsibilities for format and subject matter, all member libraries benefit by being able to provide the full gamut of communications media with the least strain on the individual library or system budgets.

As a result of system membership, the local public library will be equal to the challenge of the last quarter of the century. In return for his support of his local library, the resident of the system area will have access to rich resources in a variety of forms. He will find, because of his library's participation in the system, that he has access to a nationwide network of libraries offering undreamed-of completeness in resources never before available to him. Providing this access is the function and the responsibility of the cooperative system.

Appendixes: Examples of System Documents and Forms

A. Plan of Service

The Suburban Library System Plan of Service - 1971 Draft Revision

Objectives

The objectives of the Suburban Library System shall be to operate a system of autonomous public libraries which, through the cooperative effort of the library members and the assistance of state financing, will provide library services of a type, quality and magnitude that cannot be provided by the individual libraries. Improved library services to System residents shall always be the goal of the System. Such improvement includes assistance in establishment of library services in areas without it.

Membership

Membership in the System shall be open to any tax-supported public library in Cook County, DuPage County, Will County and neighboring areas which chooses to join. Membership shall become effective as provided in the By-Laws of the System.

Government

The System shall be governed by a Board of nine directors elected as provided in the By-Laws of the System.

There shall be an Executive Director of the System who

shall be responsible for the administration of the System and who shall be considered its chief administrative officer.

Each member library shall retain autonomy in regard to its own expenditures, operations and policies; each library cooperates with other members in following System procedures and policies involved with System services.

Services

The System shall provide the services required by the Rules and Regulations for Library Systems and State Aid prescribed by the State Librarian. Wherever applicable, all services of the System shall be conducted in accordance with the standards prescribed in Minimum Standards for Public Library Systems, 1966, and its addenda Statistical Standards, 1967, as amended or revised from time to time.

The following are current services of the Suburban Library System:

1. Development of a System Book Collection. The bulk of the collection is housed in the head-quarters libraries; namely, the Oak Park and Park Forest Public Libraries. In addition, a professional library is housed in the System Executive Office Building. Some System owned materials are on indefinite loan to member libraries.

2. Interlibrary Loan Service. Within guidelines developed by the System, mechanics and personnel will be provided to secure materials not owned by individual member libraries but requested by their patrons.

3. Central Reference Service. The System provides the mechanics and personnel to answer the informational needs of patrons of its member libraries. This service includes the acquisition of reference materials, copying facilities, microform materials and print-out facilities.

4. Audio-Visual Services. The System has developed a collection of 16mm films and a small collection of foreign language disc recordings.

5. Delivery Service. The System provides the means and personnel for delivery of materials to the requesting libraries.

6. Communications. To improve communications, the cost of telephone calls from member libraries to any System phone is absorbed by the System. A newsletter is issued monthly, and memos, bibliographies, etc. are issued when necessary.

7. System-Wide Borrowing. Library patrons who support a local member library through taxation have free

access to all member libraries in the use of printed
materials.

8. Advisory Services. Upon request, advice is rendered
    to librarians and boards of directors of member
    libraries. Included are consultant services in
    various specific fields such as administrative
    services, placement of personnel, and book collec-
    tion evaluation. The System also assists its
    members in securing expert advice beyond the
    System staff in such fields as library buildings,
    insurance and public relations. The above examples
    are not intended to be exclusive.

9. Education and Training. Through workshops the
    System attempts to increase the knowledge and
    improve the performance of trustees, administrators
    and staffs of the member libraries. Occasional
    workshops are held for community groups.

10. Centralized Purchasing. Where a substantial
    saving can be realized (i.e., film projectors)
    or sources are difficult for individual libraries
    to contact (i.e., paperback books) the System
    makes purchases on behalf of its member libraries.

11. Serving Unserved Areas. The System has accepted
    the inherent obligation to assist residents in
    promoting the development of library service in

areas where they do not exist. This may include
bookmobile service on a demonstration basis
and/or legal assistance in the formation of
library districts. The System acts as a catalyst
bringing together governmental and other
interested individuals from neighboring communities in an effort to assist in the formation of
new, adequately supported libraries.

12. Research, Innovation, Experimentation. The System
accepts the responsibility for conducting research
leading to the determination of improved methods
and technology in serving the library needs of
member library clientele. Experimental services
or techniques to provide actual testing of effectiveness of new methods and technology is a System
obligation.

Future Services

The following services are goals of the System. The availability and stage of development of related equipment and
budgetary considerations may influence the order in which
these proposed services may be inaugurated. However,
Improvement of Current Services is intended to be of first
importance.

Improvement of Current Services. It shall be the
intent of the System to frequently evaluate on-

going services and work toward their improvement.
Such improvements will include extension of System
hours of basic services.

Zoned Services. In order to take advantage of
new forms of communication media suitable to
public libraries, member libraries will be grouped
in geographical zones. Each library in a zone
may, through System assistance, provide a service
unique to the zone. Holders of system-wide
borrowers' cards may freely use the library of
their choice, thereby having a greater variety of
services and materials available at less total cost
to the System.

Centralized Printing and Art Service. To assist
member libraries in the designing, development and
production of promotional materials, the System will
provide general materials developed by the System
staff and custom materials to suit the needs of the
individual member libraries. The ultimate aim of
this service is to include signs, posters and rotating
display materials as well as printed lists, brochures,
etc.

Non-Book Media. The System will accept responsibility
for the testing, promotion, and initial acquisition
of non-book communication media which are determined

appropriate for public libraries. These may include
electronic video recordings, cassette and cartridge
tapes, 8mm films, art prints, specialized printed
materials and others.

Automation. In the broadest meaning of the term,
the System will explore the potentials and work
toward the use of the new technology in those
areas determined to be economically practicable
in rendering efficient library service to SLS
residents. Where feasible the System will acquire
equipment for the use of member libraries on a
limited basis.

Creating Larger Service Areas. Where geography
and tax base indicate, the System will encourage
existing neighboring libraries to consider the
advantages of merger and of annexations.

Inter-System and Inter-Type Library Cooperation.
In areas consistent with the Suburban Library System's
goals, cooperative ventures with other systems, as
well as special and academic libraries, will be
explored, and when determined feasible will be
proposed.

Amendments

This Plan of Service is for the guidance of the System
for the future. Changing conditions may require altera-

tions to the plan. Amendments may be made by action of the SLS Board of Directors, subject to the approval of the State Librarian one month after submission of proposed amendments to all member libraries.

B. Bylaws of a System

By-Laws of the Suburban Library System - 1968

Article I - Name

The name of the organization shall be The Suburban Library System.

Article II - Membership

Membership in the System shall be open to any tax-supported public library in Cook County, DuPage County, Will County, and neighboring areas which by appropriate action of its governing board has elected to join the System and which otherwise meets the requirements of an act of the Illinois General Assembly (H.B. No. 563), 1965, commonly called the Library Development Act and the Rules and Regulations for Library Systems and State Aid prescribed by the State Librarian pursuant to said act.

Article III - Purpose

The purpose of the System is to promote, foster, encourage, and effectuate the improvement of free public libraries, within the territory served by the System and the extension of their services to all people within such territory.

Article IV - Board of Directors

Section 1. General Powers and Objectives. The System shall be governed by its Board of Directors whose objectives shall include, but not be limited to, the following:

263

a. The development of headquarters which will facilitate improvement of present library services in the territory served by the System and expansion and extension of such services to those parts of such territory not now receiving such services.

b. The implementation of the System's Plan of Service approved by the State Librarian.

c. The continuing evaluation of said Plan of Service and the actions taken in implementation thereof and the making of recommendations for such additions to and revisions of said Plan of Service as the Board of Directors may deem necessary or advisable to better accomplish the purpose of the System.

Section 2. Number and Qualifications. The number of directors of the System shall be nine. Each director shall be a member of the governing board of a participating library. No more than one director shall be from the governing board of any one participating library at any one time.

Section 3. Election of Directors. Three directors shall be elected from libraries north of the Stevenson Expressway; three directors shall be elected from libraries south of the Stevenson Expressway; and three directors shall be elected at large, one each from libraries falling within three different population groups. Election of directors shall be as follows:

a. Each member library may nominate one director from its local governing board.

b. Directors representing libraries north of the Stevenson Expressway shall be elected by a majority vote of the libraries north of said Expressway from among nominees of such northern libraries. Each library shall have one vote.

c. Directors representing libraries south of the Stevenson Expressway shall be elected by a majority vote of the libraries south of said Expressway from among the nominees of such southern libraries. Each library shall have one vote.

d. Prior to any election the member libraries shall be ranked by population according to the latest official federal census. The list of libraries so ranked shall be divided as nearly as possible into thirds by number.

e. After the directors are elected on the basis of geographical representation the remaining nominees shall be elected, one from each of the three population groups. The director representing a population group shall be elected by a majority vote of the libraries within that population group. Each library shall have one vote.

Section 4. Term of Office. Subject to the next succeeding sentence, the term of office of directors shall be three years but no director shall serve more than two consecutive terms. At the initial election of directors, one director from each category (e.g., north of the Stevenson Expressway, south of the Stevenson Expressway, and at large) shall be elected for a

term of one year; one director from each such category shall
be elected for a term of two years; and one director from each
such category shall be elected for a term of three years. Thus
the terms of office of one-third of the members of the Board of
Directors shall expire each year.

Section 5. Disqualification. When any director fails to
attend four consecutive meetings of the Board of Directors,
the board shall declare his position vacant.

Section 6. Filling of Vacancies. Any vacancy in a
directorship occurring between annual meetings of the System
shall be filled by appointment by the Board of Directors from
the geographical or population group represented by such
directorship. Such appointee shall serve until the next annual
meeting of the System.

Article V - Officers

Section 1. The officers of the System shall be a Presiden
a Vice-President, a Secretary, and a Treasurer, who shall be
elected annually by the Board of Directors from its membership.

Section 2. There may also be such assistant officers as
the Board of Directors shall appoint or elect who need not be
members of the Board of Directors.

Section 3. The term of office of all elected officers sha
be one year, commencing at the first Board meeting following th
annual meeting of the System except that at the initial electio
of officers the officers elected shall serve one calendar year
and beyond to the next scheduled annual meeting of the Board of
Directors.

Section 4. No member of the Board of Directors shall serve as President for more than two consecutive years; nor shall any member serve as Treasurer for more than five consecutive years.

Article VI - Duties of Officers

Section 1. The President shall preside at meetings of the Board of Directors and of the System.

Section 2. The Vice-President shall preside at meetings and shall perform the other duties of the President in case of the absence or disability of the President.

Section 3. The Secretary shall have responsibility for the records of the Board of Directors and of the System and shall keep the minutes and give notice of all meetings of the Board of Directors and of the System.

Section 4. The Treasurer shall have charge of the funds of the System to the extent permitted by law. All bills of the System shall be validated by the Executive Director or some other person designated by the Board. Payment shall be made by draft or check signed by such Treasurer. In the event of the absence or incapacity of the Treasurer, the President or Vice-President shall sign the checks. Accurate books of accounts shall be kept by the Treasurer, or under his direction, showing receipts and disbursements. The Treasurer shall make monthly reports to the Board of Directors and such other reports as may be required from time to time. The Treasurer, the President, and the Vice-President shall be bonded in such amount as may be required by the Board of Directors.

Section 5. In addition to the foregoing duties, each officer shall have such power and perform such duties as are incumbent upon similar officers in corporate organizations and such additional powers or duties as may be conferred upon them by the Board of Directors.

Article VII - Committees

Committees shall be appointed by the President as the need arises or on the request of a majority of the Board of Directors.

Article VIII - Personnel

Section 1. There shall be an Executive Director of the System who shall be responsible for the administration of the System and who shall be considered its chief administrative officer.

a. The Executive Director shall appoint an Advisory Committee from among librarians of the member libraries in such number as he finds necessary to provide adequate representation of the differences among the member libraries in terms of size, location, and state of development. The Headquarters Libraries shall be represented on the Committee, but other members should be appointed on a rotating basis.

b. The purpose of the Advisory Committee shall be:

1. To promote System development

2. To consider recommendations of the Executive Director, which may affect member libraries, prior to System Board action

3. To consider and assist in drafting procedures
    which may affect member libraries

4. To initiate suggestions to the Executive
    Director

5. To be an added means of communication between
    the System administration and the membership

c. Meetings of the advisory committee are held at the
    call of the Executive Director.

d. The Executive Director shall attend all meetings of
    the Board of Directors and of the System and may take
    part in the deliberations but shall have no vote.

e. The Executive Director shall submit to the Board of
    Directors a monthly and an annual report as to the
    progress and condition of the System during the past
    month or year accompanying the same with such
    recommendations and suggestions as may seem to be
    expedient.

Section 2. A table of organization and a position
classification and pay plan shall be developed and adopted by
the Board of Directors for the guidance of its administrative
officers.

Article IX - Meetings

Section 1. The annual meeting of the System shall be held
as soon as practical after the close of the fiscal year at a
time and place to be determined by the Board of Directors, at
which meeting directors shall be elected to fill the offices
of those directors whose terms currently expire.

Section 2. The annual meeting of the Board of Directors shall be the first meeting of the Board of Directors after the annual meeting of the System and shall be at a time and place to be determined by the Board, for the purpose of electing officers, reviewing these By-Laws, reviewing the Executive Director's annual report, and considering any other business that may properly come before an annual meeting.

Section 3. Regular meetings of the Board of Directors shall be held at a time and place to be designated by the Board of Directors.

    a. No less than four meetings shall be held each year.

    b. A quorum shall consist of a majority of the members of the Board of Directors, and unless otherwise provided in these By-Laws or required by law, the act of a majority of the Directors at a meeting where a quorum is present shall constitute the act of the Board of Directors.

    c. Five days written notice of the time and place of the regular meeting of the Board shall be given to each director.

Section 4. Special meetings of the Board of Directors may be called by the President or upon the request of three directors upon five days written notice, for the transaction of such business as may be stated in such notice.

Article X - Conduct of Meetings

Section 1. Unless otherwise provided, meetings shall be conducted in accordance with <u>Robert's</u> <u>Rules</u> <u>of</u> <u>Order</u>, <u>Revised</u>.

Section 2. In the absence of a quorum the directors present may adjourn a meeting to a day that they shall fix, notice of which shall be given by the Secretary according to Article IX.

Section 3. The order of business shall be as follows, but it may be changed or suspended at any meeting of the Board by unanimous consent of the directors present.

a. The minutes of the preceding meeting

b. Communications

c. Review of bills and financial accounting

d. Reports of officers and committees

e. Report of the Executive Director

f. Nominations and elections, if any

g. Unfinished business

h. New business

i. Adjournment

Article XI - Fiscal Year

The fiscal year of the System shall be from July 1st through June 30th.

Article XII - Records and Financial Accounting

Section 1. All records of the System and the Board, including those of the Treasurer, shall be maintained at the System Headquarters.

Section 2. Copies of all Board minutes shall be sent to each member library.

Section 3. Financial records and activities shall be maintained in accordance with accepted accounting practice. The action of the Board in regard to approval of bills for payment shall be recorded.

Section 4. An audit of System and Board records shall be performed each year by a qualified independent certified public accountant or firm of certified public accountants licensed to practice public accounting in the State of Illinois. Copies of auditors' reports shall be distributed to each participating library and to the State Librarian.

Section 5. A copy of the Treasurer's, the President's, and the Vice-President's surety bond shall be filed with the State Librarian.

Section 6. System and Board records shall not be destroyed without the approval of the Illinois State Records Commission.

Article XIII - Area Expansion and Reduction

Acceptance of applications for, and withdrawals from, membership in the System shall be in accordance with the Library Development Act and the Rules and Regulations for Library Systems and State Aid.

Article XIV - Amendments

These By-Laws may be amended by a two-thirds vote of the directors present at any meeting.

C. Sample Data Sheet for Building Planners

Library Visiting Data Sheet
(to be adapted for local interests or use)

Name of library _____ Date of visit_____

Date of construction _____

Name of architect _____

Name of building consultant (s) _____

Other consultants _____

Type of construction _____

Square footage _____ Volume capacity _____

Cost per sq. ft. _____ Total cost _____

Exterior entrance

    Ramps for the handicapped _____

    Type of doors _____

    Provision for sidewalk snow melting piping _____

    Location of bicycle racks _____

    Accessibility to flag pole _____

Lobby features

    Location of plaques, if any _____

    Bulletin boards or display cases _____

    Location of public phone _____

    Location of public lockers, if any _____

    Design of book drops _____

    Location of master light switch _____

    Location of drinking fountain _____

Relationship of circulation desk to entrance and service areas

    Type of desk _____

    Work areas _____

    Storage areas _____

    Special equipment _____

Public washrooms

    Location and size _____

    Supervision controls _____

    Facilities for the handicapped _____

Treatment of interior walls _____

Location and type of clocks _____

Air-conditioning and heating

    Heat _____ Oil _____ Gas _____ Electric _____

    Location of thermostats _____

    AC control of drafts and noise _____

Fire detection system _____

Lighting

    Footcandle power _____

    Type of fixtures _____

    Shadows _____ Glare _____

Floors

    Material _____

    Color _____

    Maintenance factors _____

    Use of carpeting _____

Elevators

    Public or staff _____

    Kind _____

    Location _____

Stairways

    Location _____

    Problems in supervision _____

Stacks

    Wood or steel _____

    Treatment of end panels _____

    Arrangement _____

    Manufacturer _____

    Relationship to public catalog _____

Furniture and equipment

    Name of supplier _____

    Extent of use of lounge furniture _____

    Total seating capacity _____

    Size of reading tables _____

    Provisions for handling over-size books _____

    Provisions for magazines and newspaper storage _____

    Use of study carrels _____

    Location of audio visual equipment _____

    Type of inter-office and departmental communication

        system _____

    Type of display cases _____

Young Adult area

    Size and location _____

    Seating capacity _____

    Relationship to children's and reference rooms _____

    Type of collection _____

    Other materials beside books _____

    Office and work area _____

Children's area

    Seating capacity _____

    Extent of use of informal seating _____

    Type of picture book tables _____

    Types and heights of reading tables _____

    Use of islands _____

    Kind of picture book shelving _____

    Provision for magazines and records _____

    Office and work area _____

    Story hour area _____

    Display cases; movable or fixed _____

    Provisions for coats and hats _____

    Toilet facilities for children _____

Reference area

    Location of main information desk _____

    Number of reference desks _____

    Relation to heavy traffic flow _____

    Relation to public card catalog _____

    Location and number of telephones _____

    Location of business services _____

Types of reference tables _____

Types of consulting tables _____

Map and vertical file cases _____

Types of shelving for bibliographic aids _____

Types of shelving for encyclopedias _____

Location of copying machines _____

Location of microfilm readers _____

Seating capacity _____

Office and work area _____

Technical processes department

Types of equipment _____

Notable work-flow arrangements _____

Hot and cold water sink _____

Supply storage area _____

Receiving room

Work tables _____

Cartage and other equipment _____

Loading dock _____

Exit controls _____

Bookmobile garage

Capacity _____

Types of doors _____ Automatic _____

Special equipment _____

Drainage _____

Access to extension department _____

Staff room

Size of kitchen unit _____

Type of furniture _____

Location of staff washrooms _____

Location of staff lockers _____

Board room

Capacity _____

Type of conference table _____

Coat closets _____

Meeting room

Treatment of walls for picture hanging _____

Type of projection booth and screen _____

Number and type of chairs and conference tables _____

Coat closets _____

Chair storage area _____

Any kitchen facilities _____

Librarian's office

Size _____

Location of private lavatory _____

Location of coat closet _____

Relationship to secretary _____

Relationship to board room _____

Secretary or business office

General equipment _____

Business record storage cabinets _____

Number of visitors' chairs _____

Location of coat closets for guests or personnel _____

Custodial area

Custodian's office _____

Type of incinerator _____

Storage facilities _____

Lockers _____

Work area _____

Special features _____

Mechanical area _____

Parking

Staff _____

Public _____

Notes on special features to consider: (such as integrated art,

provisions for installation of electronic equipment, or public

typing facilities) _____

Notes of items to avoid _____

General Observations

Does the library permit smoking?_____ If so, where?_____

What type of fire exit signs are used?_____ Directional

signs?_____

What construction features relate to acoustics?_____

D. Illustrative Workshop Material Provided by System for Member Libraries

Insurance for Libraries

An Outline Prepared for Suburban Library System

by Gerald E. Myers, Insurance Consultant

I. A philosophy of insurance for our library

    A. What property (and other assets) do we own or use which is subject to loss or damage?

        1. What is its value?

        2. What perils is it subject to? (Fire, wind, explosion, theft, employee dishonesty, etc.)

    B. What are our risks of liability for accident or injury?

        1. To employees and volunteers?

        2. To members of the public?

        3. To property of others?

    C. What can we do to avoid or prevent loss or damage and accident or injury?

        1. By fire safety measures

        2. By security measures against vandals and thieves

        3. Accident prevention

    D. How do we insure against risks?

        1. Self insure the small, known losses

        2. Buy insurance for the large or catastrophe losses and the unknown

II. The technical aspects

    A. Valuation of property to be insured

        1. Buildings

2. Furniture and equipment

3. Books and periodicals

4. Index cards

5. Films, records, et al

6. Property of others in library's custody

7. Maintenance of appraisals and inventories

B. Replacement cost or actual cash value

C. Perils to be insured against

   1. Named peril:

    Fire and lightning

    Wind, hail, tornado

    Aircraft, vehicle, smoke damage

    Riot, vandalism

    Theft, burglary, hold up

    Water damage from plumbing and heating systems

    Plate glass breakage

    Boiler explosion - machinery breakdown

    VS

   2. "All risks" with exclusions of

    Flood, surface waters, sewers, earthquake

    Nuclear damage

    War and insurrection

    Wear and tear, mechanical breakdown

   3. Employee dishonesty - Blanket for all employees or individual "Faithful Performance" bonds

D. Property policy provisions

   1. Coinsurance requirements or agreed amount endorsement

   2. Deductibles and the self-insured loss

E. Liability for injuries to employees

    1. Workmen's Compensation Act - no limit policy

    2. Group insurance for "off the job" injuries

F. Liability to the public

    1. "Premises and operations" accidents

    2. Products liability

    3. Contractual agreements - hold harmless clauses

    4. "Personal injury" - slander, libel, false arrest, wrongful detention

    5. Employees as additional insureds

    6. Liability for damage to property rented or used - standard policy exclusion

    7. Auto non-ownership risks

    8. What is an adequate limit?

G. Kinds of policies

    1. By package policy these *may* be combined

        a) Fire and extended coverage and additional perils or "all risk" on buildings and contents

        b) Burglary and theft

        c) Employee fidelity

        d) Public liability

        e) Auto non-ownership

        f) Steam boiler explosion

    2. Separate policies required for:

        a) Workmen's compensation

        b) Umbrella or excess liability

        c) Individual employee bonds

H. Indirect or consequential loss

I. Losses and claims

    1. Property loss reporting and settlement

    2. Reporting of injuries and claims and cooperation
with the insurer

Glossary of Insurance Terms

Coinsurance clause: This places an obligation on the insured to
carry insurance to the stated percentage of total value which exists
at the time of the loss. For example, if the building replacement
cost is $190,000 at the time of the loss and the amount of insurance
is $160,000 with a 100% coinsurance clause, then the amount of
insurance which should be carried is $190,000 and the library will
collect only 16/19 of this loss.

Actual cash value vs. replacement cost: The standard fire
insurance or other property policy covers on the basis of actual
cash value, which contemplates a settlement of something less than
the replacement cost if the item is not new and therefore subject
to depreciation for wear and tear, obsolescence, etc. The
replacement cost endorsement modifies this standard coverage to
provide for reimbursement on an actual replacement cost basis with
no deduction for depreciation if the damaged or destroyed item is
actually replaced. The latter coverage is desirable for public
bodies such as libraries, whose financial reserves are usually
limited and which would be obliged to ask for a public referendum
for additional funds to cover a substantial financial depreciation
deduction.

Extended coverage: This is the name for an endorsement which provides coverage for the perils of wind, cyclone, tornado, hail, aircraft and vehicle damage, smoke damage, explosion, riot and civil commotion. (All of the above, of course, being subject to certain policy definitions and limitations.)

Additional perils vs. all risk: Endorsements are available extending property policies beyond the perils of fire, extended coverage and vandalism. These endorsements may cover water damage from plumbing or heating systems, collapse of buildings or equipment, burglary, theft, etc. The most desirable coverage is the so-called "all risk," which is frequently available and is subject to certain exclusions such as war damage, flood and surface or sewer water, nuclear explosion, earthquake, etc.

Personal injury vs. bodily injury: The personal injury coverage under the liability policy includes bodily injury but also includes such additional injuries as libel and slander, defamation of character, wrongful eviction, false arrest.

Non-ownership: This is an auto liability coverage which applies in the situation where an employee or agent of the library is driving his or her own car on library business and is involved in an accident where the employee or an agent may be liable but where the library also is liable under the doctrine of "respondeat superior."

Normally the auto insurance policy of the employee will protect the library but frequently the limits under this policy may be inadequate for the possible judgment. The non-ownership liability coverage is intended to protect the library only for any judgment in excess of the employee's policy. It is important to know that the library may be responsible for such accidents if the employee was engaged in library activities or business, even though the employee was violating his instructions not to use his own car.

E. Materials Selection Policy Statement (1969)

Statement of Policy for the Selection of Library Materials
North Suburban Library System

In the development of the collection of library materials which is necessary to achieve the objectives stated in the Plan of Service of the North Suburban Library System, the System recognizes the following premises, has the following goals, and is guided by the following policies.

I. Premises

    A. Library materials are defined as those materials of printed, photographic, electronic, or other form, which provide a basis for an educational or aesthetic experience, and which require the application of those techniques of acquisition, collection, preservation, and service appropriate to the public library.

    B. In developing an acquisition program to meet the educational and aesthetic needs and interests of the constituents of the System and its members, the library materials owned by the member libraries and the library material owned by the System will be considered to constitute the total resource of the System.

    C. In order to meet the objectives of the System, the development of the NSLS collection will be coordinated by the System staff.

286

D. The System assumes that the provision of library service
    adequate for the needs of today's citizens requires
    three levels of resource development:

    1. A basic collection at the local level. This broad,
        general collection of library materials includes
        current popular fiction and non-fiction, basic
        reference material, and selected retrospective
        fiction and non-fiction sufficient to meet those
        special interests and needs demonstrated by the
        community. The materials should be held in
        sufficient subject and in sufficient quantity,
        including duplication of copies, to meet, in
        accordance with standards, the local community's
        requests for regularly used materials.

    2. A comprehensive supporting collection at the system
        level. This collection, extensive both in quantity
        and in subject, complements the collections of its
        member libraries and includes in depth reference
        materials beyond the normal scope of the basic
        collection at the local level. The collection is
        sufficiently inclusive of both book and non-book
        materials so as to meet the needs of a large
        segment of the population and which according to
        standards are not the responsibility of the local
        library. It has materials in the latest and best
        editions for those with requirements for specific
        titles and also the major portion of authoritative
        materials with supporting bibliographies, periodicals,

and journals, and other publications associated
with a particular subject and which are required
for independent research in that subject. The
collection also contains materials of social
significance that may not be held at the local
level. Weeding of some obsolescent materials will
take place at this level.

3. Exhaustive collections at the state and national
level. These collections directed to a specific
subject or group of related subjects endeavor so
far as it is reasonably possible to include
everything on a subject, in all languages and
in all formats. Materials at this level are
expected to support historical research and provid
a resource beyond the limits of the comprehensive
supporting collection at the system level.

E. In developing the System's acquisition program, the
strength of the collections of member libraries will
be ascertained, and the System will build on these
strengths.

II. Goal

The goal of the NSLS selection policy is to provide a bro
collection of materials of contemporary significance and perm
value that will complement the collections of member librarie
and will contribute to

1. The objectives of the System as stated in the Plan of
Service

2. The advancement of knowledge

3. The education and enlightenment of the constituents of the libraries served

4. The availability and exchange of information

5. The aesthetic and literary appreciation of the population served

6. The individual objectives of the member libraries insofar as these objectives are consonant with those of the System.

III. Policies

A. General

1. Only library materials will be acquired which meet high standards of quality in content, expression, and form, or which, in special instances, are required to fulfill the goals and purposes of the System.

2. The selection of materials will be in accordance with the Library Bill of Rights and the Freedom to Read statement of the American Library Association.

3. Sponsored materials will be added only if they meet the same criteria as apply to materials purchased by the System.

4. The System staff will evaluate continually the needs of the System's community and will reflect this evaluation in the current selection and acquisition program.

    5.   Materials for acquisition by the System may be selected by members of the System's staff or by the System's designees.

    6.   Where it is found to be feasible and in the interest of the System, the System may contract with a member library or other institution for the selection, acquisition, and/or servicing of the System's library materials.

B. Books

    1.   The book collection shall be primarily adult, non-fiction material.

    2.   A special attempt shall be made to acquire books that are listed in standard library bibliographies and indexes.

    3.   The System normally will avoid purchasing titles which duplicate holdings of member libraries.

    4.   Books will be purchased in single copies of a title, except in cases of proven, repeated demand, in which case duplicate copies may be purchased in an effort to provide prompt service to as many member libraries as possible.

    5.   The System may suggest that a member library acquire its own copy of an item which is repeatedly requested of the System.

C. Periodicals

    1.   Acquisition will be in response to the needs of the member libraries.

2. Emphasis will be placed on acquisition of periodicals indexed in standard library indexes, and an attempt will be made to secure as complete holdings as appear to be useful to the fulfillment of the System's program.

3. Periodicals will be secured in a form that is easy to store, handle, and circulate.

4. Insofar as periodical issues can be found in System collections and they are readily available to member libraries, there will be no duplication of issues.

D. Other Non-Book Printed Materials

1. If it is necessary to provide material which has not yet been incorporated into more conventional printed sources and is in keeping with the avowed purpose of the System as a disseminator of information, such material should be added to the System collection.

E. Audio-Visual Materials

1. In keeping with the <u>Minimum</u> <u>Standards</u> <u>for</u> <u>Public</u> <u>Library</u> <u>Systems</u>, 1966, NSLS recognizes that audio-visual materials are an important part of the System's responsibility.

2. Selection of audio-visual material will follow the general policies and objectives outlined for books, with the exception that some materials will be selected to meet the demands of programming for children for public library programs.

3. Audio-visual materials will be selected for public library use and are not purchased for the classroom

or for teacher training, which are responsibilities
of the school.

4. In addition to the general criteria used as guides
in selection of materials for the System, particular
attention also will be paid to technical quality,
technique, authenticity, effectiveness of
presentation, and usefulness.

5. The content, subject matter, and treatment of films
considered for purchase will be evaluated in
relation to their lasting value, timeliness,
imagination, and originality.

F. Other Sources of Information

1. As new forms are developed, they will be appraised
by the System for possible use, and if their value
appears appropriate and useful to the purposes of
the System, the new forms will be incorporated in
the selection activities of the System.

G. Gifts

1. Materials offered to the System as gifts must meet
the System's selection standards and needs, before
these materials will be added to the collection.

2. Gifts will be accepted with the understanding
that the System has the right to dispose of the
gifts in any way the System sees fit.

H. Withdrawal of Materials

1. The withdrawal of materials from the collection
shall be the responsibility of the System's staff
or the System's designee.

2. Materials will be withdrawn from the collection
   because of poor physical condition, obsolescence,
   or failure to contribute to the stated objectives
   of the System.

3. Suggestions will be welcomed from member libraries
   on materials that should be weeded from the
   collection of which they are custodians.

4. Discarded materials may be offered to member or
   other libraries, except that if the material
   presumably would be of use to the Illinois State
   Library or other research library, such material
   will be offered to that library before the material
   is discarded.

I. Revision

1. The Statement of Policy for the Selection of Library
   Materials for the North Suburban Library System will
   be under constant evaluation, and as the collection
   grows and situations demand, the Statement will be
   altered in accordance with the findings of the
   staff of the North Suburban Library System.

F. Sample System Reference Request Form

Date:_____

Patron_____

Address_____

Phone No. _____

Scope of material needed: Introductory_____

    Intermediate_____, Advanced_____

Other comments _____

Not wanted after _____

Request _____

_____

_____

Referred by:_____ Library_____

Sources checked by library submitting request _____

_____

_____

_____

REPORT (To be filled in by System Reference Service)

Disposition of request_____

_____

Source or sources in which answer was located_____

_____

_____

Send first 3 copies of this form to:
                NSLS Reference Service
                Chicago Public Library - 5th Floor
                78 E. Washington St.
                Chicago, Illinois 60602

G. System Film Evaluation Form

Suburban Library System

Film Evaluation

Title_____Date Produced_____

Producer_____

Sources_____

Address_____

Minutes_____Color_____ B X W_____ Price_____

Summary:_____

_____

Can this film be better on other communication   Yes____ No____

    media?. . . . .

Is the continuity back and forth?. . . . . Yes____ No____

Is the subject biased? . . . . Yes____ No____

Is the approach sensational? . . . . Yes____ No____

Does the narrator try to cover too much? . . . . . . Yes____ No____

Does the narrator overlap or try to explain the

    visual?. . . . . Yes____ No____

Is the narration hard to understand? . . . . Yes____ No____

Is the music background louder than the narrator's

    voice?. . . . . Yes____ No____

Is the music background appropriate? . . . . Yes____ No____

Is the film from an original TV program? . . . . . . Yes____ No____

Is the color dull or of sharp contrast?. . . . . . . Yes____ No____

Is the photography artistic?. . . . . Yes____ No____

Is there any other film available on this subject? Yes____ No____

Does the subject control the length of the film?. No ____ Yes____

Is the interest kept up to the end? . . . . No ____ Yes____

Is color necessary? . . . . No ____ Yes____

Which group can use this film?_____

To which age is this film oriented?_____

Comments_____

_____

Notes

Chapter 1

A FRAMEWORK FOR THE REDESIGN OF PUBLIC LIBRARY SERVICE

1. First open stacks, 1885: Beaver Dam (Wis.) Public Library, as listed in "Library Firsts," in Phyllis B. Steckler, ed., *The Bowker Annual of Library and Book Trade Information* (New York: Bowker, 1968), p. 310.
2. From discussion on "Varieties of Readers and Readings in 1980," in Peter S. Jennison and Robert N. Sheridan, eds., *The Future of General Adult Books and Reading in America* (Chicago: ALA, 1970), p.34–35.
3. Carleton B. Joeckel and Amy Winslow, *A National Plan for Public Library Service* (Chicago: ALA, 1948), p.153.
4. American Library Assn., Public Libraries Division, Coordinating Committee on Revision of Public Library Standards, *Public Library Service: A Guide to Evaluation, with Minimum Standards* (Chicago: ALA, 1956), p.7.
5. Nelson Associates, *Public Library Systems in the United States: A Survey of Multijurisdictional Systems* (Chicago: ALA, 1969), p.262.
6. Ruth Warncke, "Heart of the System," *Wisconsin Library Bulletin* 64:314 (Sept.–Oct. 1968).
7. Robert R. McClarren, "State Legislation Relating to Library Systems," *Library Trends* 18:238 (Oct. 1970).
8. American Library Assn., Standards Committee and Subcommittees of the Public Library Assn., *Minimum Standards for Public Library Systems, 1966* (Chicago: ALA, 1967), p.27.
9. "Education," *Quote* 53:244 (26 March 1967).
10. Nelson Associates, *Public Library Systems in the United States,* p.242.
11. American Library Assn., *Minimum Standards for Public Library Systems, 1966,* p.21.
12. Jean L. Connor, "Role of the Medium-Sized Public Library in the 'System' (New York)," *Library Quarterly* 33:120 (Jan. 1963).

297

Chapter 2

PATTERNS OF RESPONSIBILITY AND INTERRELATIONS

1. See Table I in S. Janice Kee and M. G. Toepel, "Legal Basis of Public Libraries," in Roberta Bowler, ed., *Local Public Library Administration* (Chicago: International City Managers' Assn., 1964), p.20. See also Mildred L. Batchelder, *Public Library Trustees in the Nineteen-Sixties* (Chicago: ALA, 1969), 94p.
2. Quotation from talk presented at Allerton Park conference on "Cooperation Between Types of Libraries: The Beginning of a State Plan for Library Services in Illinois," 4–6 Nov. 1968.
3. Nelson Associates, *Public Library Systems in the United States* (Chicago: ALA, 1969), p.250.
4. Evelyn Geller, "'Think Session' at High John," *Library Journal* 93:2963–71 (1 Sept. 1968).
5. Andrew Geddes, "Managing Systems," *RQ* 9:207 (Spring 1970).
6. Nelson Associates, *Public Library Systems in the United States,* p.253.
7. Mildred L. Batchelder, *Public Library Trustees in the Nineteen-Sixties,* p.7.
8. "Duties and Responsibilities of the Director and Other Representatives," North Suburban Library System, Morton Grove, Ill. (mimeographed).
9. See "When Is a Social Issue a Library Issue: A Symposium," ed. by Dorothy Bendix, *Wilson Library Bulletin* 45:43–61 (Sept. 1970); Leonard H. Freiser, "Community, Library, and Revolution," *Library Journal* 95:39–41 (1 Jan. 1970); and Ervin J. Gaines, "Viewpoint: Faddism," *Library Journal* 95:2235 (15 June 1970).
10. American Library Assn., Standards Committee and Subcommittees of the Public Library Assn., *Minimum Standards for Public Library Systems, 1966* (Chicago: ALA, 1967), p.36.
11. American Library Assn., Public Library Assn., *Just between Ourselves* 7:3–4 (Oct. 1968).
12. Nelson Associates, *Public Library Systems in the United States,* p.247.

Chapter 3

CAPITAL IMPROVEMENTS

1. Roberta Bowler, ed., *Local Public Library Administration* (Chicago: International City Managers' Assn., 1964), p.341. Sample building program statements and campaign scrapbooks are available on loan from the ALA Library Administration Division.
2. H. G. Johnston, in review of Ruth G. Lindahl and William S.

Berner, "Financing Public Library Expansion: Case Studies of Three Defeated Bond Issue Referendums," *Library Journal* 94:49 (1 Jan. 1969).

3. James J. O'Brien, *Scheduling Handbook* (New York: McGraw-Hill, 1969), p.594–95.

4. Archives of the Oak Park (Ill.) Library.

5. Fred Kerner, ed., *A Treasury of Lincoln Quotations* (New York: Doubleday, 1965), p.239.

Chapter 4

ADMINISTRATIVE RESPONSIBILITIES

1. David Ewing, *The Human Side of Planning* (New York: Macmillan, 1969), p.11.

2. Robert E. Kemper, "Library Planning: The Challenge of Change," in Melvin J. Voigt, ed., *Advances in Librarianship* (New York: Academic Pr., 1970), p.208, 211.

3. Herbert Gans, *People and Plans: Essays on Urban Problems and Solutions* (New York: Basic Books, 1968), p.ix.

4. Arnold J. Toynbee, "Why and How I Work," *Saturday Review* 52:26 (5 April 1969).

5. *Emerging Library Systems: The 1963–66 Evaluation of the New York State Public Library Systems* (Albany: Univ. of the State of New York, 1967), p.78.

6. Alvin Toffler, *Future Shock* (New York: Random, 1970), p.416–30.

7. "Natural Library Service Zones: A Report to the North Suburban Library System, February 1969," prepared by the Institute of Urban Life, and "A Bibliographic Bank for Resource Sharing in Library Systems: A Feasibility Study," prepared for the Bur Oak, DuPage, North Suburban, Northern Illinois, Starved Rock, and Suburban Library Systems by Information Sciences, IIT Research Institute, 1969.

8. Morris S. Schwartz and G. T. Will, "Intervention and Change on a Mental Hospital Ward," in Warren Bennis, *The Planning of Change* (New York: Holt, 1961), p.564.

9. See quotation from Dr. Frederick Herzberg, in *Administrator's Digest* 6:5 (March 1971).

10. Edward N. Howard, "The Orbital Organization," *Library Journal* 95:1712–15 (1 May 1970).

11. Don Sager, "The Comfortable Pullman: Administrative Creativity on the Siding," *American Libraries* 1:587–92 (June 1970).

12. Lowell A. Martin, *Library Response to Urban Change: A Study of the Chicago Public Library* (Chicago: ALA, 1969), p.26.

13. American Library Assn., *Statistical Standards;* Addenda to be used with *Minimum Standards for Public Library Systems, 1966* (leaflet, 1967).
14. —— *Minimum Standards for Public Library Systems, 1966* (Chicago: ALA, 1967), p.36.
15. Lawrence Clark Powell, *The Alchemy of Books* (Los Angeles: Ward Ritchie, 1954), p.244.
16. Joseph L. Wheeler and Herbert Goldhor, *Practical Administration of Public Libraries* (New York: Harper, 1962), p. 174–83).
17. Roberta Bowler, ed., *Local Public Library Administration* (Chicago: International City Managers' Assn., 1964), p.152–55.

Chapter 5

COLLECTION BUILDING AND MAINTENANCE

1. See the annual report of the Corn Belt Library System, *Illinois Libraries* 51:873 (Dec. 1969), and Ray Houser, "Illinois Valley Library System," *Illinois Libraries* 52:1011 (Dec. 1970).
2. Eric Moon, "The View from the Front," *Library Journal* 89:570–74 (1 Feb. 1964).
3. Arnold Sable, "The Death of Book Selection," *Wilson Library Bulletin* 43:345–48 (Dec. 1968).
4. Helen Haines, *Living with Books* (New York: Columbia Univ. Pr., 1935), p.23.
5. Carl B. Roden, "Theories of Book Selection for Public Libraries," in Louis R. Wilson, *The Practice of Book Selection* (Chicago: Univ. of Chicago Pr., 1940), p.11.
6. Francis K. W. Drury, *Book Selection* (Chicago: ALA, 1930), o.p. Quoted in Mary D. Carter and Wallace J. Bonk, *Building Library Collections* (2d ed.; Metuchen, N. J.: Scarecrow, 1964), p.30.
7. Dan Lacy, "The Library and New Creative Literature," *Pennsylvania Library Association Bulletin* 19:20–22 (May 1964).
8. Margaret E. Monroe, "Library's Collection in Time of Crisis," *Wilson Library Bulletin* 36:372–74 (Jan. 1962).
9. Kathlyn C. Adams, "Collections in a Capsule," *The Bookmark* 27:117–18 (Dec. 1967).
10. Regional History Project of the North Suburban Library System, Morton Grove, Ill.
11. James F. Fixx, "The Library Goes to Market," *Saturday Review* 45:14–15 (7 April 1962).
12. Robert Oppenheimer, "Prospects in the Arts and Sciences," *Perspectives USA* 11:10–11 (Spring 1955).

13. See *Freedom of Book Selection* (Chicago: ALA, 1954), 132p.; and Robert B. Downs, ed., *The First Freedom* (Chicago: ALA, 1960), 469p.
14. Judith Krug, "Intellectual Freedom," *American Libraries* 1:20 (Jan. 1970).
15. Virginia Haviland, "Search for the Real Thing," *Library Journal* 86:4332 (15 Dec. 1961).
16. Sister M. Claudia Carlen, "Expanding Resources: The Explosion of the Sixties," *Library Trends* 18:52 (July 1969) (an article directed to college librarians but of interest to public librarians).
17. Dan Herr, *Stop Pushing* (New York: Hanover, 1961), p.144.
18. American Library Assn., *Minimum Standards for Public Library Systems, 1966* (Chicago: ALA, 1967), p.40.

Chapter 6

ADMINISTERING SERVICES FOR PEOPLE

1. Robert D. Leigh, *The Public Library in the United States* (New York: Columbia Univ. Pr., 1950), p.99–100.
2. *Emerging Library Systems: The 1963–66 Evaluation of the New York State Public Library Systems* (Albany: Univ. of the State of New York, 1967), p.42.
3. "Library Rights of Adults," adopted by the membership of the Adult Services Division of the ALA, July 3, 1970.
4. Eleanor T. Smith, "The Federal Government and Libraries," *New Jersey Libraries* 1:18–19 (Summer 1968).
5. Jean Connor, "Role of the Medium-Sized Public Library in the 'System' (New York)," *Library Quarterly* 33:120 (Jan. 1963).
6. Research project completed by George Babcock for North Suburban Library System 1968, Morton Grove, Ill. (unpublished).
7. American Library Assn., *Minimum Standards for Public Library Systems, 1966* (Chicago: ALA, 1967), p.31.
8. Lowell A. Martin, *Library Response to Urban Change: A Study of the Chicago Public Library* (Chicago: ALA, 1969), p.21–22.
9. Eleanor Quin, *Last on the Menu* (New York: Prentice-Hall, 1969), p.87.
10. Robert T. Jordan, *Tomorrow's Library: Direct Access and Delivery* (New York: Bowker, 1970), p. 76.

Chapter 7

CONTINUING EDUCATION FOR LIBRARIANSHIP

1. "The Civilization of the Dialogue," *Center Occasional Paper* 2: verso cover (Dec. 1968).

2. Marie Davis, "In-service Training for Adult Service Librarians," *Adult Services Division Newsletter*: 4–6 (Spring 1966).
3. Bergen Evans, *Dictionary of Quotations* (New York: Delacorte, 1968), p.494.
4. Elizabeth W. Stone, "Continuing Education: Avenue to Adventure," *School Libraries* 18:43 (Summer 1969).
5. Estelle Brodman and Doris Bolef, "Printed Catalogs: Retrospect and Prospect," *Special Libraries* 59:786 (Dec. 1968).
6. Irving A. Verschoor, "Planning for Personnel," in *Statewide Long-Range Planning for Libraries;* report of conference, 19–22, Sept. 1965, Chicago, Ill. (Washington, D.C.: U.S. Dept. of Health, Education and Welfare, 1966), p.41.
7. Jacques Barzun, "The New Librarian to the Rescue," *Library Journal* 94:3963–66 (1 Nov. 1969).

A Selected
Bibliography

1960–1970

Advances in Librarianship, v.1. Ed. by Melvin J. Voigt. New York: Academic Pr., 1970. 294p.

American Library Assn. Adult Services Division. *Library Service to an Aging Population;* an Institute presented by the American Library Assn. Adult Services Division and the American Library Assn. Office for Adult Education; ed. by Ruth M. White. (Public Library Reporter No. 10) Chicago: ALA, 1960. 60p.

—— —— Committee on Reading Improvements for Adults. *Literacy Activities in Public Libraries: A Report of a Study of Service to Adult Illiterates,* by Bernice MacDonald. Chicago: ALA, 1966. 50p.

—— American Assn. of State Libraries. Standards Revision Committee. *Standards for Library Functions at the State Level.* Chicago: ALA, 1970. 48p.

—— Library Administration Division. *The Small Public Library: A Series of Guides for the Community Librarian and Trustee.* Chicago: ALA, 1965.

—— —— Personnel Administration Section. Personnel Publications Committee. *Personnel Organization and Procedure: A Manual Suggested for Use in Public Libraries.* 2d ed. Chicago: ALA, 1968. 59p.

—— Library-Community Project Headquarters Staff. *Studying the Community: A Basis for Planning Library Adult Education Services.* Chicago: ALA, 1960. 128p.

—— Library Technology Project. *Protecting the Library and Its Resources: A Guide to Physical Protection and Insurance.* (LTP Publication no.7) Chicago: ALA, 1963. 322p.

—— Library Technology Program. *Work Simplification in Danish Public Libraries: The Report of the Work Simplification Committee of the Danish Library Association,* by Henning Gimbel, Study Director. An abridged version, tr. from the Danish by Rudolph C. Ellsworth. (LTP Publication no.15) Chicago: ALA, 1969. 256p.

—— Public Library Assn. Committee on Standards for Work with Young Adults in Public Libraries. *Young Adult Services in the Public Library.* Chicago: ALA, 1960. 50p.

—— —— Standards Committee and Subcommittees of the Public Library Assn. *Minimum Standards for Public Library Systems, 1966.* Chicago: ALA, 1967. 73p.

—— —— Subcommittee on Standards for Children's Service. *Standards for Children's Services in Public Libraries.* Chicago: ALA, 1964. 24p.

—— ——Subcommittee on Standards for Small Libraries. *Interim Standards for Small Public Libraries: Guidelines toward Achieving the Goals of Public Library Service.* Chicago: ALA, 1962. 16p.

Bendix, Dorothy. *Library Service for the Undereducated.* (Drexel Library School Series no.15) Philadelphia: Drexel Pr., 1966. 54p.

Biel, Audrey, ed. "Young Adult Service in the Public Library," *Library Trends* 17:115–220 (Oct. 1968).

Bowler, Roberta, ed. *Local Public Library Administration.* Chicago: International City Managers' Assn., 1964. 375p.

Conant, Ralph W., ed. *The Public Library and the City.* Cambridge: MIT Pr., 1965. 216p.

Connor, Jean L. "Role of the Medium-Sized Public Library in the 'System' (New York)," *Library Quarterly* 33:115–27 (Jan. 1963).

Coplan, Kate, and Castagna, Edwin, eds. *The Library Reaches Out.* New York: Oceana, 1965. 403p.

Curley, Marie. *The Buckram Syndrome: A Critical Essay on Paperbacks in Public Libraries of the United States.* (Public Library Reporter no. 13) Chicago: ALA, 1968. 65p.

Dennis, Donald D. *Simplifying Work in Small Public Libraries.* Philadelphia: Drexel Institute of Technology, 1965. 80p.

Dougherty, Richard M., and Heinritz, Fred J. *Scientific Management of Library Operations.* Metuchen, N.J.: Scarecrow, 1966. 258p.

Gans, Herbert J. *People and Plans: Essays on Urban Problems and Solutions.* New York: Basic Books, 1968. 395p.

Gaver, Mary Virginia, ed. *Background Readings in Building Library Collections.* 2v. Metuchen, N.J.: Scarecrow, 1969. 1357p.

Hensel, Evelyn, and Veillette, Peter D. *Purchasing Library Materials in Public and School Libraries.* Chicago: ALA, 1969. 150p.

Hiatt, Peter, and Drennan, Henry T. *Public Library Service for the Functionally Illiterate: A survey of Practice.* Chicago: ALA, 1967. 67p.

Jansen, Guenter A. *Univac Electronic Data Processing in the Public Library Systems of Long Island.* Bellport, N.Y.: Suffolk Cooperative Library System, n.d. 16p.

Jordan, Robert T. *Tomorrow's Library: Direct Access and Delivery.* New York: Bowker, 1970. 200p.

Lee, Robert Ellis. *Continuing Education for Adults through the American Public Library, 1833–1964.* Chicago: ALA, 1966. 158p.

Lindahl, Ruth G., and Berner, William S. *Financing Public Library Expansion, Case studies of three defeated bond issue referendums.* (Research Series no. 13) Springfield, Ill.: Illinois State Library, 1968. 64p.

Martin, Lowell A. *Baltimore Reaches Out: Library Service to the Disadvantaged.* (Deiches Fund Studies of Public Library Service no. 3) Baltimore: Enoch Pratt Free Library, 1967. 54p.

——— *Library Response to Urban Change: A Study of the Chicago Public Library.* Chicago: ALA, 1969. 313p.

Merritt, LeRoy Charles. *Book Selection and Intellectual Freedom.* New York: Wilson, 1970. 100p.

Minder, Thomas. *The Regional Library Center in the Mid 1970s: A Concept Paper.* Pittsburgh: Univ. of Pittsburgh Pr., 1968. 41p.

Molz, Kathleen. "The Public Library: The People's University?" *American Scholar* 34:95–102 (Winter 1964–65).

Monroe, Margaret E. *Library Adult Education: The Biography of an Idea.* Metuchen, N.J.: Scarecrow, 1963. 550p.

——— "The Library's Collection in a Time of Crisis," *Wilson Library Bulletin* 36:372–74 (Jan. 1962).

Moon, Eric, ed. *Book Selection and Censorship in the Sixties.* New York: Bowker, 1969. 421p.

Moore, Everett T., ed. "Intellectual Freedom," *Library Trends* 19:3–168 (July 1970).

Nelson Associates. *Public Library Systems in the United States.* Chicago: ALA, 1969. 368p.

New York Library Association. Personnel Administration Committee. *Outline of a Personnel Organization and Policy Manual.* New York: New York Library Assn., 1969. 11p.

New York (State) University. *Emerging Library Systems: The 1963–66 Evaluation of the New York State Public Library Systems.* Albany: Univ. of the State of New York, State Education Dept., 1967. 291p.

Parker, Ralph H., and Price, Paxton P., eds. "Aspects of the Financial Administration of Libraries," *Library Trends* 11:341–451 (April 1963).

Pearson, Mary D. *Recordings in the Public Library.* Chicago: ALA, 1963. 153p.

Prentiss, S. Gilbert. "The Evolution of the Library System (New York)," *Library Quarterly* 39:78–89 (Jan. 1969).

Profiles of the Public Library Systems in New York State. 2d ed. New York: Univ. of the State of New York, 1966. 143p.

Shaffer, Kenneth R. *Library Personnel Administration and Supervision.* Hamden, Conn.: Shoe String, 1963. 214p.

Shaw, Spencer G. "Children's Services Operating under 'Systems' Organization," *Library Trends* 12:38–51 (July 1963).

Sinclair, Dorothy. *Administration of the Small Public Library*. Chicago: ALA, 1965. 173p.

Smith, Hannis S., ed. "Regional Public Library Systems," *Library Trends* 13:275–381 (Jan. 1965).

Stebbins, Kathleen B., and Mohrhardt, Foster E. *Personnel Administration in Libraries*. 2d ed. Metuchen, N.J.: Scarecrow, 1966. 373p.

Stenstrom, Ralph H. *The Emergence and Development of Public Library Systems in Illinois*. Springfield, Ill.: Illinois State Library, 1968. 98p.

Stevenson, Grace T., ed. "Group Services in Public Libraries," *Library Trends* 17:3–108 (July 1968).

Wheeler, Joseph L., and Goldhor, Herbert. *Practical Administration of Public Libraries*. New York: Harper, 1962. 571p.

Whitney, Stephen. "The Library System Trustee," *Library Journal* 95:636–39 (15 Feb. 1970).

Wight, Edward A. "Precursors of Current Public Library Systems," *Library Quarterly* 39:23–40 (Jan. 1969).

Wulfekoetter, Gertrude. *Acquisition Work: Processes Involved in Building Library Collections*. Seattle: Univ. of Washington Pr., 1961. 268p.

Young, Virginia G., ed. *The Library Trustee: A Practical Guidebook* New York: Bowker, 1969. 242p.

Index